Hegland Study & Pr Laws NS-1

INTRODUCTION
TO THE
STUDY and PRACTICE OF LAW

IN A NUTSHELL

SECOND EDITION

By

KENNEY HEGLAND
Professor of Law
University of Arizona

ST. PAUL, MINN.
WEST PUBLISHING CO.
1995

Nutshell Series, In a Nutshell, the Nutshell Logo and the WP symbol are registered trademarks of West Publishing Co. Registered in the U.S. Patent and Trademark Office.

COPYRIGHT © 1983 WEST PUBLISHING CO.

COPYRIGHT © 1995 By WEST PUBLISHING CO.
610 Opperman Drive
P.O. Box 64526
St. Paul, MN 55164-0526
1-800-328-9352

Library of Congress Cataloging-in-Publication Data

Hegland, Kenney F., 1940–
Introduction to the study and practice of law in a nutshell / by Kenney Hegland. — 2nd ed.
p.   cm. — (Nutshell series)
Includes index.
ISBN 0-314-05933-4 (softcover)
1. Law—Study and teaching—United States.   2. Practice of law—United States.   I. Title.   II. Series.
KF273.H4   1995
340'.071'173—dc20   95-5907
                                                     CIP

ISBN 0-314-05933-4

TEXT IS PRINTED ON 10% POST CONSUMER RECYCLED PAPER

PRINTED WITH
SOY INK

In memory of

>Arthur Leff and Grant Gilmore,
>Hall of Famers

And dedicated simply to lawyers,

>In good times, great jokes;
>In bad, great friends

*

PREFACE

This book will make you a better law student and, down the road, a better lawyer. I'm thrilled to be a part of your professional development.

Standing on the shore, about to depart, you have doubts, questions.

"What lies ahead?"

"Will I make it?"

"Have I found my life's work?"

"Will I be happy?"

"Do I have to read the whole book?"

Well, no . . . at least not now.

To begin, read only the first fifty pages. You'll learn the key skills: legal analysis and argument. Don't leave home without them; otherwise your first weeks in law school will be a blur.

But maybe you aren't a law student; maybe you just picked this book up in hopes of learning something about the law and something about the profession. Maybe you are thinking about law school in the future ("What's it like and will I like it?") or maybe some of your best friends are lawyers ("What ever happened to them?"). Maybe, like George, you're just curious.

What is it "to think like a lawyer"? How are lawyers trained? Why are they trained that way? What are the premises of the adversary system? What are the ethical and psychological pressures on lawyers? What is the "common law" and what is the relationship between courts and legislatures? How do judges decide questions of law? How do juries decide questions of fact? And which is which and which came first?

Whatever your goal, be you a beginning law student or a liberal arts reader, this book will provide you with a unique "hands on" experience in the art of lawyering.

You will throw pots. I will describe and illustrate the key skills: legal analysis, legal argument and, oh yes, exam taking. Then I will give you an opportunity to develop and practice those skills: cases to analyze, arguments to construct and exams to take.

Throw pots and you will soon be "thinking like a lawyer" (and perhaps even mixing metaphors like one). The more you put into your pottery, the more you will teach yourself about the art of lawyering. As for me, I'll stick around, offering encouragement, a few words of advice and, of course, an occasional joke.

But we have many miles to ride before we sleep. Which woods should detain us?

Again, Part One, on legal analysis, is essential. Because Part One is essential, **reread** it later in your first semester, after five or six weeks. You will be amazed with how much you have learned and, on second reading, you will simply understand things at a much deeper level. This is important stuff.

Part Two of this book focuses on "Studying Law." You will practice fundamental law school skills: reading and briefing cases and taking law school exams.

Part Three takes you through a typical lawsuit, from late night TV advertising to closing argument. Law students will see how classroom materials play out in the real world; liberal arts readers will be able to astonish, amaze (and eventually disgust) friends and relations by pointing out petty flaws in Perry Mason.

Part Four deals with basic law school skills, legal writing, legal argument (Moot Court) and legal research. Don't read this part in advance; it will make more sense when you face the actual tasks in law school.

Part Five deals with the "Great Hereafter," the second and third years and career choices. One chapter discusses what to take and what to do in the second and third years of law school. It includes a short history of legal education, a description of underground activities such as Law and Literature, and offers suggestions as to *pro bono* activities in law school.

The chapter "Career Choices" deserves an early peek. During your first year of law school, don't be overly concerned with what you will eventually do. However, a little thought now might help you find the perfect job later, a job which puts a smile on your face and a spring in your step.

The last chapter, "Lawyers Talk What They Do," should be of interest to both law students and the liberal arts reader.

———

I have many debts to acknowledge.

First, to my students, at Arizona, Harvard and U.C.L.A. What a delightful job it is to be with curious and energetic folks at the beginning of a major new task; we meet temporarily but intensely. Thanks for inspiring me; thanks for perplexing me.

Second, to people who helped me write this book: Mohyeddin Abdulaziz, Charles Ares, Bill Boyd, Dan Hobbs, Jamie Ratner, Andy Silverman, Tom Sullivan, David Wexler and Winton Woods. I would like to particularly thank Barbara Atwood, Carol Eliot, Toni Massaro and Karen Waterman for their review of particular chapters.

Then there is Kay Kavanagh. She read the entire manuscript, made great suggestions and was marvelously supportive. (Struggling authors, send her your stuff.)

I would also like to thank Jamie Ratner for all of his wonderful insights into legal education and for his spirited resistance to most of mine.

My sister, Sherina Cadmun, read the manuscript and, as always, helped in many ways and at many levels. Of course, if any poetry is misquoted, it's her fault. My parents, Edwina Kenney and "Heg", taught me so much about writing; even though they are now gone, their insights are part of me. My wife Barbara and my three older sons, Robert, Alex and Caleb, read chapters, made wise cracks, and offered advice and encouragement. As to Little Ben, frankly, he has yet to play his part.

When it came time to get down in the trenches of manuscript preparation, spelling words, if not correctly, at least consistently across hundreds of pages, Sandy Beeler was there. Thanks to her good cheer and competence, we got through.

I wish to thank the authors and publishers who have given permission to reprint copyrighted material:

Turow, *One L.* Excerpts reprinted with permission of G. G. Putman's Sons.

Mueller and Rosett, *Contract Law and Its Applications*. Excerpt reprinted with permission of Foundation Press.

Noonan, *Persons and Masks of the Law*. Excerpts reprinted with permission of author and Farrar, Straus and Giroux.

Along these lines, I note that the chapters on legal writing and on legal argument are pretty much the same as those chapters in my other Nutshell, *Trial and Practice Skills 2d. Ed* (West, 1994). That book is designed for second and third year students so not to worry, you will have probably already forgotten what I say in this book.

———

Finally, I would like to kick a little sand in the faces of my two dear friends at U.C.L.A., David Binder and Paul Bergman. Perhaps they are spending too much time at the beach. I believe, he said reluctantly, that this makes for two unanswered books (but, hey, who's counting?).

KENNEY HEGLAND

March, 1995

OUTLINE

INTRODUCTION

TO THE

STUDY and PRACTICE OF LAW

IN A NUTSHELL

SECOND EDITION

*

PROLOGUE

LAW SCHOOL

It is the best of schools, it is the worst of schools. And it won't be the same old stuff.

As an undergraduate you sat and took notes while the professor lectured. You left, often inspired, occasionally depressed, but with the feeling that your life had advanced, that you had actually *learned* something, such as:

> "That Sartre believed essence precedes existence" (or vice versa—I'll look it up for the final).

> "That the Second Law of Thermodynamics suggests that the universe will eventually run out of energy."

> "That Sartre, had he known of the Second Law of Thermodynamics, would have been even more depressed."

Naturally, when you get to law school, you expect to go to class, sit back and *learn* the law.

> "That murder is the unlawful killing of a human being."

> "That minors don't have contractual capacity."

> "That torts are not English muffins."

It is not to be. Law professors generally do not explain or supplement the assigned reading—their mission is to put you to work. You don't mull over the readings, you tear them apart, testing their coherence, exposing their assumptions and pondering their implications.

It can be exhausting.

Often you leave class convinced that you lost ground: "Before class, I worked real hard and finally learned what 'murder' is. I felt good about myself. Then came class—people to the left of me, people to the right of me ... getting called on ... and questions, questions, questions. Never any answers! And confusion. What was the professor getting at? I no longer know what murder is * * * frankly, I don't think I even know what a human being is, much less an English muffin."

Preparing for class isn't a cakewalk. You don't skim the material looking for central ideas nor do you sit long hours attempting to memorize key points. In law school you struggle with the ideas—expect, at first, to be whipped by a two page case.

You think that's hype? Okay, try out this case; it's only a paragraph:

Nichols v. Raynbred

Nichols brought an assumpsit against Raynbred, declaring that in consideration, that Nichols promised to deliver the defendant to his own use a cow, the defendant promised to deliver him 50 shillings: adjudged for the plaintiff in both Counts, that the plaintiff need not to aver the delivery of the cow, because it is a promise for a promise. Note here the promises must be at one instant, for else they will be both nuda pactum.

That's the entire case.

Yes, it does has something to do with a cow. Good for you.

Stop trying to figure it out. It drives seasoned law students bonkers. But I have given it to you to illustrate an important point.

Much of your first year is not (optimistically) "learning how to think like a lawyer", nor (pessimistically) exposing yourself as the simpleton you know, deep down, you are. Much of the first year is simply vocabulary building, as in:

Stand up.

Spell "assumpsit."

Now use it is a sentence.

Don't beat yourself when you find yourself bewildered the first several weeks. You are not dumb; you just speak the wrong language. Picture yourself on a Greek island, in a crowded restaurant. People are talking, apparently about events of great moment, and you don't understand a word.

"Oh, no ... I'm an idiot. I should never have come. I'm going to flunk out of Greece."

Lighten up and get a dictionary.

As to law exams, they're different too. Usually, you will not be asked to recite what you have learned ("Define murder.") Nor will you be given broad essay questions such as "Is Law Just?" Law exams require you to apply the law you have learned to new factual situations. They are great fun to take and you will be surprised at how much you have learned and how competent you are becoming. (Sometimes, admittedly, it is not great fun to **think** about exams, particularly in the predawn hours.)

These differences are bewildering, threatening, challenging and exhilarating. It is the worst of schools, it is the best of schools.

You will read of real murders, of real scoundrels and of real heroes: of seven-year-olds who pull chairs out from their aged aunts, of neighbors who fight over water wells, of New York executives who manipulate stock prices, of old fogies who cut off ungrateful kids (hopefully, the chair pranksters) and of lawyers who stand tall in the fight against injustice. And you will share this dizzy ride through human experience with marvelous classmates and professors, folks with different lives and different outlooks.

You will learn to read carefully—more carefully than ever before—and you will become sensitive to the ambiguities of language (almost to the point of losing old friends who prefer familiar sloth, their "Can you pass the salt?" to your "Will you pass the salt **to me**?"). You will learn to suspect the rush to judgment and will appreciate that even the most despised among us have things that can be said on their behalf. Eventually, you'll even find it hard to get mad at the plumber.

A law professor (from Harvard ... get out your high-lighter) once said that the best thing about legal education is that it teaches "Yes, but ... ". For all good points, there are competing points. Perhaps thinking like a lawyer is no more than training your Little Voice to whisper "Yes, but ..." every time your Big Voice waxes profoundly.

Finally, and perhaps most exhilarating, you will discuss and debate things that **matter**. The endless, meandering undergraduate discussions of good and evil, of human nature, of free will and of the just society suddenly hit a wall: real life. The accident victim either recovers or she doesn't; the accused either goes to prison or he doesn't; the schools will remain segregated or they won't.

Theories, evidence, counter-examples and clever retorts, all crash into the lawyer's only question: "What shall we do next?"

Exciting stuff. It is the best of schools!

Welcome.

All good law schools are alike. Go to any law school in the country, and, once inside, once you sit down in class, you could be anywhere. Same cases, same books, same questions. (And, thankfully, same Nutshells). This uniformity should solace those who didn't get in their "first choice"; it should (but probably won't) humble those who did. But this is not a book of therapy.

What does the standard method of teaching law have to do with the practice of law? Sure, lawyers will need to know the rules of law, but what of the method of instruction? Why not have students read books stating the legal rules rather than forcing them to extract those very same rules from judicial opinions? In short, what does the case method have to do with the practice of law?

Everything.

Day in, day out, trying murder cases, negotiating widget contracts, drafting franchise agreements, and counseling divorce clients, lawyers focus on the **interplay of law and fact**. And that is exactly what you will be doing, staying up late reading cases and struggling through class.

The uniformity of American legal education means something else as well. I don't care if your hero is Earl Warren, William Rehnquist, Thurgood Marshall or Sandra Day O'Connor; I don't care if your hero prosecutes vicious criminals or defends the downtrodden; I don't care if your hero is the most trusted advisor of the President or, indeed, is the guy advertising on the late show.

All of them once sat where you sit; they read the cases you will read; they too cursed the profs and marveled at their own growing competence.

You are now with them, part of them.

Let's go.

PART 1

LEGAL ANALYSIS

CHAPTER 1

THE SECOND CASE IN THE WORLD

In law school, there is only one game worth playing: I call it the "Second–Case-in-the-World." It is the key to your legal education; indeed, it may be the key to everything!

There you have it, you have learned something profound in the very first paragraph! You're going to love this book.

"Is it enough for us to know that the Second–Case-in-the-World is the only game worth playing or must we know *why* it is the only game worth playing?"

Knowing why is knowing what.

Knowing why is knowing what, even if you forget it. This is the essence of legal study.

"Wow, an incomprehensible, Zen-like sentence on the first page! This is gonna be great!"

Once you learn how to play the Second–Case-in-the-World, once you know its rules and appreciate

7

its deep structure, you will know everything you
need to know about law. It shouldn't take more
than an hour. As to the remainder of your first
year, indeed, as to the next three years, it is simply
review ... and filler.

It is not, however, silence.

Back to the Game.

A core concept in our jurisprudence is that of
"precedent" or "stare decisis"—in reaching decisions courts should follow the rules laid down in
prior cases. This concept explains casebooks—as a
student you will learn law by reading judicial opinions. Those opinions are "the law"; today's cases
will be decided upon the rules developed yesterday.

Note this as well: under the doctrine of "stare
decisis," tomorrow's cases will be decided upon the
rules developed in today's cases. Judges are not
just deciding current controversies; *they are also
creating tomorrow's law*.

When you become a lawyer, you will continue to
read cases, no longer to pass tests, no longer to
avoid crushing humiliation in class, but rather to
advise clients, to negotiate deals and to try lawsuits.
Frankly, it's a lot more fun.

Let's start by examining the basic notion: *should*
courts follow precedent? (Aside: Never, not once,
assume that the status quo makes sense, that a
group of wise folks sat down and planned things out
and that they had "their reasons"—a lot of what we
live is simply historical accident. It is only by
questioning the "wise lessons of the past" that we

can either embrace them or liberate ourselves from them. Don't simply memorize yesterday's Wisdom in order to pass a test—you owe your kids that much.)

To sharpen our inquiry as to "precedent", consider an alternative system. When folks get into a dispute, they go to the designated Wise One, tell their stories and then the Wise One decides, free of any consideration of what other Wise Folks have decided in similar disputes. What would the costs and benefits be of such a system? What are the costs and benefits of a system that requires the Wise One to decide the same way as previous Wise Ones?

A Note on Learning

Often it is helpful, in approaching a topic, to assume a point of view. If one takes the position, say, that following precedent is a great idea, one is likely to get more involved in the issue, to see more of its ramifications, than if one hikes up the mountain, assumes the Lotus Position, and muses, "I will now think about whether precedent is a good idea. Ooommm."

Positioning is the root notion of the Adversary System (the clash of mad dogs) as opposed to the Inquisitorial System (one very nice dog, sniffing). The idea is that truth is more likely to emerge from conflicting positions rather than from the most well-meaning of neutral investigators.

Whether the adversary system leads to truth is a question you should consider during the leisure of the next three years. Right now, I merely suggest that positioning is a great way to learn legal doctrine—put yourself in the position of **either** the person advancing the doctrine or in that of the person resisting it.

Here's the rub. *Always consider what your opponent will argue and how your opponent will respond to your points.* Remember "Yes, but,": there are always good points on both sides and that we must, to understand our own position, test it in the hot fire of competing positions.

Another device to help you think through your positions, to develop their complexity, is to **write them out**. I will repeat this again and again and again and some of you might actually try it once, probably sometime in November. I am a person of few illusions. However, know this now: writing slows the mind and deepens analysis.

Lastly, as to law study, we tend to get a tad abstract. "Precedent: Yes or No?" I think it is well to approach issues in terms of your own experiences. Following past cases is a familiar concept, no doubt employed by your parents ... sometimes ... and no doubt you employed by yourself ... sometimes. Take an example from your past. What are the costs and what are the benefits of following prior cases?

Back to the Game

After you consider whether courts should follow precedent, Round Two of the Game is designed to see how the doctrine works in the everyday world of lawyers and judges.

Assume that we have decided to follow precedent. Assume further that we have a Case I which laid down a certain rule of law. Now assume we have a new case, Case II. Should the judge in Case II follow the rule of law that was laid down in Case I? He, or she, should, under the doctrine of precedent, but **only if** Case II is sufficiently **like** Case I that it would make sense to follow the rule of Case I.

In lawyer talk, the question is "Does Case I (and the rule of law it laid down) control Case II?" This question introduces the art of legal analysis and legal argument; they are key. The ability to apply the law you learn to new situations is the essence of "thinking like a lawyer" and you will spend much of your first year in developing that skill.

Our final inquiry will go to the situation where there is no controlling law and the judge must decide the controversy as a matter of "first impression." What kinds of arguments should a judge consider? What goals should be sought? We will focus on a particular controversy: should a court, for public policy reasons, refuse to enforce a specific contract clause? This, in turn, introduces a major theme of your Contracts course—the interplay between personal autonomy and community welfare.

The Second–Case–In–The–World

Of course, to play "Second–Case," we need a First–Case.

Assume Paradise. People mind their own business and everyone is happy. No one sues anyone, not for anything. Then, alas, Trouble in Paradise. Someone sues. It results in the FIRST CASE in Paradise. Here is a "brief" of that case:

Globe v. Credit Bureau, 1 Paradise Reporter 1

Facts: Plaintiff Globe hired defendant Credit Bureau to run a credit check on a man named Jones who wished to borrow money from Plaintiff. Due to defendant's neglect, it failed to find a mortgage that was on Jones' property; it reported that Jones' credit was good; had it found the outstanding mortgage, it would have labeled Jones a bad credit risk. Based on this favorable, yet erroneous, report, plaintiff lent Jones money which was not repaid. Plaintiff now sues Defendant for negligence. "If it weren't for your negligence, I would not have lent the money and thus I would not have lost the money."

Defendant moved to dismiss Plaintiff's case based on a clause in the contract between Plaintiff and Defendant wherein Plaintiff agreed not to sue Defendant for negligence. In response to this, Plaintiff argued that the agreement "not to sue" should not be enforced by a court because it would violate "public policy" to do so. The court rejected Plaintiff's argument, enforced the clause and threw Plaintiff out of court. (Ouch!)

Rule: In Paradise, exculpatory clauses do not offend public policy.

Rationale: The Court stressed the importance of freedom of contract. The court wrote that if parties who make contracts cannot agree to limit the extent of liability, it is difficult to see where such a ruling would lead.

We are now on the verge of the First–Litigation– Explosion in history (bad for our friends and neighbors, great for us). The SECOND CASE in Paradise involves a Ms. K who fell down the back stairway in her apartment house and was severely injured. She sues Landlord for negligence in maintaining the stairs (allegedly there was a defective step). In the lease, we find an exculpatory clause:

Tenant hereby agrees, covenants and promises, not to sue the Landlord for any or all injuries received due to the Landlord's neglect.

At court, Landlord will argue: "Tenant cannot bring this case because she signed a lease agreeing not to sue me for negligence and that's exactly what she is about, your Honor." Tenant will respond, "Agreements not to sue should be unenforceable as a matter of public policy" and Landlord will respond "The *Globe* case has held that exculpatory clauses are *not* against public policy."

Tenant will make three arguments. First, whatever *Globe* said doesn't matter because the courts in Paradise should decide controversies on the basis on fairness and not on the basis of precedent. Second, even if the court decides to adopt the doctrine of "precedence," whatever the *Globe* case had to say about exculpatory clauses does not matter because

Globe involved a very different kind of case and thus is **"distinguishable."** It does not **"control."** Third, finally getting to the moral merits of the thing, Ms. K will argue that exculpatory clauses are such a bad thing the courts should refuse to enforce them on the basis of public policy.

An Aside: On the Need to See the Relationship Between Arguments

Legal arguments get complicated. A lawyer (or judicial opinion) may make four basic points: it is essential that you not only understand the points but the relationship between them. Does the lawyer need to win all four points to win the case? Or will one victorious point carry the day?

To raise your math anxiety, there are several possibilities:

$1 + 2 + 3 + 4 = $ VICTORY

Here the lawyer must prevail on all four points in order to win; lose one and it's back to late night advertising.

$(1 + 2)$ or $(3 + 4) = $ VICTORY

Here the lawyer doesn't have to win all the points, only a certain combination.

1 or 2 or 3 or 4 = VICTORY

Here, Hog Heaven.

There are several other combinations. In our case, Ms. K makes three points: 1. Precedent shouldn't matter; 2. *Globe* is distinguishable; and

3. As a matter of public policy, agreements not to sue should be rejected. Fill in the blanks:

1 __ 2 __ 3 = VICTORY

Reading law, focus on both the points **and their relationship**.

A Review and an Assignment

To review the issues:

First Issue: In deciding Case Two, should the judge be at all concerned with what another judge did in *Globe*, the first case? In other words, should the courts of Paradise follow "precedent" or should they decide each case as if it were **a case of first impression?**

Pick a side and write out your argument. Writing deepens thought (Repetition Number 2) and be sure, in developing your own arguments, to anticipate those of your opponent (Repetition Number 3).

Of course, you need not do this. You can keep on reading, confident in the knowledge that, after bluffing, I will tell you the answer. If I do, and frankly I'm not sure if I will, then when you read it you will know something * * * at least for the next 15 minutes. Then you will probably forget it. From me, knowledge is lifeless and dead, something to be memorized and forgotten. From you, it is a triumph.

Second Issue: Assume that the judge in Case Two, after argument, decides that she will follow "precedent" and "treat like cases alike." Does the "rule" of the first case, *Globe*, ("exculpatory clauses do not offend public policy") **control** Case Two? It would, under the doctrine of Precedent, **if** the cases are "alike." But are they?

Here take the position of Ms. K. Prepare what you will say when you stand before the Judge, swallow once, and argue:

*"Your Honor, the Globe case is distinguishable on its facts from this case and hence this court need not apply the rule in Globe. The reasons Globe is distinguishable, the reasons it is not "alike" are as follows * * * "* (Fill in the blanks; that's the crucial part.).

Note: Arguing a case is distinguishable is basically the same as arguing that someone has taken a quote out of context: "Yep, they did say that, alright, but they said it in a very different context than the one we find ourselves in. Had they been in our situation, they would never have said that."

To distinguish a case, you must not only point to factual differences in the two cases but also point out why those factual differences should make a difference in the rule of law to be applied. For example, the names of the parties are different, but **so what**? (Thinking like a lawyer is more complicated than I indicated in the Prologue: in addition to "Yes, but," your little voice must be trained to repeat, and repeat, **"So what?"** whenever your big voice comes up with something it takes as quite profound.) "Your Honor, in *Globe* there was merely a financial loss; here we have a physical injury!"

All together now: "So what?!"

Third Issue: Assume that the judge is free to decide the Second Case as if it were the First Case, either because she rejects the notion of following precedent or because, accepting the notion of precedent, she finds *Globe* "distinguishable," not sufficiently "alike" Tenant's case to control it. (Reread that last sentence—particularly if you didn't do your math assignment. Don't just underline and think you "got" it.)

The math of it is:

(1 or 2) + 3 = Victory

Should courts ever disregard what the parties agreed to and hold that it is unenforceable? What are the pros and cons of complete "freedom of contract"?

At this point, **STOP!!!** Don't read the next chapter until you have written on the three issues. Looking ahead is cheating and, as you full well know, you wouldn't be cheating me * * * unless, of course, you stole this book.

CHAPTER 2

LEGAL ANALYSIS MADE SIMPLE

Well, not that simple. You got to read Chapter One first.

Ping Pong and the Law

In appellate argument, each side advances arguments that support their side and respond to arguments offered by their opponent. It is all quite dignified and borderline pompous (on this side of the Atlantic, however, we don't get wigs).

The best analogy is ping pong.

To illustrate, ping ponging the Second Case in the World would go something like this:

Landlord: *You can't sue me because, in the lease you signed, you promised not to sue me.*

Tenant: That's true enough. However, even though I made that promise, it should not be enforced because such promises, not to sue for harm caused by another's negligence, will encourage negligence. Hence such promises should be voided as against public policy.

Landlord: *That argument was made in Globe and the court rejected it. Exculpatory clauses are not against public policy and are enforceable.*

Tenant: *Globe* is distinguishable because it involved a financial loss and not a personal injury, and, second, *Globe* involved a contract signed by two business people while our case involves a landlord and a tenant.

Landlord: *Sure, there are factual differences between the two cases. But the rule of Globe should apply no matter the kind of injuries or the kind of contract. It establishes that the citizens of Paradise have the right to freedom of contract; what they agree to, short of illegality, will be enforced by the courts. There is no Big Brother in Paradise. The court in Globe stated, and here I quote, "the parties must be free to make their own contracts and once the courts start rewriting them there will be no end to it in sight."*

Tenant: I disagree; the facts of *Globe* are pivotal. It is one thing to agree not to sue for financial harm but quite another to agree not to sue for personal injury. The public has a great interest in preventing physical injury; allowing landlords to exempt themselves from liability will encourage them to be negligent, thus leading to more injuries.

And who the parties are is pivotal. *Globe* glorifies personal autonomy and well it should. However, unlike business folks dealing at arms length, what bargaining power do tenants have? Likely Ms. K never read the lease or, if she did, likely she would not have known that it meant that if the landlord caused her severe injuries, she could not sue. However, assume such knowledge. Could she have insisted the landlord change the term? No; she would have been forced to find another place to stay. Freedom of contract is based on the notion of free choice; here Ms. K had none.

Now when lawyers actually argue a case, they don't go back and forth like this; usually they get up and make all their points at one time. Not to worry— there is a chapter on Legal Argument later.

Note what happens when judges write their opinion. It's as if they thought of all the points themselves.

K v. Landlord

2 Para. Rptr. 1

Flintstone, J. This case involves the validity of an exculpatory clause in an apartment lease where the tenant is suing for personal injuries caused by the alleged neglect of the landlord. **While it is true** *that this court, in* **Globe***, upheld an exculpatory clause, we note that was in the context of a commercial contract and involved only financial loss.* **Even though** *we quite properly give contracting parties great freedom to fashion their own agreements, and* **despite the fact** *that we are fearful of where voiding such agreements will lead us, we feel we must invalidate this agreement. We note that there is inherent unequal bargaining strength between landlords and tenants and that, in this case, the tenant is seeking recovery for* *personal injuries. A landlord, under traditional doctrine, has a duty to take reasonable steps to keep common areas safe; if we allow landlords to escape this duty by the simple expedient of a standard lease term, physical injuries that could have been avoided will not be.*

Note that **legal writing is marked by words of contrast**:

On the one hand * * *

Although this is so, that is so

Even though * * *

However * * * .

While X is true, so is Y.

Judges write "down the middle." They collapse the competing arguments and often it is not clear which side made which argument. It's as if the judges made it all up themselves.

A character in Gilbert and Sullivan, who became the "Ruler of The Queen's Navy," sings of how he rose through the political ranks:

"I never thought of thinking for myself at all"

Judges are like this: **every case they cite, every point they make, they stole from one of the lawyers!**

[Ed. note: Professor Hegland wants to assure all judges, particularly those he might appear before, that he has the highest opinion of them. They have very difficult jobs. The notion that they "steal" points is simply an analytical ploy, not a value judgement.]

A great device to help you understand appellate decisions is to force yourself to figure out which party raised which point and why. To get a feel for this, go over the opinion in *K v. Landlord* and jot down the points Flintstone makes. Flintstone discussed:

Globe

commercial loss

freedom of contract

Then figure out which side made the point. Which side brought up *Globe* and why? Which side brought up "commercial loss" and why? Which side argued "freedom of contract" and why?

In short, deconstruct the opinion and restage the ping pong game.

An Aside on Judicial Thievery

It is a good thing, not a bad thing, that judges rest their decisions on points raised by the lawyers. This is a manifestation of the adversary system and its commitment to have all positions considered in the heat of battle.

Say that Judge Flintstone decided *K* on the basis of a point not argued by counsel. Assume that K's lawyer argued only the personal injury aspect and did not bring up the matter of unequal bargaining. Now, if Flintstone, on her own, after the case was submitted, thought up that point and decided the case upon it, it would not be fair to the landlord because the landlord would not have had the opportunity to argue against it. And it might lead to a bad decision because, without someone developing the contrary side, we don't really know how good the point actually is.

But, and here I use "Yes, but", on the other hand, if judges use only the arguments developed by counsel, injustice can result: Ms. K hired a dullard as a lawyer who overlooks key arguments. Should she lose a substantial case simply because she hired an incompetent?

The Third Case

Now we have two cases in Paradise, *Globe* and *K* and, in St. Paul, some smart Norwegians have just incorporated the West Publishing Company.

When the third case arises, it will be resolved by reference to the first two. Note that the second case did not **overrule** the first.

On Overruling and the Appearance of Permanence

Sometimes Courts overrule prior cases, come out and admit that they (or, more likely, their predecessors), got it wrong. The most famous overruling was in *Brown v. Board of Education* which overruled the "separate but equal" doctrine of *Plessey v. Fergeson* and held segregated schools to be unconstitutional.

Once a case is overruled, it can't even come to the party: had *K* overruled *Globe*, the third case in the world would be decided only in reference to *K*.

Courts are reluctant to overrule prior decisions—it is upsetting to their conservative nature and represents a big "in your face" to stare decisis. If their predecessors were wrong, why then ....

Courts prefer to "distinguish" prior cases. One of the real joys of law study is to note how the world changes while apparently, on the surface, it stays the same. The world of *Globe* was likely a world where giants walked the earth and stern judges let the chips fall where they may. The world of *K* is likely the world of judges committed less to freedom of contract and more to judicial intervention in the name of fairness. These are radically different worlds but to read the opinion in *K*, which merely distinguished *Globe*, no one would know it.

Now if Judge Flintstone had come right out and overruled *Globe*, "The doctrine of 'hands off' is wrong," then we could easily see that the world had changed. Clearly the world of *Brown v. Bd. of Education* is not the world of *Plessey*. But, because of judicial reluctance to overrule, it seems, on the surface, that the world remains pretty much the same.

Practice

Because *K* did not overrule *Globe*, both are still **good law**. To practice playing the Third–Case-in-the-World, I give you two cases:

A Paradise statute (Yes, Virginia, there are Legislatures in Paradise), provides that tenants must be given 30 day notice before they can be evicted. Joe, a single father earning a low wage, moved into an apartment house with his 2 children. He signed a lease waiving his right to 30 day notice. The landlord has brought an eviction action which could not be brought under the Paradise Statute. The Landlord asserts that the protection was waived.

Under *K* and *Globe*, who wins?

At a tyrannosaurus riding stable (this gets boring for me too), a rider (a lawyer) is eaten and the heirs bring suit based on the owners' negligence (they forgot to feed it). Needless to say, as part of the riding agreement the lawyer signed on that fateful day, there was a clause providing "Riders cannot sue for negligence."

Under *K* and *Globe*, who wins?

Case Synthesis

The process of putting two or more cases together is known as **"case synthesis."** You can expect to do a lot of it during your first year. A casebook will have a couple of cases, usually from different jurisdictions, which face the same general issue but which come to apparently different results.

"Consistent or inconsistent?" puffs the professor.

There will be a longing to make them consistent. Human beings (lawyers are not the only ones) hate inconsistencies. We long for a world that we can understand, a world that we can explain. William James once wrote of "our pleasure at finding that a chaos of facts is the expression of a single underlying fact" and that, in our chaotic world, "each item is the same old friend with a slightly altered dress."

> *Who does not feel the charm of thinking that the moon and the apple are, as far as their relation to the earth goes, identical; of knowing respiration and combustion to be one; of understanding that the balloon rises by the same law whereby the stone sinks.*

I recall reading an autobiography of someone who went to Harvard where he hoped to learn the Grand Generalization that Explains Everything.

How does a scientist reduce the world of complexity? By finding a "law" that explains apparently different phenomenon. An apple falls and the moon circles the earth: both are following the law of gravity. How do lawyers reduce complexity? By stating a rule of law that explains what appear to be inconsistent cases.

At the level of rule, *Globe* (exculpatory clauses are **valid**) is inconsistent with *K* (exculpatory clauses are **invalid**). But we can fashion a rule that explains both?

Exculpatory clauses are valid unless they relieve from physical injury liability and (or?) are signed by a party of unequal bargaining strength.

or

Exculpatory clauses are not valid unless they are signed by parties of equal bargaining strength and (or?) involve matters of financial, as opposed to physical, loss.

Neat. But we have paid a price. The longer the rule, the more cumbersome to apply and the less predictive it is. When there was but one case, *Globe*, we could have a short rule—"Exculpatory clauses are valid"—which could be easily applied because it applies to all contracts. It also had great predictive power: lawyers, knowing the rule, could advise clients: "Yep, they're valid." Now, with our new rule, with its "unless" and "and/or" clauses, things get more complicated: what exactly is meant by "physical injury" (does it include mental breakdown?) and when does a party have "unequal bargaining power"?

The rule can grow in complexity to the point where it explains nothing but the phenomenon and predicts nothing:

Exculpatory clauses are valid if one of the parties is named Globe and involves reporting on credit risk but are invalid if they appear in an apartment house lease and one of the parties is the sister of someone who once appeared in a Kafka novel.

This is akin to a law of nature describing what happened to an apple on Grandma's farm and to the moon on New Year's Eve. It doesn't take human understanding very far and doesn't get one tenure.

We are dealing with the dilemma of the general versus the particular. They more general a law is, the more cases it will apply to and the more people can plan their lives around it. However, the more general the law is, the more likely injustice will result: allow tenants to sign away their protection from physical injury.

A study tip: You will soon be "briefing" cases and one of the things a "brief" does is to state the "rule" of the case. The real art is in stating it somewhere between too general (always valid) and the too specific (K's sister). More of this later in the book.

Best of luck in life.

Pause to consider what happens if *K* and *Globe* are inconsistent. Oliver Wendell Holmes once said that to him law was simply a prophecy as to how a court will rule. If courts are inconsistent, then what becomes of the law? Will lawyers be able to predict what a court will do? Is it a matter of "sometimes yes, sometimes no"?

And what of a root notion of the common law system: that human reason can come to correct solutions? What happens if it gets out that human reason can come to inconsistent solutions?

Take a moment to figure out how the quest for consistency is motivated by the same desire as is the reluctance of courts to overrule prior decisions. Both are old friends, in slightly altered dress.

Know this, however. Making inconsistent cases consistent is great fun (akin to "Find 6 things wrong with this picture"). It will sharpen your analytical abilities: you will have to think real hard. However, don't be fooled. There are inconsistent cases out there: total understanding will continue to allude our grasp, even if we go to Harvard.

One last comment on inconsistency. Sometimes lawyers admit to the fact of inconsistent cases but quickly conceal the troubling implication that human reason can lead us to radically different conclusions. We slap a label on the inconsistent cases **(Majority Rule, Minority Rule)** and happily proceed as if all is right in our cozy world of reason.

Had scientists thought of this ploy, their lives would have been a lot easier too:

Laws of Nature

Majority Law: Apples fall.

Minority Law: Sometimes they don't.

Thus far we have looked at the Second and Third cases in Paradise. I hope that you have noticed that we are on some horrible regress. If we decided the third case based on the first two, and, if we decided the second based on the first, how is it possible ever to decide the first?

Which came first, the chicken or the egg?

The First Case in the World:
The Use of Hypothetical

Assume we have to decide whether to enforce an exculpatory clause and there are no cases, one way or the other. Woe is us.

Cases of "first impression" are decided upon **notions of justice and policy**. In *Globe*, the court put forth two justifications for its decision: furthering freedom of contract and avoiding "slippery slopes" ("if we void this term, then we don't know when we will stop rewriting contracts"). Later in this book, I will have a lot to say about "slippery slopes," none of it charitable.

As to "freedom of contract," note that it is a slogan. Behind it lies a whole range of philosophic and policy concerns, such as the commitment to individual autonomy and the economic theory that individual choice is the best mechanism to produce efficient allocations.

Note how Ms. K responds when "freedom of contract" is thrown in her face. Rather than simply admitting to her socialistic tendencies, she makes an end run and gets to the policies behind it:

> "Yes, freedom of contract is very important! But it doesn't apply to this contract as I didn't have any choice in the matter and 'freedom of contract' is premised on individual choice."

Two important practical lawyering tips here. First, it is often better to deflect your opponent's jabs rather than try to block them. That is to say, Ms. K admits to the importance of "freedom of contract" and argues it doesn't apply; that is a different kind of argument than one which denies the importance of "freedom of contract".

The second piece of practical wisdom, never admit you are a socialist.

Lawyers argue policies and justice; they often do so by putting **hypotheticals** and **arguing by analogy**. Let me show you how this works.

The issue in *Globe* is whether to refuse to enforce a contract provision. Can you think of a contract, or a provision in one, which, **obviously,** a court would refuse to enforce? **STOP!!!** Make up such a case before you see mine.

———————

My case of non-enforcement: A six-year-old promises to give his allowance, every week, to his big brother. No court is going to enforce that deal.

Now make up a contract which a court would **obviously** enforce.

What about a contract signed by two major corporations after months of negotiation by competent lawyers?

Now we have two cases, neither of which happened, but so what. The next step is to decide whether our case, the one involving the exculpatory clause, looks more like the kid's contract or more like the corporation's?

"Your Honor, this is basically like a case where a six-year-old agrees to give up his allowance; that agreement would not be enforced and neither should this one."

"No, Your Honor, it's more like an agreement between two corporations, one we would surely enforce. You should enforce this one as well."

How do we decide which it is more like? We articulate why the hypothetical cases are easy ones. Why, exactly, is the six-year-old an easy case? Once we understand that, then we can look and see if those reasons (policies) apply in the case at issue.

"We don't enforce kids' contracts because we don't think they know what they are agreeing to. Ms. K didn't know what she was agreeing to."

"No," replies the other side, "We don't enforce kid's contracts because we feel that they are not capable of understanding what they are agreeing to. Ms. K, as an adult, surely is capable of knowing what she agreed to; if she didn't take the trouble, that's not our concern."

What we have done is to make up an easy case and, by asking ourselves why it is easy, we have, in effect, written the supporting opinion. *We have created a new first case, along with its rationale. Presto, what was the First case now becomes the Second and we land safely on familiar ground.*

Neat trick.

As to the chicken/egg quandary, the egg came first, created a hypothetical chicken and the rest is history.

Or maybe, come to think of it, it could have been the other way around. I guess we still don't know the answer * * * but at least now we know how they did it!

On Trusting, but Testing, Your Intuitions

Don't be confused about law. While logic is important, intuition is key.

Split brain research suggests that the right side of the brain is the intuitive side: it sees relationships, creates moments and sings. Unfortunately, it has grunts for words. The left side is organized, logical and has a brilliant vocabulary: alas, it has nothing much to say, pretty much limited to such things as "Pass the salt."

Whether the research is correct or not, I think it is helpful in understanding how we think. Prize both your intuitions and your logic.

Facing a new problem, our mind throws out, "Gee, this is like X, an old problem I previously solved." This is the brain's right side, grunting. It is up to the left side, with its logic, to ask: "Oh yeah, how is X just like the new problem?" That way it can test and apply the intuition.

My sense is that law students either back off their intuitions ("Well, I guess it isn't like X") or dogmatically assert them ("It is too like X"). *Intuition is not the solution: it is an invitation to do the hard analysis needed to get to a solution.* Give your right side credit and have your left side get to work.

Further Thoughts on the Second Case: Statutory Construction

Statutory interpretation is a variation of The Second Case (**everything** is).

Assume a statute in the following form: "No vehicles in the Park." Ben, age 4, drives his Big-Wheel in the Park. Has he violated the statute?

Obviously the question turns on the meaning we attribute to "vehicle." Now had the rule been announced in a case, we would have the *facts* of the case to guide us. If the rule was announced in the context of a dispute over heavy trucks in the park, then we might conclude that the court, in using the word "vehicle," meant things of that ilk—things that could run people over and things which pollute the air and things that make loud noises. Ben's BigWheel does none of these things and hence is not that kind of "vehicle."

Note again: distinguishing cases is like arguing something is quoted out of context. "Sure, the Court said no 'vehicles' but that was in the context of discussing heavy trucks; surely the judges were not thinking in terms of BigWheels."

And, if the rule were announced in a case, we would have the court's *rationale or justification* to guide us. Assume the judges said:

> *Public safety, noise abatement and pollution control all require us to prohibit vehicles in the Park.*

We would then have some sense of how the judge was using the word "vehicle". Occasionally a judge might use language that resolves the case:

We stress that this does not include BigWheels.

or

We stress that this does include BigWheels.

Statutes come to us (usually) without facts and without rationale, they simply appear, like the ghost of Hamlet's father. How are we to resolve ambiguities that appear? But, before that, a few paragraphs on statutes and case law.

Both statues and case law are sources of law—judges must follow controlling statutes and controlling cases. As a general matter, statutes trump: legislatures can overrule the rules laid down in judicial opinions by simply passing a statute (unless the judicial rule rested on the United States Constitution, which trumps everything, or on the State Constitution, which trumps state law—but not Clubs). Judges can throw out statutes **only** if they contravene the Constitution.

To illustrate, if a court said "Exculpatory clauses in leases are valid," the legislature could change that result by simply passing a statute saying they were void. On the other hand, if the legislature passed a statute saying "Exculpatory clauses in leases are valid," a court **could not** change that rule unless it found it to be unconstitutional.

Bottom line, in terms of what you want to be when you grow up, if you want to change the world, become a legislator, not a judge. (This sentence entirely ignores the Civil Rights Movement and other great moments in our legal history but Nut-shell Writers have to make tough choices).

It is also worth noting that judicial and legislative styles differ. Courts **justify** their decisions in terms of precedent and/or reason. They do not simply announce rules. At least in theory, and I believe often in practice, they are not free to simply exercise their will; theirs is a limited power. Legislators, elected by the people and subject to ouster, simply pass statutes declaring rules. They generally do not feel compelled to state the reasons, at least in written form. In democratic theory, political decisions can be "irrational" as long as they are the majority's.

Returning to the question of how to interpret an ambiguous statute, our quest is to find the "legislative intent." **"Intent" is our quest when we interpret any language.** In a interpreting case, "When the judge stated the rule as X, what exactly did she intend?" In interpreting a contract, "When the parties said in the contract X, what did they intend?"

The first move is to look to **context** and we have seen a lot of that: judicial rules are announced in a specific factual context and justified by certain rationales. Often it is possible to find the context in which a statute was announced:

1. Sometimes there will be **legislative history** in which the legislature writes out what it has in mind.

2. Sometimes what appears to be an isolated statute was in fact a part of a larger legislative package. Perhaps "No vehicles in the Park" was part of a "Clean Air Act" and, if it was, one could argue that, in using "vehicles," the legislature intended only those that pollute the air.

3. Sometimes statutes amend prior statutes. If the old statute was "No cars or truck in the park," one could argue that, in substituting the word "vehicle," the legislature intended an inclusive definition.

In your Legal Research class, you will learn how to check out all of these possibilities. Here I want to assume that none bears fruit. All you have is "No vehicles in the Park." Does it include Ben's Big-Wheel?

Having successfully solved the chicken and egg problem, we know how to proceed. We **posit a legislature and then posit its purposes**.

Your Honor, the legislature must have intended, not only to abate noise and pollution in the park, but to prevent clutter and to protect public safety. A park filled with BigWheels is not a pleasure place for adults to be and BigWheels do in fact present a risk of injury.

Of course, the opposing lawyer would posit different legislative purposes.

As in the case of distinguishing cases, here too lawyers put **hypotheticals**:

Surely the statute would prohibit tanks (unless, perhaps, it was driven by a Presidential candidate). On the other hand, the statute would not prohibit a child's model truck. Which is the BigWheel more alike?

Why I am going on and on about this? Isn't my example simply an instance of bad legislative drafting? Okay, let's clear it up.

"No vehicles in the Park and this includes Big-Wheels!"

Ben drives his BigWheel in the Park and gets busted. Easy case? You don't know Ben.

He will argue: "My BigWheel was **on the road**, not **in the park** and the purpose of the rule is to prevent damage to lawns and flowers. The rule reads '*in* the Park' and not '*on* the road.' The very precision of the rule in other respects shows that the legislature was drafting very carefully. Besides, I had only *one* BigWheel. The rule specifically says 'BigWheel*s*'. Probably the rule was aimed against vendors or people putting on races. So there!"

Let the Legislature throw some more words at the problem; soon we will have an Internal Revenue Code—much too big to fit on a Yellow Sign. Park signs will read:

Warning: Certain rules may or may not apply. Read them!

Legal training is training in the fine art of finding ambiguities. You will be forced, again and again, to focus on the precise meaning of language.

We tend to read sloppy, skimming over language, getting its gist, assuming that close is good enough.

But law is written tight.

We tend to write sloppy too and this does not bode well. What lawyers do most is to write: briefs, contracts, bylaws and, yes, even statutes. Welcome our endless nitpicks and infuriating quibbles as vaccines against ambiguity in your own writing.

Everything we do, after all, is for you.

CHAPTER 3

THOUGHTS ON STARE DECISIS, RELATIVE VALUE AND ETHICS

The Mechanics of Stare Decisis

Several years ago a Juvenile Court judge in Florida was asked to decide the right of a surrogate mother to retain custody of her child. Paid to carry the father's baby to term, she changed her mind and wished to keep the child. The father filed an action to gain custody. It was the first such case ever, the ultimate case of first impression.

The press wrote as if the trial judge's decision would conclusively establish the respective rights of surrogate mothers nationally and for all time.

Not so.

Under the doctrine of **stare decisis**, courts are **obligated** to follow **only** the law set down by higher courts in their own state and those of the United States Supreme Court. These cases are known as **"controlling authority"** as opposed to **"persuasive authority**." (**"Primary"** authority are the cases and statutes themselves; **"secondary"** authority is what commentators say about them, in law reviews, in legal reference books, but not on talk radio). Trial courts in, say, Iowa **must** follow the law laid down by the Iowa Supreme Court; they are not obligated to follow the law as laid down by other state courts. Note that, even in Florida, the judge in the next courtroom could ignore the surrogate decision until it was affirmed by a higher Florida Appellate Court.

This does not mean the Florida decision would have no impact elsewhere. If a judge were faced with a similar case in Montana, the Florida decision could be cited as "persuasive" or "secondary authority". It is significant, but not conclusive, that a judge in Florida came to a particular decision. There are several sources of "persuasive authority" (things that lawyers can cite to judges in support of their positions): decisions from other states, statutes from other states, Restatements, law review articles, and state Bar journal articles. However, as I was forced to once tell an outraged first year student, not the *I Ching*.

The Philosophic Underpinnings

Herein we will take a quick look at natural law, relative value, and the conflict between the abstract and the concrete. Who said law isn't philosophic?

Why should courts follow precedent? Three possible justifications come to mind. First, the prior decision is "right" and it would be a waste of time to retry it: the next judge would decide the same way. This view rests upon a notion of natural law or, at least, on a view that human reason is constant and comes out the same way across peoples and times.

Second, even if the first decision wasn't "right," the new judge should follow it in order to allow people to plan their lives. Landlords will want to know whether exculpatory clauses will be enforced; if not, they will buy more liability insurance and perhaps raise rents.

Curiously, the view stressing the need for predictability rejects the philosophic underpinnings of the first: we need precedent because there is no natural law and human reason is arbitrary: without the doctrine of precedence, judges would be all over the lot and there could be no predictability.

The third justification goes to the effect of the doctrine on current decision making. Because the judges will realize that they are not only deciding the case before them, but cases to come after, they will tend to think in terms of universals, rather than specifics. The question will not be so much as what is fair between Ms. K and her particular landlord, but what is fair between all tenants and all landlords—what the judges decide will become precedent for future disputes.

Let's take a deeper look at these three justifications.

Universalization

There is always the chance that judges may cheat. They may find for Ms. K, for example, not on the merits of her case but because they don't like the race, or politics, or sexual orientation of the landlord. How can we prevent this from happening?

The philosopher Kant urged us to universalize our decisions. Decide not between Ms. K and her particular landlord, but choose between all tenants and all landlords. The doctrine of precedence forces this mindset and it does well in removing personal biases from decision making. But there is a downside (Yes ... but).

Justice may not reside in the abstract but only in the specific. This is a classical dilemma in the law. The more abstract a rule of law, the more work it can do, the more cases it can resolve. But should the same rules that govern nice tenants and nasty landlords be used to determine fights between nasty tenants and nice landlords? More broadly, should the same rules that determine controversies between widget merchants determine who wins surrogate mother battles?

Take mandatory sentencing. No doubt, when judges had wide discretion, some misused it and gave different sentences to blacks and to whites, to rich and to poor. To correct for this, legislatures adopted mandatory sentences: Armed robbery, 5 years. But this uniformity created its own injustices: the mentally handicapped individual who waves his pocket knife as he shoplifts a six-pack from his local convenience store.

5 years.

Predictability

Today most folks justify stare decisis, not on the basis that prior cases are somehow "right," but rather on the basis of predictability: people need to plan their lives. Why do we need stare decisis to achieve predictability? The argument is that, without it, judges would come out differently, some holding "X," others holding "not X." This argument, however, assumes that values are relative and that human reason cannot come to correct solutions. If people shared values and if human reason can lead people to correct solutions, there is simply no need for the doctrine of stare decisis. Judges, deciding each case as the first case, would all hold "X" (or hold "not X.")

Take exculpatory clauses in apartment house leases. If judges were free to decide the issue without reference to prior cases, would some uphold them and others throw them out? If they would generally come to the same conclusions, if the matter of whether such clauses are a good or bad idea is something other than the matter of whim, then we would not need a doctrine of stare decisis to assure predictability. Landlords, planning their lives, would simply know whether or not these clauses would be enforced.

We will return to the question of relative value momentarily. Note here, however, another soft spot in the argument that stare decisis is needed assure predictability: maybe it simply can't deliver it.

"The devil can cite Scripture for his purpose."

So Shakespeare tells us. If so, what is the good of Scripture?

We have already discussed how cases can be distinguished, how statutes can be interpreted. Given these techniques, can judges decide any case any way they want to? If so, then the whole house of cards comes crashing down: stare decisis cannot deliver on its promise of predictability.

In the case of Ms. K, the court **could have** enforced the lease she signed based on *Globe*. Once we have the decision in *K v. Landlord*, can lawyers safely predict whether such clauses will be enforced?

The degree to which cases and statutes control judicial behavior is a central jurisprudential (and practical) issue. The practical aspect is that lawyers are hated. They can never give a clear answer. "Will this clause be upheld if we litigate?"

"Maybe."

Thanks to modern research techniques, the unpredictability of law may be getting even worse. When the common law system of precedence was being developed, there weren't that many cases. Stroll in your law library: that is no longer true today. When you had a few cases **on point**, the system worked; when you have scores, it starts to break down.

Professor Grant Gilmore argued that the Restatement Movement and the Uniform State Law Movement stemmed from a breakdown of the case method—there were too many cases pointing in too many directions for it to work. Now we have Restatements of such things as Torts and Contracts—a group of law professors and leading practitioners sat down and distilled the common law rules (case rules) of their subjects. We also have Uniform State Laws such as the Uniform Commercial Code. It was written by the same kinds of folks and is adopted, modified or not, by state legislatures.

Now, with computer retrieval systems, research becomes cheap and easy and lawyers in San Diego can quickly access cases from Boston: the flood of relevant authority has expanded vastly. Who knows what eventful effect this will have on our system.

Natural Law, Right Answers

In discussing stare decisis with countless law students, none, never, once, said that courts should follow prior cases because those cases were "right." This is curious. We don't even consider the possibility of "natural law" or the possibility of human reasoning coming to correct solutions.

Ours is a world of relative value and power politics. We rejoice in debunking ideas and authorities, and love to point to political or psychological factors as the "real" reasons behind decisions. As undergraduates, we analyzed Marx in terms of Freud and Freud in terms of Marx.

It is difficult for us to believe that judicial decisions are "right" in any strong sense of the word. But others have so believed.

Once people believed in "natural law," that law somehow exists "out there", independent of us. Under this view, judges don't make law, they discover it. Scientists, after all, did not invent gravity. We don't buy this anymore. We believe that judges are not discovering the law; they are making it up as they go along.

The relationship between invention and memory/discovery, is a fascinating one. The child psychologist Jean Piaget wrote that children confuse invention and memory: they make something up and think that they are remembering it. Once my eldest son, then around four, declared that "Scientists know everything." When I asked how he knew, he replied, "God packed it there, like a suitcase."

But who is Piaget to say? Perhaps, as I sit here, typing away, I am not really creating these thoughts, these relationships; perhaps I am merely remembering them.

What do you think about this? What do you remember about this? Maybe there is more to the old way of thinking than we think. Maybe there are "inborn" ideas of justice which can be thought of as "natural law," that judges, thinking long and hard on a problem, discover, rather than "make up."

Evolutionary theory would tend to support the notion that the theory of relative value, at least that of radical relative value, is incorrect. People, all over the world, look pretty much the same; there is no radical relativism when it comes to body type. Although languages differ, people, all over the world, talk. From an evolutionary standpoint, would it make sense to allow the matter of morals to swing radically between: "Be nice to your kids" and "Steal their candy"?

It is very hard to get a good discussion going in law school over such topics as "fairness". Is it fair to enforce (or to refuse to enforce) exculpatory clauses? Some students think that these kind of discussions are doomed from the start: "Well, whether it is or isn't, that's just someone's opinion; values are relative so what's the use discussing them?" A curious twist on this argument is given by other students who view such discussions, not as a waste of time, but as occasions for ringing declarations of principle: "I think it is fair (or unfair) and that's that."

The root notion in both views is that nothing intelligent can be said about values. They are subjective, arbitrary and just matters of opinion. Careful thought and analysis will shed no light on them * * * they simply are and that's that.

A major argument in favor of relativism is the **fact** of relativism: that people have different values. Curiously, we don't throw up our hands and admit defeat when people disagree about matters of scientific truth.

> *"Well, folks in the middle ages thought the world was flat and that **proves** there is no truth about the shape of the world. The shape of the*

world is not worth talking about [or] I think it's flat and that's that."

Rather we assume that careful thought and careful observation can lead us to a true understanding of our physical world; we assume that you can be right or wrong about the shape of the earth.

The traditional rejoinder to this argument is "Yeah, well, that's science. Morals and ethics are different. Careful thought and observation don't help in these areas."

How do you know?

Everyone knows.

They also knew the world was flat.

My point is not necessarily that the doctrine of relative value is wrong. My point is that, even if it is correct, and all values are relative, careful thought can **help**.

First, even if long and careful analysis may never lead us to the "right" answer, it can expose "wrong" answers. Here the analogy to science helps. While there is doubt whether science can lead us to a perfect understanding of nature, there is no doubt that it can expose our errors. We were wrong when we thought the earth was flat. We were in error as to that even though we may never know if the earth is made up of atoms or quarks. We know that uncooked pork is not good for us even though the ideal diet may forever elude our palate.

Second, the quest's the thing. Professor Grant Gilmore, one of my heroes, believed that we will never understand the law. His analogy was to baseball: even if we knew all the rules, all the players, all the fans, we would not know baseball. Why? Because baseball isn't something you know, it is something you do. Law, thought Gilmore, is like that: ultimately, the law is not something that we know, but something that we do.

This is a rather dismal view for an academic to take: It's our job to **know** things. But, if Gilmore is right, that when it comes down to it, human understanding will fail.

Professor Arthur Leff, another hero, wrote of Gilmore's philosophy. Reluctantly he conceded that Gilmore may be right. Final defeat does not, however, entail despair. He writes, citing to the corpus of Grant Gilmore's work:

> *All right, all right, amen. But at least there is this: on the way to those final defeats, there are, at least for some, some beautiful innings.*

So ends our discussion of the doctrine of precedent, how it works and why we use it. I will close showing how your classroom experience teaches you how to operate the doctrine and then, as is so typical of law professors, tack on some questions of ethics that we probably won't get to.

On Legal Education

In the Prologue I told you that, in class, professors generally do not explain or supplement the assigned reading: they put you to work—in exploring the coherence, the assumptions and the implications of the assigned readings. Maybe now you will see why.

Assume the very first law school, the SNU College of Law (State of Nature University). Again, we have only one case, *Globe*. What the professor will do is to call on a student to recite the facts and law of the case. Now, rather than saying "How about that?" the professor will veer off into insanity.

"Freedom of Contract? What does that mean? What assumptions about humans, about the good life, does it rest on?"

"This was a credit report. What if it were an X-ray report?"

"Why shouldn't courts rewrite contracts? We know better than these people. We did better on the LSAT. Besides, they live in caves!"

The professor will ask questions and the students will mumble responses and it will never be clear whether the student was right or wrong or what the answer is and then, wham, the class is over and it is 15 pages for tomorrow.

"I don't get it. Are exculpatory clauses valid or not; I knew before class but, frankly, now, I couldn't tell an exculpatory clause from an English muffin."

Why do we do this to you? To teach you how to be a lawyer. Lawyers work with legal rules and doctrines: you must learn how to use them. Had you learned only the "law" of *Globe*, had Ms. K hired you, you would have given her incompetent advice: "Sorry, you signed an exculpatory clause and they are valid, now go home and suffer."

Some Matters of Ethics

Two remarkable things. Students who have graduated and have become lawyers,

1. Still talk to me, and
2. Find the hardest part of their practice is dealing with ethical problems.

In the hurly burly of law study, we tend to forget what it is to practice. Every now and then, put yourself in the role of a lawyer and ask yourself tough questions:

1. If a landlord comes and asks you to draft a form lease, do you automatically include an exculpatory clause (assuming they are legal in your jurisdiction)? Should you discuss the issue with the landlord, expressing your feelings about the propriety of the clauses?

2. Assuming exculpatory clauses have been held nonenforceable in your state, what if the landlord says "Draft one anyway. Maybe the courts will change their minds; in any event

most of my tenants don't know the law and won't sue."

3. Assume that exculpatory clauses are valid in your state. A landlord who has been quite negligent and whose negligence has seriously injured a tenant seeks your representation. Reviewing the store-bought lease, you find an exculpatory clause buried on the second page. Would it be proper for you not to raise the defense? If you do raise it, should you tell your not-too-bright opponent that similar clauses have been found invalid in other states?

4. Should you decide these issues yourself or should you do whatever the official lawyer ethics dictate?

Someday, out there, you will have to resolve these issues. Best to think about them now, before the crush of phone calls and memos.

*

PART 2

STUDYING LAW

In this part, I discuss the art of studying law. Chapter 4 answers the question "What should I be learning?" Believe it or not, this question haunts first year students throughout the first semester and, perhaps, even thereafter.

Chapter 5 suggests approaches to how you should read cases and gives you one to work on. The next chapter discusses how to brief cases and, it too, gives you one to work on. Do the work; you will most likely encounter both cases during your first semester Contract's class—you are only helping yourself.

Chapter 7 offers general study tips, from how to get the most out of class to study aids and outlining. Chapters 8 and 9 discuss law school exams. You will be given a typical exam question and then two model answers to analyze. You will then be invited to answer the question yourself as a way of practicing the fine art of legal writing.

Chapter 10 is therapy.

CHAPTER 4

STUDYING LAW: LOOKING BUSY IS NOT ENOUGH

Staying awake is the main thing. Law's difficult, sometimes boring. And there is a lot of it. The temptation to close up shop will be constant.

Stop it! Let me rest! Just underline for a while. I don't care. Use pens with different colored ink. Come back later and figure it out. Buy an outline. The person behind me has an outline. All these words. Where was I? How many more pages?

To determine the best way to study, begin with an idea of your goal. Let's put aside our loftier goals, those you wrote of on your law school application, and descend to the bottom of Maslow's pyramid: "My goal is to pass the test."

Fair enough.

Surprise Test

These are the most dreaded words in the English language, except, of course, "Tyrannosaurus just broke loose!"

Take this test **only if** you read the first three chapters, the ones about the first cases in the world.

If you haven't read those chapters, you have no business being here. Go back.

If not a typical law school exam question, what follows is definitely in the ballpark. Note (and appreciate) the attempt at humor. Read the question. What is the main issue? What factors might a court consider in resolving it?

Little Orphan Annie was a happy child, however, she had one problem: she had no dots in her eyes. Her rich friend, Daddie Warbucks, planned to give her enough money to pay for the operation (about $100,000). Unfortunately, he died.

But Warbucks had met with his lawyer, Mr. Quibble Weaver, and rewrote his will to provide Annie with $100,000. Alas, Quibble was negligent and made a mistake; after Warbuck's death, the will was thrown out. Annie got nothing. She was crushed and ended up suffering a mental and physical breakdown.

Annie now files suit against Attorney Quibble, seeking recovery for his neglect.

In the contract between Warbucks and Quibble, one finds the following clause:

"Daddy Warbucks agrees that he will not sue Quibble for negligence."

Assume that if the clause is binding on Warbucks, it would be binding on Annie.

Annie is suing both for the $100,000 Warbucks attempted to give her and $50,000 for mental and *physical injuries she suffered when she learned she would not be getting the money.*

Discuss.

Take about half an hour, maybe more. First, jot down your thoughts. Then write them out.

Don't blow this off: "Oh, that's easy ... I'll look ahead and see the answer."

On the other hand, don't freeze up: "I have no ideas; I can't do it." Yes, you can.

Discussion

I gave you this exercise to illustrate a very important point: **you learn law by struggling with it**, not by memorizing it, not by buying commercial outlines.

Previously we worked hard on the *Globe* and *K* cases. We were not trying to "learn" law; we were struggling to understand the cases: why did the judges come to the conclusions they did? The law we learned was a by-product of hard legal analysis.

When you read of Annie's plight, the **issue** of the validity of the clause jumped out at you. "Hey, is that enforceable? Maybe it isn't." You weren't "looking for" the issue and it wasn't on a checklist. It just suddenly appeared. That's what happens, when you have law in your bones.

Thinking about the issue, you recalled that sometimes the courts invalidate exculpatory clauses. But what times?

From the dark recesses of your mind came something about financial loss as opposed to physical injury. "There was a case that threw out the clause when the person was suing for physical injuries." How does that apply to Annie? Well, she is suing for financial loss and mental and physical suffering. Perhaps the clause would be valid for the financial and not the other.

Yes, but * * * (there goes your Little Voice), in the lease case, wasn't there something about unequal bargaining power? Well, how does that cut? On the one hand, Daddie Warbucks had a lot of bargaining power given his wealth. On the other hand, maybe the court would feel that the lawyer's expertise gave him the upper hand. Maybe a court would feel that lawyer/client relationship are always unequal. Why was it that courts were concerned with unequal bargaining and does that reason apply here?

You are well on your way to a very good answer, indeed, perhaps, a great answer. You "spotted" the issue and began to analyze it as would a court. **You are applying the law you learned to a new fact pattern: you will do this on exams and you will do this as a lawyer, day in, day out.**

Would the clause be enforced or not? We don't know. There are no right answers (except, of course, that there are no right answers).

A cartoon shows a teacher talking to a sheepish student standing forlornly at the head of the class. "Johnnie, there are no wrong answers.

But if there were, that would have been one of them."

On law exams, you **discuss** issues more than you **resolve** them. If you ever find yourself saying "Clearly, the plaintiff will win * * * " more than likely your are in deep trouble. More of this in the chapter on exams.

How did you learn the law? **By struggling with it** (**not** by sitting down and attempting to memorize it).

How can you, each night, maintain the struggle? How can you keep awake?

Teaching Yourself

Now you know what you must do: stay awake. What can you do to be involved with the material? What is likely to distract you? What's worked and what hasn't worked in the past? Spend a few minutes jotting down your ideas.

I want to involve you with this. If you can't be passive studying law, you can't be passive studying about studying it. You know about learning. It has probably been your main job up until now. Rather than asking me about how to study, you should be up in front of the room, acknowledging the warm applause, putting on the gold watch.

Everyone knows that the most important thing to learn is how to teach yourself. I have two suggestions. First, going into a new topic, realize that you probably already know something about it and then access that information. "What do I already know (about study techniques)? What don't I know? What would I like to know?"

Second, once you have completed a task, make a habit of reviewing it. How did it go? What could have gone better? After a few weeks of law study, and later, every now and then, step back and take a look at your study techniques. Do you feel that you are engaged with the material? Are you staying awake and struggling? If so, what are you doing right? If not, what's wrong?

To get you started on this life-long process of self-reflection, take a few minutes and think about what you learned from working with the surprise test. What did you learn about legal study? About how to approach exams?

Let me flag here what I think is central to the whole enterprize: **the need to write your thoughts**. To illustrate this, when I asked you to jot your thoughts about what study techniques worked for you in the past, most likely you didn't do it ... if it were me, probably I wouldn't have. I would have thought either one of two things:

"No, I really don't know much about studying, surely not very much about law study. I am going to keep on reading."

or

"That's an interesting idea. I bet I do know a great deal about studying. Let's see. Well, you should turn off the radio and get a good light. I'm sure I know a lot more than that but I want to

finish the chapter so now I'll stop doing my own work."

Take my word for it. Once you start writing, you will be amazed at how much you already know. Slow down. Think. Write. Think. Write.

Later I will give you some specific study tips. In the next two chapters, I want to stress the most important two: reading carefully and briefing cases.

CHAPTER 5

READING CASES

"Who's on first?"

"No, Who's on second."

"What?"

"What's on third!"

"Who's on third?"

"No. I already told you. Who's on second!"

Reading cases is like that. Figuring out who's who is sometimes impossible. ("No it isn't. Who's a ballplayer.") After great struggle it finally hits you that the plaintiff and the respondent aren't two different people; they are the **same** guy! ("Why didn't they just say so?") Another flash: "That must mean the defendant and the appellant are the same too." You write it down:

Plaintiff = respondent

Defendant = appellant

You have learned something! You stride confidently to the next case.

Bonkers. Now the plaintiff is the appellant and there is no respondent, only an "appellee".

Expect to reread a case several times to understand the basics:

Who is appealing?

On what theory?

Who wins and why?

What happens next?

Write it down and let's stride on.

I'm a basketball fan. A highly touted high school All–American comes to the University. After a few months, the coach is quoted as saying, "He's got great talent but he has to learn to play with intensity."

"Play with intensity? I've been playing with intensity for years. I can't play harder and better than this."

But he can ... and he will.

We all have levels of competence that we cannot ever fathom. With a good teacher, and hard work, we can amaze ourselves.

In your first weeks of law school you will work very hard and spend long hours struggling with the cases. You will read closely and with great care.

"I just can't read with greater concentration."

But you can ... and you will.

At first you will read cases as short stories, get their drift, lament or celebrate their result and then close up shop. But cases are not short stories: they are legal constructions that you must tear apart.

What follows is a rather famous case, known as *Walker–Thomas*. I want you to read it and then answer some questions about it. Part of the difficulty you will encounter in reading cases is that you will meet with a new vocabulary and come across procedures that you are unfamiliar with. To help you in this regard:

— **Appellee** (also known as **respondent**) is the party who is responding to the appeal. That party won the point in the **court below**. The party taking the appeal, the loser below, is the **appellant**.

— For the District of Columbia, Congress acts as would a state legislature. That is why we will see it dealing with a contract law question, usually a matter left to the states.

— The **Uniform Commercial Code**, the **UCC**, is a code written by various experts covering, among other things, the subject of **sale of goods**. That Code covers much (but not all) of the same ground as the **common law** (court made law) of contracts. Most states, and as you will see, Congress for the District of Columbia, have adopted the UCC.

— **Statutes trump common law**: once you have a statute covering an area, it is the primary source of law.

With these things in mind, read *Walker–Thomas*.

WILLIAMS v. WALKER–THOMAS FURNITURE CO.

U.S. Court of Appeals, District of Columbia Cir., 1965.
121 U.S.App.D.C. 315, 350 F.2d 445.

J. SKELLY WRIGHT, CIRCUIT JUDGE. *Appellee, Walker–Thomas Furniture Company, operates a retail furniture store in the District of Columbia. During the period of 1957 to 1962 each appellant in these cases purchased a number of household items from Walker–Thomas, for which payment was to be made in installments. The terms of each purchase were contained in a printed form contract [which provided that] in the event of a default in the payment of any monthly installment, Walker–Thomas could repossess the item.*

*The contract further provided that "the amount of each periodical installment payment * * * **shall be credited pro rata on all outstanding bills** * * * ." Emphasis added. The effect of this rather obscure provision was to keep a balance due on every item purchased until the balance due on all items, whenever purchased, was liquidated. As a result, the debt incurred at the time of purchase of each item was secured by the right to repossess all the items previously purchased by the same purchaser * * *.*

On April 17, 1962, appellant Williams bought a stereo set of stated value of $514.95 [1] *She * * **

1. *At the time of this purchase her account showed a balance of $164 still owing from her prior purchases. The total of all the*

defaulted shortly thereafter, and appellee sought to replevy all the items purchased since December, 1957. The Court of General Sessions [the trial court] granted judgment for appellee. The District of Columbia Court of Appeals [the first level appeals court] affirmed, and we [top dogs] granted appellants' motion for leave to appeal to this court.

Appellants' principal contention, rejected by both the trial and the appellate courts below, is that these contracts, or at least some of them, are unconscionable and, hence, not enforceable. [T]he District of Columbia Court of Appeals explained its rejection of this contention as follows:

Appellant's argument presents a more serious question.

The record reveals that prior to the last purchase appellant had reduced the balance in her account to $164. The last purchase, a stereo set, raised the balance due to $678. Significantly, at the time of this and the preceding purchases, appellee was aware of appellant's financial position. The reverse side of the stereo contract listed the name of appellant's social worker and her $218 monthly stipend from the government. Nevertheless, with full knowledge that appellant had to feed, clothe and support both herself and seven children on this amount, appellee sold her a $514 stereo set.

We cannot condemn too strongly appellee's conduct. It raises serious questions of sharp practice

purchases made over the years in question came to $1,800. The total payments amounted to $1,400.

and irresponsible business dealings. A review of the legislation in the District of Columbia affecting retail sales and the pertinent decisions of the highest court in this jurisdiction disclose, however, no ground upon which this court can declare the contracts in question contrary to public policy * * *. We think Congress should consider corrective legislation to protect the public from such exploitive contracts as were utilized in the case at bar.

We do not agree that the court lacked the power to refuse enforcement to contracts found to be unconscionable. In other jurisdictions, it has been held as a matter of common law that unconscionable contracts are not enforceable. While no decision of this court so holding has been found, the notion that an unconscionable bargain should not be given full enforcement is by no means novel. In **Scott v. United States**, *79 U.S. (12 Wall.) 443, 445, 20 L.Ed. 438 (1870), the Supreme Court stated:*

*" * * * If a contract be unreasonable and unconscionable, but not void for fraud, a court of law will give to the party who sues for its breach damages, not according to its letter, but only such as he is equitably entitled to. * * * "*

Since we have never adopted or rejected such a rule, the question here presented is actually one of first impression.

Congress has recently enacted the Uniform Commercial Code, which specifically provides that the court may refuse to enforce a contract which it finds to be unconscionable at the time it was made. 28

D.C.Code § 2–302 (Supp.IV 1965). The enactment of this section, which occurred subsequent to the contracts here in suit, does not mean that the common law of the District of Columbia was otherwise at the time of enactment nor does it preclude the court from adopting a similar rule in the exercise of its powers to develop the common law for the District of Columbia. In fact, in view of the absence of prior authority on the point, we consider the congressional adoption of § 2–302 persuasive authority for following the rationale of the cases from which the section is explicitly derived. Accordingly, we hold that where the element of unconscionability is present at the time a contract is made, the contract should not be enforced.

Unconscionability has generally been recognized to include an absence of meaningful choice on the part of one of the parties together with contract terms which are unreasonably favorable to the other party. Whether a meaningful choice is present in a particular case can only be determined by consideration of all the circumstances surrounding the transaction. In many cases the meaningfulness of the choice is negated by a gross inequality of bargaining power. The manner in which the contract was entered is also relevant to this consideration. Did each party to the contract, considering his obvious education or lack of it, have a reasonable opportunity to understand the terms of the contract, or were the important terms hidden in a maze of fine print and minimized by deceptive sales practices? Ordinarily, one who signs an agreement without full knowledge of its terms might be held to assume the risk that he has entered a one-sided bargain. But when a party of little bargaining power, and hence little real choice, signs a commercially unreasonable contract with little or no knowledge of its terms, it is hardly likely that his consent, or even an objective manifestation of his consent, was ever given to all the terms. In such a case the usual rule that the terms of the agreement are not to be questioned should be abandoned and the court should consider whether the terms of the contract are so unfair that enforcement should be withheld.

In determining reasonableness or fairness, the primary concern must be with the terms of the contract considered in light of the circumstances existing when the contract was made. The test is not simple, nor can it be mechanically applied. The terms are to be considered "in the light of the general commercial background and the commercial needs of the particular trade or case." Corbin [the academic guru of contract law] *suggests the test as being whether the terms are "so extreme as to appear unconscionable according to the mores and business practices of the time and place." We think this formulation correctly states the test to be applied in those cases where no meaningful choice was exercised upon entering the contract.*

Because the trial court and the appellate court did not feel that enforcement could be refused, no findings were made on the possible unconscionability of the contracts in these cases. Since the record is not sufficient for our deciding the issue as a matter of law, the cases must be remanded to the trial court for further proceedings.

So ordered.

————————

Discussion

If you were reading the case with the intensity that is required (and the intensity that you are capable of), you would be able to answer the questions that follow with at most a quick glance back to the case for reference. I don't expect that you will be able to do so now; in fact I hope you can't; if you can, I told the basketball story to the wrong person!

1. What was the precise issue before this court?

2. Which side cited the case of *Scott v. United States*. What argument was made based upon that case?

3. Why didn't the court simply apply the UCC to this case? Congress had passed it and made it the law.

4. What argument did the store make based upon the fact that Congress passed the UCC?

5. Assume that a customer proves that he had "no meaningful choice" in agreeing to a certain term in a contract because every store in his area had the same contract term in their contracts. Under the doctrine of **unconscio-**

nability as developed by the court, would that customer win?

Reread the case to find the answers.

Reading law is a skill, one which must be developed. Seldom do you have to read with such great attention. As my colleague Dan Dobbs says, you must read with the same intensity as you would read a difficult poem, a scientific report or a mathematical proof. Usually, when we read, we are passive; it's like watching television (although we feel more self-righteous). Reading judicial opinions, you must be an active participant; you must take them apart and turn the materials in your own hands.

No doubt I have caused a minor panic: "I'm supported to learn all that from each case? Like who cited which case?"

No ... you're not!

I am talking about the care with which you must read cases; I am **not** talking about what you want to take away from a case; that is the subject of the next chapter on case briefing. A careful reader would know, as she read along or with a moment's reflection, which side cited *Scott* and for what purpose; a careful reader would not, however, try to "learn it". Who cited *Scott* in terms of legal doctrine doesn't matter.

Are you going to insist on answers?

1. The precise issue was whether the courts of D.C. had the **power** to refuse to enforce parts of contracts if they were **unconscionable**. The court below didn't think it had the power. This case **does not** decide whether the particular clause was unconscionable; the case is sent back to the lower court to make that determination.

2. The customers cited *Scott* in support of their argument that the courts have an inherent power to refuse to enforce contracts, at least not to their "letter," if they are "unconscionable."

   A somewhat plausible "wrong answer" would be that the store cited *Scott* for the proposition that the courts enforce, even if not to their "letter," unconscionable contracts. The problem with this answer is that the store, given the tenor of the lower court opinion, knows that the "letter" the court would refuse to enforce is the clause in question.

3. The court couldn't just apply the UCC to the case because the contracts in question were signed **before** the UCC was passed. Statutes, generally, cannot have **retroactive effect**.

   This raises a fascinating jurisprudential issue: Congress can't retroactively change the rules on Walker–Thomas ("unconscionable contracts will not be enforced") but, apparently, the courts can ("unconscionable contracts will not be enforced"). To save us from this embarrassment, we might argue that the common law in D.C. always had a doctrine of unconscionability; never mind that no one knew about it.

But what happens when a court overrules prior decisions. Aren't they changing the rules, upsetting apple carts, **retroactively**? Ask your profs.

4. This one is harder because you must **infer** the Store's argument. The Store uses Congress' passage of the UCC to make the argument that, prior to its passage (and when the contracts were signed), the courts of D.C. **could not** refuse to enforce contracts on the basis of unconscionability: if they already could, why would Congress have to pass the UCC?

Note here the **reversibility** of many legal arguments. The court, adopting something of an "in your face" style, writes:

> *The enactment [of the UCC] * * * does not mean that the common law of the District of Columbia was otherwise at the time of enactment.* ***In fact*** * * * *we consider congressional adoption persuasive authority for following the rationale of the cases from which the section is explicitly derived.*

5. To show a contract provision unconscionable, the customer must show **both** lack of meaningful choice **and** terms unreasonably favorable to the other party.

> *Unconscionability has generally been recognized to include an absence of meaningful choice on the part of one of the parties* ***together with*** *contract terms which are unreasonably favorable to the other party.*

It is critical that you focus on the relationship between elements. In our prior math notation, this is a 1 + 2 = victory, not a 1 **or** 2 = victory.

A Few Tricks to Reading Closely

1. First, figure out what the **issue** is: what legal point must the court decide in order to resolve the case?

2. Be clear on the basics:

   What happened in the court below?

   Who is appealing?

   On what theory?

   Who wins and why?

   What happens next?

3. As to each case cited, and as to each argument the judges make, ask **"Who did they steal that one from?"** Remember that judges don't think for themselves at all. Who cited the case to the court and for what purpose? This question forces you to restage the ping pong game that legal argument is.

4. Be clear about the **relationship between arguments and between elements**. If the court is making two points, the relationship can be:

$$1 + 2 = \text{Victory}$$

   or

$$1 \text{ or } 2 = \text{Victory}$$

   Again, to prevail on unconscionability, the customer must show "lack of meaningful choice" **and** "unreasonable terms": one is not enough.

5. **Play loser.** Pretend you are the lawyer representing the losing side in the case and that the court's opinion is simply your opponent's argument. How will you respond to it?

Often opinions seem so clearly right that we ask ourselves, "Why did the losing side even bother?" **Always remember that the losing side thought that it would win!** Judicial opinions are **"winners' history."** To recall a previous concept, they are the **Yes**: play the part of the losing side and fill in the **but**.

CHAPTER 6

BRIEFING CASES

In law school, you "brief" cases. That sounds mysterious, difficult and terribly grown-up. I recall, on my first day in Junior High, being told by one of the Big Kids:

"Everyday, and I mean everyday, you have to bring a pencil."

Oh well ... one of these days ....

Now I want you to brief a case.

"You can't do that. You haven't told us **how**!"

A better point: I haven't told you **why**.

You brief cases partly for the same reason you take notes, **to review** later on. Given the large number of cases you will read, ***brevity will be a virtue***. However, the main reason you brief cases is to force yourself to grapple with them, to reduce them to their core. Brief well and you will **understand.**

Case briefing is a brilliant educational device.

Of course you want to learn the "law". As we have seen, however, the "law" is more than the blackletter statements of rules ("exculpatory clauses are valid"). The law, according to Justice

77

Holmes, is a prophecy of how a court will resolve a particular controversy. Will the court apply the rule "Exculpatory clauses are valid"? We don't know unless we know something of the **factual context** in which the rule was announced and the **rationales** offered for it. Recall the "surprise test" in the last chapter. You could not simply apply the "rules" of *Globe* and of *K v. Landlord*; you had to get behind the rules, to facts and rationales, to see how they would apply in the case of Little Orphan Annie.

At its core, a case is **rule, facts, rationale.** The traditional briefing format uses these categories of analysis:

1.   Statement of Facts
2.   Issue/holding (the "rule" which emerges)
3.   Rationale

For a model, take a look at the "brief" of *Globe* in the first chapter, pages 12–13.

You don't need to know anymore; no more excuses; time to brief a case.

The case you will brief is a classic. Written by a famous judge, Justice Cardozo, whose prose helps a case. It involves a marvelous character, Lucy, Lady Duff–Gordon (who is seen, alas, not at her finest). Lucy was a very "high profile" designer and, leading the way for today's superstars, was one of the first to endorse products. Whether she was a role model is lost in the historical record. She did, however, survive the Titanic (whether there were self-congratulatory T–Shirts is also lost in the sands of time).

But we are not here to gossip.

To help you understand the case, one piece of background. As you will learn in your Contracts course, there is a doctrine called "mutuality of obligation" which requires that both sides to a contract must be bound or **neither is**. In this case Lucy, who is the defendant, made a promise to Wood, who is the plaintiff. She broke her promise to Wood and defends on the basis of "mutuality of obligation":

"I may have made a promise but Wood never promised me anything. If you look at what he 'promised,' he wasn't bound to do anything at all. Because he didn't have to live up to his promise, I don't either."

Your brief shouldn't be more than a page. Follow, for now, the traditional format. After you have done the brief, we'll critique it together.

WOOD v. LUCY, LADY DUFF–GORDON

New York Court of Appeals, 1917.
222 N.Y. 88, 118 N.E. 214.

CARDOZO, J. *The defendant styles herself "a creator of fashions." Her favor helps a sale. Manufacturers of dresses, millinery, and like articles are glad to pay for a certificate of her approval. The things which she designs, fabrics, parasols, and what not, have a new value in the public mind when issued in her name. She employed the plaintiff to* help her to turn this vogue into money. He was to have the exclusive rights, subject always to her approval, to place her indorsement on the designs of others. He was also to have the exclusive right to place her own designs on sale, or to license others to market them. In return she was to have one-half of "all profits and revenues" derived from any contracts he might make. The exclusive right was to last at least one year from April 1, 1915, and thereafter from year to year unless terminated by notice of 90 days. The plaintiff says that he kept the contract on his part, and that the defendant broke it. She placed her indorsement on fabrics, dresses, and millinery without his knowledge, and withheld the profits. He sues her for the damages, and the case comes here on demurrer.

The agreement of employment is signed by both parties. It has a wealth of recitals. The defendant insists, however, that it lacks the elements of a contract. She says that the plaintiff does not bind himself to anything. It is true that he does not promise in so many words that he will use reasonable efforts to place the defendant's indorsement and market her designs. We think, however, that such a promise is fairly to be implied. The law has outgrown its primitive stage of formalism when the precise word was the sovereign talisman, and every slip was fatal. It takes a broader view today. A promise may be lacking, and yet the whole writing may be "instinct with an obligation," imperfectly expressed (Scott, J., in McCall Co. v. Wright, 133 App.Div. 62, 117 N.Y.S. 775; Moran v. Standard

Oil Col., 211 N.Y. 187, 198, 105 N.E. 217). If that is so, there is a contract.

The implication of a promise here finds support in many circumstances. The defendant gave an exclusive privilege. She was to have no right for at least a year to place her own indorsement or market her own designs except through the agency of the plaintiff. The acceptance of the exclusive agency was an assumption of its duties. Many other terms of the agreement point the same way. We are told at the outset by way of recital that:

"The said Otis F. Wood possesses a business organization adapted to the placing of such indorsement as the said Lucy, Lady Duff–Gordon, has approved."

The implication is that the plaintiff's business organization will be used for the purpose for which it is adapted. But the terms of the defendant's compensation are even more significant. Her sole compensation for the grant of an exclusive agency is to be one-half of all the profits resulting from the plaintiff's efforts. Unless he gave his efforts, she could never get anything. Without an implied promise, the transaction cannot have such business "efficacy, as both parties must have intended that at all events it should have." Bowen, L.J., in the Moorcock, 14 P.D. 64, 68. But the contract does not stop there. The plaintiff goes on to promise that he will account monthly for all moneys received by him, and that he will take out all such patents and copyrights and trademarks as may in his judgment be necessary to protect the rights and articles affect-

ed by the agreement. It is true, of course, as the Appellate Division has said, that if he was under no duty to try to market designs or to place certificates of indorsement, his promise to account for profits or take out copyrights would be valueless. But in determining the intention of the parties the promise has a value. It helps to enforce the conclusion that the plaintiff had some duties. His promise to pay the defendant one-half of the profits and revenues resulting from the exclusive agency and to render accounts monthly was a promise to use reasonable efforts to bring profits and revenues into existence. For this conclusion the authorities are ample.

*The judgment of the Appellate Division should be reversed * * *.*

Discussion

Before you can begin to brief a case, you must read it all, probably more than once. Never just start writing; you must think long and hard about a case before you begin to brief it.

Focus first on **"issue/holding"**. Without knowing what the fight is about, you won't know what facts are significant. What **issue** must the court resolve to decide the case? How the court resolves the issue its **holding**. (The "holding" is also known as "the rule of the case" and, occasionally, as the "blackletter.")

Unfortunately, usually courts don't come right out and tell you what the focal point is. Sometimes they do: "The issue we have to resolve is * * * "or "We therefore hold that * * *." When they do, hog heaven. But generally they don't; you have to root around some. (Sorry for the imagery).

In *Lucy*, the issue was whether the court would imply a promise on the part of Wood to use "reasonable efforts" in marketing Lucy's endorsements. Under the "mutuality of obligation" doctrine, if that promise was not implied, Lucy would not be held to her promise. The court **held** that the promise would be implied and thus Lucy would be held to her promise.

There is no magic way of stating the issue/holding. Good lawyers can differ as to their statements of it. For your purposes, what you want to come away with is the notion that, sometimes, courts can imply promises to save ("create"?) contracts and that *Lucy* is one such instance.

> **Issue**: Should the court imply a promise of reasonable efforts to make the contract valid?
> **Held**: Yep.

Take a look at the issue that you stated. Does it come close to stating the main fight? Coming close is, in this business, a cigar.

Knowing the issue, you can tackle the "Facts". What key facts led the court to decide the issue as it did? Some folks call these the **"operative facts"** and we will too.

You are already very familiar with the notion of operative facts: they are the facts used to distinguish a case. The court in *K v. Landlord* distinguished *Globe* on the facts of *Globe*: it involved a financial loss and the agreement was between people of equal bargaining strength.

While reasonable folks can argue as to which facts are operative, we can all agree that some are not: that Lucy designed parasols, that the contract was dated a certain date or, alas, that her favor helps a sale. Reread your statement of facts: have you included things that don't matter? Things that played no part in the court's decision?

To include the kitchen sink, is a sin worse than simply taking up space; it shows that you are not concentrating on the case.

Does it matter that Wood promised to "account monthly"? Is it an operative fact? If he hadn't made that promise, would the court still have implied the promise of "reasonable efforts"? I think so. As I don't think the court's decision would have been different, I don't think "monthly accounting" was an operative fact.

But who am I to say? Perhaps, down the road, a court might distinguish *Lucy* on that very basis. As you may recall, what is, and what isn't, an **operative fact** is very much at issue in applying and distinguishing cases.

Given uncertainty as to centrality (Ed. note: Great phrase), there may be a tendency to err on the side of inclusion. Don't; it's too easy. "Well

I'm not sure if that fact matters, so I'll put it in." Do the work now: "Is this fact important or isn't it?" If you can't decide now, you won't be able to decide when you review.

You brief cases, not to get them right, but as a way of forcing yourself into the thick of things. You may go to class and discover that others (alas, perhaps the Prof) saw things different-ly, saw things that you took as collateral as pivotal, and things you thought central as not being worthy of mention. **No matter**. By forcing yourself to work hard on the question "Which facts matter?", you are becoming a lawyer.

If you are simply writing "facts" down, **you ain't briefing**.

The court's **rationale** are those reasons it gives in support of its decision. Sometimes they are somewhat hidden: courts don't always say "We are doing this for the following reasons." Again, you may have to root around.

In *Lucy*, the court's rationale seems to go to the common sense notion that, "Come on, the parties obviously intended that Wood would sing for his supper." Sometimes a court will wax philosophical rather than lyrical. In *Globe*, we read of "freedom of contract" and we saw how Ms. K attempted to distinguish *Globe* on the basis of its rationale: "Sure, freedom of contract is a great thing, but I had no choice."

Perhaps a good way to think of a brief is:

We decided X (holding) because

1. Operative facts and

2. Good reasons (rationale).

Use the formula in checking your briefs. If you apply, it you may find some strange constructions:

We decided to imply a promise of "reasonable efforts" on Wood's part **because** Lucy designed parasols.

That is all I can say about briefs. The rest is work. Your work.

Okay, a few more points.

Try putting the issue/holding **first**. The traditional format, Facts, Issue, Rationale, makes little sense. You only know which facts are important if you know what issue is to be decided. Let's say the issue is "Is Lucy a woman of few talents?" Now what had been just an interesting tidbit becomes the smoking gun.

We decided that Lucy was a woman of many talents **because**, among other things, she designed parasols.

Good legal writing always involves the **interplay of law and fact**. Never have long recitations of the "facts": always ground them in the law. Never have long discussion of "law": always ground it in facts. It should always be clear to the reader (and to you) why you are discussing a particular legal principle or a particular fact. The way to achieve this clarity is to ground *facts in law* and *law in* *facts*. When you are discussing law or fact, ask **"So what?"** This will take you to ground.

Discussing the court's rationale, **don't copy**. Some students simply copy (or closely paraphrase) what the court had to say. Unless you put a doctrine in your own words, there is no guarantee that you understand it.

> *The law has outgrown its primitive stage of formalism when the precise word was the sovereign talisman, and every slip was fatal. It takes a broader view today. A promise may be lacking, and yet the whole writing may be "instinct with an obligation," imperfectly expressed.*

I don't care how many times you underline that, how many times you copy it over. To understand it, you simply must try to express it in your own words. What does it mean? Talk about "imperfectly expressed"!

I know: you have a lot to do and the case does seem to be going on and on and maybe this weekend you can get back to it . . . .

One possible exception to "no copying" is when a case turns on specific statutory (or Restatement) language. Because statutes are drafted with precision, each word tells, and copying the actual words of the statute will increase your attention.

Is it important to include the date of a case and the name of the judge? Is the procedural history of the case important?   And what of this distinction between *dicta* and *holding*?

Aside on Holding and Dicta

Holdings are statements of law necessary for the decision in the case; *dicta* are statements of law which aren't necessary for that decision.   Take the case of *Brown v. Finney* which involved two men meeting in a bar and, after a few drinks, making a supposed contract for the sale of coal.   The evidence disclosed that the seller may have been joking.   The appellate court reversed the judgment for the buyer on the basis that the jury should have been instructed that if the seller was joking he should not be held to the contract.   Suppose, in the course of that opinion, the court stated:

> We reverse this case on the basis that the jury should have been instructed as to the issue of seriousness.   We also note that intoxicated persons do not have contractual capacity.

Was the statement about intoxication necessary for the court's decision?

No, it wasn't.   The court reversed on the seriousness issue. Compare the situation where the court reverses on the intoxication issue:

> We reverse this case on the basis that the jury should have been instructed that if one of the parties was intoxicated at the time the contract was made, that party cannot be held to it.   We also note that persons who are not serious at

the time of the contract can defend on those grounds.

Here the **holding** is the intoxication point, the **dicta**, the seriousness point.

Why do we split these hairs?

It has to do with the doctrine of **stare decisis**. When something is really at issue, when the case turns on it, likely the court thinks long and hard before deciding. Compare to that a statement of law that has the quality of "Oh, by the way, did you know that * * *."

Dicta is not ("are" not, for you real hair splitters) worthy of the same respect because it is not ("they are not") the product of serious thought; nothing in the case turned on them.

Thus, in a case after *Brown*, a drunk, wobbly on his feet, slurs:

Your Honor, *Brown* is a controlling decision here. It says "Intoxicated folks don't have the capacity to contract." So there! I win! Let's celebrate! Drinks on me!

Here, "My Learned Opponent" stands and with great sobriety, sneers:

This court is not obligated to follow the statement in *Brown* that "Intoxicated persons do not have contractual capacity." It is merely dicta. It was not necessary for the decision in that case. Brown involved pranksters, not drunks. It held that pranksters should be able to get out of their contracts. Its comments about drunks are totally beside the point. Hence this court is not obligated to follow the statement in Brown.

Such stark realities drove our friend to drink in the first place.

For a law student, the distinction between holding and dicta is a useful analytic ploy. Which statements of law are absolutely necessary for the result reached? Which are not. However once you determine something is dicta, don't skip it. Much of the law you will learn will come from judicial asides. Both drunks and pranksters have defenses.

Back to briefing.

_____

Citation and Dates: should they be included?

A typical caption might be:

BROWN v. FINNEY

Penn. Supreme Court 1866.
Opinion by Judge Tompson.

Is this information necessary in your brief?

No, hardly ever. It won't help you review and does not further your understanding of the case.

If you were citing *Brown* to a judge in an actual case, the information *might* be important. Like the pigs of *Animal Farm* (I seem to have a pig thing in this chapter), some courts are more equal than others. In the development of common law principles, for example, the New York Court of Appeals (the highest state court in New York) with Justice Cardozo and the California Supreme Court under Justice Traynor led the way. Opinions of those courts carry particular weight. (To continue the animal metaphor, I'm not letting the cat out of the bag by suggesting that the 1866 Pennsylvania Supreme Court was not such a court; even if I am, it is too late as the horse is already out of the barn).

In Constitutional Law courses, it's interesting to see how a particular Justice's philosophy plays out in several areas. However, in most courses, who wrote the opinion is of little interest.

Dates are important *if* you are studying the historical development of a particular legal doctrine. Sometimes you are. *Usually* you aren't. Most cases are included in casebooks not to show you what the law **was** but to show you what the law **is**. The "Rule" of *Brown v. Finney* is as good (or as bad) today as it was in 1866.

An aside and a lament. Legal education has been justly criticized for its ahistonical approach. The sense the student gets from reading old cases as current law is that the problems facing the law have always been the same and that the law itself is above history, that it is the product of neutral rational principles rather than the clash of competing philosophical, economic and political positions.

Science is taught that way as well. The text will present a scientific problem and trace the path leading to its ultimate (our) solution. There will even be a picture of Sir Isaac Newton. Thus it appears that scientists have always been working on the same problems that we find of interest. Not so. Did you know that Newton was an alchemist? And that alchemy wasn't as silly as it seems today? If you could turn metal into gold, turn impermanence into permanence, you might be able to eventually achieve immortality.

"Science" has not always focused our concerns; scientists are influenced by their times and their politics. Why, for example, in our own day, has so little work been done in developing male contraceptives? The way science is taught, and the way law is taught, conceals the politics.

As to the law's neutrality, Oliver Wendell Holmes, in his great essay, "The Path of the Law" (10 Harv.L.Rev. 457, 1897), wrote:

I cannot but believe that if the training of lawyers led them habitually to consider more definitely and explicitly the social advantage on which the rule they lay down must be justified, they sometimes would hesitate where now they are confident, and see that really they were taking sides upon debatable and often burning questions.

As to the law being above history:

The life of the law has not been logic: it has been experience. The felt necessities of the time, the prevalent moral and political theories, intuitions of public policy, avowed or unconscious, even the prejudices which judges share with their fellow-men, have had a good deal more to do than the syllogism in determining the rules by which men should be governed.

Law cannot and should not escape its historical context. Yet we teach law as a set of timeless principles.

I, of course, lament this with great fanfare, wringing my hands and even bringing up Newton and Holmes. Bottom line, however, I am part of the problem. Don't include dates. Include them **only if** you think it important. And be explicit as to why is it important. Do you feel the case would not be followed today because it reflects different "felt necessities"?

Procedural history of the case: Should it be included?

Some profs **insist** on it and, well, it's their nickel (*Buffalo* Nickel).

I am less sure. I do not think you should routinely include the procedural history of the case.

Jury found for plaintiff. Defendant appeals on basis of improper jury instruction. Appellate court reversed and plaintiff appeals. Affirmed.

This tells you nothing about the law and simply takes up space. Your interest is in what the error was in the jury instruction.

This is not to say, however, that procedural history is irrelevant. I return to the notion that I developed in the last chapter. There are things that you should understand about a case (such as which party cited which case) that you need not "take away" from the opinion. The procedural history of a case is one such things. Forcing yourself to sort it out will help you understand how courts operate and will help you understand which party is arguing what.

The procedural history of a case can tell you some very interesting things. **Lucy won at the lower court**. Reading the flowing prose of Justice Cardozo, we are swept along, "But of course a promise should be implied." Cardozo was working a major shift in the law but he doesn't seem to be making a ripple. Courts of the time were reluctant, in the name of party autonomy, to "imply terms" to contracts. A case can be made for such a position.

What if Wood really did not want to promise Lucy that he would take "reasonable efforts"? His frame of mind, entering into the deal, was that he would get around to helping Lucy but he didn't want to make any promises. He knew that if he promised "reasonable efforts," no matter how hard he tried, she could sue him claiming that he had been "dogging it". Sure, he might win down the road but he would be facing a lawsuit.

Would Lucy ever agree to give him exclusive rights if he promised nothing? Sure ... if Wood was good at what he did. Lucy would realize, for all the reasons Cardozo noted, that Wood would mostly likely work hard on her behalf ... to make money, not to live up to his promise.

In addition to the procedural history of a case, consider its **procedural future**. Always ask: **"What happens next?"**

Recall *Walker–Thomas* from the last chapter. The appellate decision did not end the controversy. It just sent it back to the lower court to take evidence as to whether the cross-collateral clause was unconscionable. Who will have the burden of proof as to that issue? What kinds of evidence could be introduced to support it?

Has Wood won his case against Lucy? No, the case simply held that Lucy cannot get out of her promise simply because of the apparent defect in Wood's. At trial, Wood still must prove that she broke her promise and, indeed, she might be able to defend her own breach on the basis that Wood breached first, by "dogging" it.

After an appellate case is decided, the lawyers always plan their next move. By putting yourself in their shoes, by asking "What next?" you will reread the case with greater care and will begin thinking like a lawyer.

Because I think the **procedural history** and the **procedural future** of a case may be important, I include a space in my ideal briefing format. It is more of a reminder: is there anything important to learn about the law from these matters? Do I need to understand the procedural history to understand the case?

Some Final Pointers on Briefing

1. Leave wide margins so that you can add points from class discussion and make further notes when you review.

2. Don't expect to write your brief the first time you read the case.

3. Some advise *not* to brief a case until you have read all of the cases in the same assignment. This helps you see how the particular tree fits.

4. Include a "puzzling points" section at the end. What don't you understand about the case? Do you agree with it?

Here is a format you might try out. If you find that doesn't always work (and it won't), this discovery doesn't make me an idiot; it makes you a genius. It shows that you not mechanically filling in the blanks; it shows you are struggling with the material.

1. Issue/holding

2. Operative facts (don't include the kitchen sink ...unless the case is about a plumber)

3. Rationale (in your own words)

4. Procedural history and future (when of interest)

5. Puzzling points

"That's it? The end of the chapter? I'm puzzled. Why would anyone end a chapter here?"

CHAPTER 7

GENERAL STUDY TIPS

Learning By Writing

Write in the margins; when you run out of room, draw arrows to the top and write upside down ... a well used casebook is a mess.

Reading, we skim along and all is right with the world. Put pen to paper and the mind slows. "Wait, that point really doesn't make sense. And how did the court get from point A to point C? I thought I understood that."

Underlining and decorating your book with various color markers gives you a sense of accomplishment but leaves the real work of understanding to a later day.

Do your own stuff even though you will make mistakes. Canned briefs and commercial outlines may be more accurate. But you're not learning the law at the level of memorization; you're learning it at the level of understanding and application.

Expect to be wrong. Rejoice in being wrong. Even Shakespeare had rough drafts. ("To hang in there or not * * * ").

In order to *write* you need room. Leave *sufficient margins* on your briefs, class notes, and outlines.

When you review your outline the night before the exam, you will still have new questions and you will still see new relationships and **you should still be writing new things.** (Better yet, the night before, go to a movie).

Attending Class

Elsewhere I write on the sheer terror of it. ("How I Stopped Worrying and Came to Love Civil Procedure!"). Here a few brief points.

Just before class, spend five minutes skimming your briefs; you'll hit the floor running. Take notes, but not verbatim. A key phrase often will do if you go over your notes soon after class. If you try to take everything down, you will lose the thread of the discussion. At first you're current, then you slowly fade into the past, a minute behind, three minutes behind, five minutes behind, here comes College, now high school, now that Big Kid warning about pencils . . . .

After class, as soon as possible, spend five or ten minutes going over your notes—filling in the gaps and generally reviewing what went on. If you do this, then if won't be so bad if you don't get everything down in class.

Outlines and Old Exams

"Outlining" is a law school tradition. It is the stuff of nightmares:

"Have your started your Contracts outline yet?"

> "Contracts! Oh no .... I forgot **to go** to Contracts."

"Outlining" is the stuff of dreams:

> "Hello. I am the head of the Law Book Division of West Publishing. A copy of your Contracts Outline came into my possession and, if you haven't sold it to Foundation or Little Brown, we are prepared to ...."

Outlines combine case briefs, class notes, and any outside reading you have done. For the major categories, consider using the Table of Contents of the casebook.

There is nothing magical about outlining except doing it. Its value is not the product but the production. It is yet another way to be actively involved with the material. ("Where does this interesting tidbit fit? Should it go under Topic A or Topic B?")

My next topic is "old exams". (Does this topic really fit with "Outlines," which are something you produce? Perhaps it should be a separate topic or maybe it should go with the discussion of "study aids." Like study aids, old exams have been prepared by others but, then again, they are different.)

Some students find it very helpful, toward the end of the semester, to review old finals. Many schools maintain files of them. There are also books giving typical exam questions. (Maybe it does fit better with Study Aids.) As a student I didn't get much value out of them. I would look at an old exam and simply freeze—there was simply no way I could answer it. In the real test situation, of course, I had to overcome this panic and go ahead and answer the question.

Like other study devices, going over old test questions is helpful to many, but not all, students.

Study Aids, Canned Briefs, and Commercial Outlines

Most professors advise not to rely on canned briefs or commercial outlines. I will join this chorus—knowing full well that you will believe the second year student sitting across the table in the library who assures you that someone in his class used nothing but canned briefs ("Didn't even buy the book!") and did great. **Believe second year students at your own risk.**

Study aids **work** while you **snooze**. That's not good.

Another problem with study aids is that they may teach you more than you need to know, may teach you more than it is possible to know and, indeed, may drive you crazy. Learn from a story by Ray Bradbury:

> *A man commits murder in the victim's living room. "I must wipe my fingerprints off the glass I was drinking from!" Fair enough, he does. "What about the table? Did I touch it?" Why take a chance?*
>
> *"Maybe I went into the kitchen! I don't think I did but I can't be too sure; it will take just a few minutes!"*

*The next morning, the murderer is found in
the attic * * * slavishly wiping off old trunks.*

First year courses do not cover "everything"
about Torts, Civil Procedure or whatever. Treatises and hornbooks do. Use them and risk falling
into the abyss. You may get further and further
afield from the topics covered in class; eventually
you may end up in the attic * * * where, to your
delight, you find your old Junior High Yearbook and
are pleased to see that Big Kid signed it, in pencil,
"You are really swell!" (This stuff can drive you
crazy).

If you don't use outside materials to do **your
work** and are aware of their dangers, they can be
valuable. If you are having a particularly difficult
time with an area, a treatise might help. Go to one,
however, only after you have struggled. Treatises
can also help you review. After you have worked
through a topic, it is helpful to read a Nutshell or
commercial treatise *as a method of coming at the
material from a different perspective.* Once you
have done your own work, you will learn more by
seeing how others have organized the material,
reading how others describe the rules, and thinking
about examples others have used to illustrate the
doctrines. Treatises can also help overcome the
discreteness of the case method by showing where a
particular topic is in the forest.

Study Groups

Most lawyers spend a great deal of their time
working with others. There are times when you

work alone, doing research, drafting documents or preparing a cross-examination. One of the real joys of law practice, however, comes in discussing difficult cases and problems with your colleagues. After law school I practiced with a Legal Services Program. Every Friday afternoon, we sat around the table in our small law library and talked "cases."

"How is your feedlot case going?"

"I am moving for an injunction next week."

"But won't you have a problem with the *Knowles* case?"

"Well, I think I can get around it by arguing X."

"Yeah, But what if they come back with Y?"

"Then I'll argue Z."

"I dunno. Do that and they'll come back with W."

These were intellectually exciting times, hard-headed legal analysis on the run. Lay folks may not, however, recognize our elegance. A reporter, who once sat in, summed up:

"They've overrun the Nitpicks * * *. Retreat to the Quibbles!"

————————

Many students find study groups productive. There is an additional hurdle and benefit.

Working with others is a tricky business. Some may dominate, others may seek free rides. Legal education has been criticized for its emphasis on individual work: study groups will require you to negotiate, often implicitly, the critical dynamics of working with others, including, perhaps, some explicit breaks:

> "Let's stop for a few moments. This group doesn't seem to be working out. We never get as far as we plan. There are too many distractions. What can we do to improve this?"

> "George, shut up!"

A few tips:

1. Agree to ask "dumb questions" and to admit confusion. Learn, don't maintain image.

2. Structure the sessions. Will you go over more than one subject? Will you review by discussing the cases or by working on problems, possibly old exam questions? How much time will be spent?

3. Consider having discussion leaders. Rotate them. "Next week, you do Property, I'll do Contracts." One effective way to learn is to teach: planning and conducting a review session can be quite educational. Rotation shares this learning experience.

4. It is **not** a good idea to divide the first year curriculum among the group to prepare outlines. "Kingsfield, you take Contracts." The true value of outlines comes in putting them

together. Each person should outline each course.

Study groups are not for everyone. Some people work better alone. So be it! But "talk law" with other students before class or over coffee. I think discussing law with other students is simply essential.

The Forest/Tree Problem

You face a real forest/tree problem. Usually your focus will be quite narrow, a particular case or, indeed, a particular paragraph. Every now and then, step back and try to get an orientation as to where you are and how a particular case fits with the others you have read.

A good Table of Contents helps. Assume that you have just read a case by the name of *Kulzmiak v. Brookchester* and want to know where it fits. Turn to the table of contents and see where the case is. The following is from Mueller and Rosett, *Contract Law and Its Application,* 2nd Edition.

Chapter One

CONTRACT AS A CONCEPT AND AN INSTITUTION: WHAT PROMISES ARE LEGALLY ENFORCEABLE AND WHY?

To ground a case, begin with it and expand outward along the book's outline.

a. What does *Kuzmiak v. Brookchester* add to your understanding of "Illegal Promises" that the *McConnell* and *Allen* cases did not? Was *Kuzmiak* added to the casebook to show the same rule of law in a different factual

context? To show a variation on the rule of
law? Or to simply show off or to allow the
authors to fulfill their contract to produce a
book of X pages? (And why did I throw in
that last question?)

b. How does the subsection "Illegal promises"
relate to the one of equal rank: "Relationships that the do not call for contractual
recognition"? How are the cases in those
two sections the same? How are they different? And how do those to subsections, relate
to the larger topic of Roman Numeral III?

Note that you can use this technique to go where
no one has gone before: the future.

Wow, look here. Next we'll read about "Vague
and Indefinite Promises." I wonder what they
will be like. How might they be different from
"illegal promises"? How will they fit into the
topic of Chapter One?

The periodic journeys into the vast unknown
shouldn't take very long, only a few minutes. I
don't even suggest you write anything: just sit, look
at the table of contents and ask yourself questions.

At first it will be difficult to even begin to answer
the questions I have suggested and indeed some
may be without rational answer. (Some cases seem
to be in casebooks simply "Because they're there.")
Still the questions take you beyond the narrow
focus of the particular case and, ever so slowly, the
overall picture clears. The trick is knowing both

the particular and the general, in seeing both the tree and the forest.

How Much Time?

Law study is demanding. A study of over one thousand students at seven law schools indicated that *on average* first year students spent about 36 hours a week in study, compared to 27 by second year students and 24 by third year students. These figures do *not* include time spent in class. For each group, study time was slightly over two and one-half hours for each hour spent in class (upper-year students spent less time in class). Again these figures represent averages and hence should be used simply as rough guidelines.

Structure your time. Some find that they study well in the early morning hours and that, come 9 p.m., they are blurry eyed. Set specific study times; study at times you are most productive and *don't* study at other times. It is quite possible to "study" 80 hours a week but this is neither necessary nor productive. Without limits, expect to wake up one morning in the attic, dust rag in hand.

Keep A Journal

I have a chapter on writing; others have books. Much can be said which can improve your writing. However the best advice is to write, write, write, and, of course, edit, edit, edit.

Keeping a journal will give you an opportunity to write. There are other benefits.

Law study is turbulent and overwhelming. Expect moments of exhilaration and expect moments of deep self-doubt. Every now and then, quit the hurly-burly and step back to reflect on what is happening to you.

Keep a journal. Take 20 to 30 minutes a few times a week to be with yourself and your thoughts.

I require my students to do this. Afterwards, they tell me they got a great deal out of keeping a journal. Graduates tell me that they reread what they had to say as first year students and rejoice.

Write your thoughts, because until you write them you really don't know what they are. In your head they are just vague impressions and fragments of ideas; on paper they take shape and content. Write *now* while you are experiencing what will be an intense and highly significant period in your life. Next year it will be too late:

"First year? I liked it, at least some of it, I think."

Many journal entries will be "bitching" and gossip. But occasionally force yourself to attempt something in the nature of an essay.

- *Reflections on a particular case or legal doctrine.* Did you find it just? Were there certain aspects of the case that you found of special interest which your classmates and professor did not?

  Once an anthropology graduate student was sitting in a Torts class. The case was on "assumption of risk." It was a 1935 case. The plaintiff went to the circus in Ames, Iowa, and, as fate would have it, an elephant backed up and, there is no nice way of saying this, defecated on him.

"The question I had," the student told me later, "was why would someone at that time and place be so upset so as to sue."

I like that story; it reminds me of how narrowing legal education can be.

- *Reflections on law school.* How is it affecting you? Is it what you thought it would be? How does law school compare with undergraduate education? What about competition? What of male/female reactions in the classroom? Do the males tend to dominate discussions? Do you participate in class? Why or why not?
- *Reflections on lawyering.* Based on what you see, do you think you will like being a lawyer? What do you think the lawyers who handled a particular case were feeling? Were thinking? Could they have done something to avoid litigation?

Sit right down and write yourself a letter. Address it to yourself as a third year student. What will you want to tell that person about you? "Why I came to law school" might be a good topic. In two or three years, when you are considering what kind of job to take, it will be well to recall why you came to law school.

Finally, what if you think keeping a journal is a waste of time? Write an essay: "Why keeping a

Hegland Study & Pr Law NS—5

journal is a waste of time." You can't win. It's my book.

Bottom Line: Getting Better

After the dust has cleared, students will come to discuss their finals.

"I thought I would do better. I really know Contracts."

That might be the problem. I have taught Contracts a long time and I don't "know" Contracts. Contracts, like all law, is not something that is static; it is not something we memorize and store. Law is something lawyers use and law exams are simply your opportunity to use the law to solve problems and resolve conflicts.

As you hear Finals' winged chariot hurrying near, and as you go through your notes for the very last time, it should be a dumpy ride. You will feel elation when you see relationships between doctrines that you have not seen before and you will feel terror when, in the face of a sudden, nagging, question, your "understanding" of an entire area seems to crumble.

If you push yourself, if you refuse to be satisfied with easy understandings and insist on asking difficult questions, you will never walk away from a subject: you'll simply run out of time.

Law is like baseball. As Professor Gilmore points out, knowledge of the rules is not knowledge of the game: baseball is not something we know, it is something we *do*.

View your studies (reading cases, briefing, outlining, going to class and arguing law with classmates) as Saturday morning practice. You'll never know Contracts, but you'll get a whole lot better doing Contracts.

Guaranteed.

CHAPTER 8

WRITING LAW SCHOOL EXAMS: THE ONLY SKILL WORTH HAVING!

The first thing you'll notice is that law school exams are written in Greek. You will confront an indistinguishable mass of words, all blurred, all running together. Let me give you an example.

Question 1

allkdfj pqwiur nbvmznx kdk ieur pire jdjo ghjhgfiyr oiyu re otjhg lkpqyr pqlxh plvhgfd qwert yuiop asdf fgh zxcvb mjuik opk kiuy juyhgr dqwsxcgy plmbht fdghj qmpzwno hyde nhyu cdew mkoiy asdfqwer. Discuss. Be concise but don't overlook anything. Pay particular attention to kuzt op mdzopor yuiopt.

You look around the room. Everyone else has already started writing. Sweat runs into your eyes and drops onto the page, smudging the only words you understood.

Take a deep breathe. Remember this: All law school exam questions relate to, are somehow about, the material you covered in the course. Eventually you will be able to understand the question and you will be able to answer it. The folks who have started writing are writing home.

And don't worry that you didn't get "enough" sleep the night before—while advisable, sometimes sleep just doesn't come. No one has ever, not ever, gone to sleep during a law school exam.

What follows is a typical (at least for me) law school exam question. In the first edition of this book, I advised students to answer it before they read my discussion of it. I now think it would probably work better the other way around. Read the question, then the two model answers and my discussion of them. **Only then** should you return to the question and write your answer. This way you can immediately apply what you have learned.

Isn't that kind of cheating? No. It is one thing to read something and say "That's good". It is even something to go through the material and focus on why it is good. It is quite another, however, to **do it**. I advise my writing students to find a good piece of legal prose and **copy it** just to get an operational sense of how it is put together.

This is the way art is taught. It is not enough to recognize good art or even to describe what makes it good. You must **do** good art and that involves actually doing it. Students copy the masters.

The first question is how do we know why something is good? Do we define the characteristics and then run them against the work or do we do the reverse?

In Pirsig's *The Zen of Motorcycle Maintenance*, a college English instructor is asked by his class "What is good writing?" Rather than discuss the hallmarks of good writing, he simply read two student essays.

"Which is better?"

Almost all agreed on the second.

"Why?" he asked.

The class began to articulate the hallmarks of good writing. Let's do it the Zen way.

　　a. Some Rules of Law to Apply in Answers to Questions
　　　　1. In order for there to be an enforceable contract, there must a valid offer and acceptance. What if one of the parties makes an offer she is not serious about? What if she is joking or is simply "off-the-cuff?" Take the King who says "My Kingdom for a horse!"? Can a mere peasant ascend to the throne with a mere "I accept! Here, take mine!"? The law protects the *reasonable* expectations of the person accepting an offer. If the peasant reasonably believes the King is making a serious offer, then the acceptance is valid, even if the King can later convince us that he was really wasn't. On the other hand, if the peasant knows or should know the King was not making a serious offer, then his acceptance does not a contract make. And how does the law judge what a reasonable peasant would believe? By looking at the circumstances surrounding the offer—was it made at the height of battle, for example, or during a drunken party?

2. There is something in the universe which is called the Statute of Frauds, which requires that some, not all, agreements be in writing. It generally goes something like this:

The following contracts are invalid, unless the same, or note or memorandum thereof, is in writing and signed by the party to be charged:

1. An agreement for the sale of real property.

2. * * *

Cases interpreting the Statute of Frauds have indicated that it fulfills two purposes. The first purpose is to protect against false claims. A writing is good evidence that the parties actually agreed and that no one is making things up. The second purpose of the Statute is cautionary. People shouldn't enter into important legal transactions, such as the sale of realty, orally. Written contracts ensure greater reflection on the part of the contracting parties.

3. Contracts for an illegal purpose are void and unenforceable. For example, a "contract" as in "there is a contract out on the Godfather" is unenforceable. Even if the assassin does his part, he can't sue to recover his promised fee. Such contracts are illegal on their "face," that is, the illegality appears in the agreement itself: "I'll shoot Jones for $5,000."

THE EXAM QUESTION

Sleazy Sam and Billy Bigmouth ran into each other at the Lazy J Bar. After several drinks, Billy says, "You know, I think I'll blow this town and get into pictures."

"Oh yeah? How are you going to support yourself in Hollywood until they discover your major talent?" asked Sam.

"Why I'll sell my house. You can have it for $60,000. Last week it was appraised at $120,000."

"You must be joking, that deal is too good to be true," replied Sam, having another drink.

"Man, it's just that you don't have the money."

"Look, I can have $60,000 cash at the end of the week."

"Bring it by."

"Are you serious?"

"Sure." laughed Bigmouth.

"Well, I need a new place for my bookmaking activities."

"That's illegal but what you do with the place is your business," said Bigmouth, "Let's shake." The men shook and left the bar.

Three days later Sam received the following letter from Bigmouth:

Dear Sam,

Of course I was joking when I promised to sell you my house for $60,000 cash at the end of the week. In any event I don't want to do it. So there.

> Yours truly,
> Billy Bigmouth

MUST BILL MAKE GOOD ON HIS PROMISE TO SAM? DISCUSS HIS LEGAL POSITION.

———

You might want to jot down some ideas about how you would go about answering the question. Make a rough outline. Try filling in the following blanks.

Issue One:

   Controlling law:

   What P will argue:

   What D will argue:

Issue Two:

   Controlling law:

   What P will argue:

   What D will argue:

Issue Three:

   Controlling law:

   What P will argue:

   What D will argue:

Again, my advice is not to write your answer until after you read the model answers and my discussion of them.

Two quick points before beginning. Funny names like "Sleazy Sam" and "Billy Bigmouth" are a law school tradition. If you find absolutely nothing humorous in your exams, you are taking them too seriously. Loosen up.

Note too that law profs do not have a good ear for dialogue.

MODEL ANSWERS

Which is the best answer and why? You already **know** what makes for a good exam; you must force yourself to access this information.

Answer Number 1

This case is about Sam and Bill who met in a bar and began to talk about the selling of Bill's house to Sam for $60,000. The issue is whether the alleged contract is enforceable or not.

First, Bill was clearly drunk.

Second, Bill was joking. He said as much in his letter to Sam. Who on earth would sell an $120,-000 house for $60,000 in order to go get into pictures? Sam was going to use the house for book-making activities and that's illegal. And remember that Sam didn't think Bill was serious because he asked him "Are you serious?" Sam knew Bill was joking.

Because this deals with the sale of real property, the Statute of Frauds applies. The first English Statute of Frauds was enacted nearly 300 years ago to prevent fraud. In California the Statute is Civil Code § 1624. Many commentators in law reviews have argued that the statute, which has been adopted with modifications in many states, causes more fraud than it prevents. That is, it allows people who have made promises to get out of them simply because they are not in writing. Courts often try to get around the Statute of Frauds. One way around the statute is part performance. Had Sam built a garage or some other structure on Bill's property, then he could claim part performance and raise an estoppel. Realtors always require things to be in writing and there must be a legal description of the property. What if Bill had two houses?

Bill will clearly win.

Answer Number 2

There are several issues to be considered in this question:

1. Did Bill make a serious offer to sell his house to Sam?

2. Assuming that the Statute of Frauds applies, does the letter of Bill to Sam satisfy it?

3. Is the contract void because Sam intended to use the house for an illegal activity?

The first issue is whether or not there was a valid offer. **Even though** Bill may have been joking in making the offer, the question is whether he appeared to be serious. The law is designed to protect the reasonable expectations of people accepting offers: was it reasonable for Sam to think Bill really wanted to sell him the house? Bill will claim he was joking and that Sam either knew it or should have known it. He will point out that both men accidentally met in a bar. There is no indication that they met to discuss the sale of the house. He will also point out that both men were drinking. (If Bill had been drunk, and Sam knew he was drunk, that would be another defense.) He will argue that no reasonable person would believe he wanted to sell a $120,000 house for $60,000 in order to go into pictures. Note that there was nothing put in writing—it is reasonable to assume that if Bill were seriously thinking about selling a house, it would be in writing.

On the other hand, Sam will argue that Bill appeared to seriously want to sell his home. First, Bill initiated the discussion. Second, he mentioned that the house had been recently appraised—one does that when one is planning to sell. Third, Bill told Sam he was serious and both men shook hands, a traditional way to conclude a deal. If Bill had been joking, he would have told Sam just that rather than shake hands. Finally, Bill himself thought the deal serious because he wrote the letter to Sam—had the joke been clear, he wouldn't have thought to write claiming it was a joke. On balance, it seems that Sam will have the better argument here.

Even if it was found that Bill was serious, **however**, the agreement might be unenforceable because of the Statute of Frauds. The Statute applies because the deal concerns the sale of real property. Was there a note or memorandum signed by the party to be charged? The original agreement was oral. However, Bill wrote Sam saying he wanted out of the deal. He signed that letter. The question becomes, then, can a letter denying the seriousness of a promise be used to satisfy the Statute of Frauds? On the one hand, it seems as if it might. One of the purposes of the Statute is to prevent fraud—by signing the letter, Bill admits he made the promise to sell the house. Sam didn't make up the agreement. On the other hand, another purpose of the Statute is cautionary—to insure that people reflect before committing themselves to important deals. Obviously a letter trying to get out of a deal cannot be said to fulfill any cautionary function: it comes too late.

Even though the letter might be used to satisfy the Statute, I don't know how specific the letter would have to be. Must it describe the property? Must it say when delivery is to be made? I really don't know the answer.

Assuming Bill was serious in making the offer and **even if** his letter satisfies the Statute of Frauds, **there is another** possible defense, that of illegality. The law states that contracts illegal on their face are unenforceable. However, this contract isn't illegal on its face—it is not for bookmaking, it is for the sale of a house. Assuming a seller knows that the buyer is to use what is purchased for an illegal activity, can he, must he, refuse to go ahead with the deal? I assume that contracts for illegal acts are not enforced in order to deter illegal activity. That policy would apply here and make the contract unenforceable.

To summarize, I think a court would find that Bill made a serious offer but that the agreement would not be enforced because of illegality. The court could go either way on the Statute of Frauds issue.

Which of the two answers is best?

If you guessed "One," there are great opportunities in telemarketing.

Why is Number Two so much better than Number One? The more you try to answer that question, the better writer you will become. Before looking at my analysis, try doing your own.

THE MODEL ANSWERS ANALYZED

A. ANSWER 1

Answer One begins:

This case is about Sam and Bill who met in a bar and began to talk about the selling of Bill's house to Sam for $40,000. The issue is whether the alleged contract is enforceable or not.

How is that for an opening? If you were the prof, what would you tell the student who wrote it?

This is a weak opening because it tells the reader nothing that is not already known and does not focus the issues at all. The issue "is the contract enforceable" is so broad as to be meaningless.

The major fault, however, is that it seems that the student just started writing without **analyzing** the problem. While student approaches vary, you must spend some portion of your allotted time thinking about and organizing your answer. If you simply start writing after you read the questions, you have definitely started off on the wrong foot. **Plan**.

Now examine the opening paragraph in the second answer:

There are several issues to be considered in this question:

1. *Did Bill make a serious offer to sell his house to Sam?*

2. *Assuming that the Statute of Frauds applies, does the letter from Bill to Sam satisfy it?*

3. *Is the contract void because Sam intended to use the house for an illegal activity?*

Why is this such an improvement?

The student who wrote this **planned** before writing. The student has a good sense of the issues to be discussed and probably a sense of how they all fit together.

In terms of style, it is **not** necessary to list all of the issues you are to discuss up front. You can start:

The first issue is whether Bill made a serious offer.

However, even if you don't list all the issues you are going to discuss, be sure you have a fairly good idea of them before you start writing. It is a mistake to suddenly take off on the first issue you see.

Stating all of the issues up front does have some advantages. It forces you to organize your thoughts and gives instant credibility to your answer (as long as you have listed most of the issues the prof is looking for).

Answer One continues:

First, Bill was clearly drunk.

There are two problems with this. First the student has manufactured facts—the question did not say Bill was drunk, simply that he was drinking. Be **very** careful to get the facts straight. An important lawyer skill is careful reading and an acute awareness of the critical distinction between **observed data** and **inference**. Exams often test for this awareness. Don't jump to conclusions.

The second problem is that the statement is **implicit**: So what if Bill was drunk? If Bill was drunk, it would make a legal difference—**but** it is the **student's** job to tell us what that difference would be.

Observe that the second answer avoids both of these problems:

Had Bill been drunk, and Sam knew it, that would be another defense.

One problem in answering exams is the "collateral" issue. You want to focus your efforts on the main issues but, in the heat of battle, you may be unsure what the main issues are. You don't want to omit an important issue; on the other hand, you don't want to devote a great deal of time on what you suspect to be a collateral matter.

Bill's intoxication is collateral in this case, but it would be something a careful lawyer might examine. Note that the second answer deals with the problem of the non-issue by simply noting the issue. There is no lengthy discussion, yet there is a recognition that it is a possible issue.

Second, Bill was joking. He said as much in his letter to Sam. Who would sell an $120,000 house for $60,000 in order to go get into pictures? Sam was going to use the house for bookmaking activities and that's illegal. And remember that Sam didn't think Bill was serious because he asked him "Are you serious?" Sam knew Bill was joking.

There are multiple problems here. First, it appears that the writer is **taking sides**, looking only at Bill's position. Had the student asked the right question—"What would the other side say when Bill's lawyer argued Bill was joking?"—all the counter facts would have jumped out. The problem with "taking sides" is that you fail to see the other side's point of view: **without rubbing contention against counter-contention** your analysis is doomed to remain superficial.

Always ask "How will the other side respond?" Your analysis will go deeper and get better.

"What will the other side say" is a long way of saying "**Yes * * * but**".

Second, in the example above, the writer is making an **implicit** argument. **So what** if Bill were joking? The reader is forced to guess the legal relevance of that factual conclusion. Always ask yourself "So what?" and then tell the reader your answer.

Third, the writer mixes legal categories—the business of illegality is thrown into a discussion of seriousness. Not good. Legal analysis is **analysis by category**. "Illegality" and "seriousness" are **separate** legal categories; each, on their own, could make the contract unenforceable. Always keep categories separate.

Finally there is no basis in the facts recounted to conclude "Sam knew Bill was joking." When one takes sides, when one becomes contentious, one is more likely to manufacture facts.

Because this deals with the sale of real property, the Statute of Frauds applies. The first English Statute of Frauds was enacted nearly 300 years ago to prevent fraud. In California the Statute is Civil Code § 1624. Many commentators in law reviews have argued that the statute, which has been adopted with modifications in many states, causes more fraud than it prevents.   That is, it allows people who have made promises to get out of them simply because they are not in writing. Courts often try to get around the Statute of Frauds.   One way around the statute is part performance.   Had Sam built a garage or something like that on Bill's property, then he could claim part performance and raise an estoppel.

This paragraph reads like a good undergraduate essay and that's its fatal flaw.

Before focusing on this paragraph, however, a few words on the critical matter of relationship between issues. Most questions trigger several issues. Let's take two: "seriousness" and "Statute of Frauds". The question is always, **what is the relationship between issues?** To prevent the contract from being enforced, must the defense show

Lack of seriousness **and** violation of the Statute

or

Lack of seriousness **or** violation of the Statute

This is obviously a very important matter. Good legal writing not only discusses the issues, it shows how they are related as it goes along. Here a good, effective transition might read:

"Assuming that Bill made a serious offer, the Statute of Frauds may prevent enforcement."

This formulation flags the **"or"** relationship.   If the relationship were **"and,"** you might show it by

"Even if Bill were not serious, it must also be shown that the Statute of Frauds was violated before the contract will be denied enforcement."

Spend some time getting clear on this: the relationship between issues (doctrines, elements) is crucial, as is the use of effective transitions in expressing them. More on this will be found in the chapter on legal writing.

Returning to the example, why is writing like an undergraduate a flaw? Writing law always **involves the interplay of law and fact**. Recounting on the history of the Statute of Frauds is showing off. *Or* desperation! No one, least of all Bill and Sam, is interested in a history lesson. The question is whether the statute will prevent Sam from successfully suing Bill. That some courts have been hostile to the Statute of Frauds *may* be relevant to this but again there is the need to be explicit: "Because the courts have been hostile to the Statute, it is likely that they will interpret it to allow for enforcement of promises by holding that a letter denying the obligation satisfies the Statute."

Fortunately, there is usually little need, in law exams, to cite specific code sections ("Civil Code § 1624") or, for that matter, specific case names. Case names may be important in some courses, such as Constitutional Law. In most first year courses, however, case names are not significant. Ask your professor.

Now the business about Sam building a garage is unabashed showing off—Sam didn't build a garage.

One gets the idea that the student is simply trying to fill up space because the student does not know what else to do. This is a dangerous idea for your prof to get about your exam.

Realtors always require things to be in writing and there must be a legal description of the property. What if Bill had two houses?

Answers should reflect what you learned in the course, not interesting tidbits that you picked up elsewhere. The paragraph does contain two choice kernels which, unfortunately, are not developed.

What of this matter of the "legal description?" And what if Bill had two houses? If the student had asked "**So what**?" perhaps these interesting points would have led to deeper mines. For example, the student might think, "If Bill had two houses, then the failure to describe the house he meant to sell may mean that his offer is too ambiguous. How specific must offers be, anyway?" Great. And what if the student doesn't know how specific offers must be? Don't chicken out! Mention the issue and move on.

Finally:

Bill will clearly win.

If it were that clear, the question would not have been asked.

B. ANSWER 2

The first issue is whether or not there was a valid offer. Even though Bill may have been *joking in making the offer, the question is whether he appeared to be serious. The law is designed to protect the reasonable expectations of people accepting offers: was it reasonable for Sam to think Bill really wanted to sell him the house? Bill will claim he was joking and that Sam either knew it or should have known it. He will point out that both men accidentally met in a bar (there is no indication that they met to discuss the sale of the house). He will also point out that both men were drinking. (Had Bill been drunk, and Sam knew it, that would be another defense.) He will argue that no reasonable person would believe he wanted to sell a $120,000 house for $60,000 in order to go into pictures. Note that there was nothing put in writing—it is reasonable to assume that if Bill were seriously thinking about selling, it would be in writing.*

This is really good. I wonder who wrote it?

It starts off discussing the law. **Precise statements of law** are not required. You need **not** memorize the language of statutes or Restatements or the key language from opinions. In fact, as a matter of learning, it is best to put thoughts in your own words—it is possible to memorize without understanding and **understanding** is what you must achieve.

The seriousness issue requires the student to apply a relatively clear legal standard to an ambiguous fact pattern. The paragraph shows good factual analysis. For example, note the use of the fact that the deal was not put in writing. There is a **separate** issue concerning the Statute of Frauds but here the fact of no writing is skillfully used as evidence of lack of serious intent. Well done!

On the other hand, Sam will argue that Bill appeared to seriously want to sell his home. First, Bill initiated the discussion. Second, he mentioned that the house had been recently appraised—one does that when one is planning to sell. Third, Bill told Sam he was serious and both men shook hands, a traditional way to conclude a deal. If Bill had been joking, he would have told Sam just that, rather than shake hands. Finally, Bill himself thought the deal serious because he wrote the letter to Sam—had the joke been clear, he wouldn't have thought to write claiming it was a joke. On balance, it seems that Sam will have the better argument here.

This paragraph answers the essential question "What will the other side say?" (or, to state the matter differently, employs **"Yes * * * but"** analysis).

After you state each side, is it necessary for you to reach some conclusion as to who has the better argument? Generally, **maybe**. A conclusion is appropriate as a way of indicating that you know some arguments are better than others. Once you become adept at arguing both sides, you will always be able to come up with some argument, even if it is unconvincing. If you simply state "Of course the defendant could argue that the plaintiff should not have come to California in the first place," the prof may think you actually find this convincing. Hence, weighing of the arguments is often essential.

This demands further elaboration. Physicians often don't make good law students as they have been trained in a system where coming to the right answer is crucial: "Does the patient have TB?" In law, it is our analysis, not our conclusions, which matter. Take the issue of whether Bill's letter satisfies the Statute of Frauds. The competing contentions would be:

> *Bill:* *My letter could not satisfy the Statute of Frauds because the goal of the Statute is to force people to reflect before they enter into important deals. My letter was written after I made my hasty promise. To allow it to satisfy the Statute would defeat its purpose.*

> *Sam:* *Not so. The main purpose of the Statute of Frauds is to prevent false claims from being made. It requires that before one person can sue another for the breach of certain kinds of promises, that that person produce written evidence that the promise was made. And there is that evidence, Bill's letter.*

Developing the competing contentions is your main work. It shows that you know how to analyze problems as would a lawyer. To further that analysis it is often proper to reach a conclusion, not because it is necessary to reach the "right" conclusion, but rather to round off the analysis, to show the reader that you have a legal sense that some arguments are better than others. Two important learnings come from this discussion:

1. *Don't freeze up in fear you won't reach the proper conclusion.*

2. *Don't simply assert your conclusion; always justify it.*

If you have analyzed the problem properly, don't fear that the professor may disagree with your ultimate conclusion. Most exam questions are close questions; you will not be dealing with two plus two. That conclusions are not solutions but are rather analyses will also teach you that unsupported conclusions count for little or nothing. Take the following conclusion:

I think that Sam will win the Statute of Frauds issue.

Well and good. Perhaps, in a real court, he would. Yet, as written, the conclusion tells us nothing about the only thing we are really interested in: the student's ability to analyze problems. Perhaps the student simply made a lucky guess—after all, the odds aren't all that bad. Compare:

I think Sam will win the Statute of Frauds issue. Although Bill's letter was written after the promise, and hence could not fulfill any cautionary function, it seems that the main thrust of the Statute is to prevent false claims. Here we know Bill made the promise because we have his signed letter to prove it.

Here we know the student understands.

In sum, while analysis may stand without conclusion, conclusion can never stand without analysis.

*Even if it was found that Bill was serious, **however**, the agreement might be unenforceable because of the Statute of Frauds. The statute applies because the deal concerns the sale of real property. Was there a note or memorandum signed by the party to be charged? The original agreement was oral. **However**, Bill wrote Sam saying he wanted out of the deal. He signed that letter. **The question becomes**, then, can a letter denying the seriousness of a promise be used to satisfy the Statute of Frauds? **On the one hand**, it seems like it might. One of the purposes of the Statute is to prevent fraud—by signing the letter, Bill admits he made the promise to sell the house. Sam didn't invent this. **On the other hand**, another purpose of the Statute is cautionary—to insure that people reflect before committing themselves to important deals. Obviously a letter trying to get out of a deal cannot be said to fulfill any cautionary function: it comes too late.*

Another job well done. Nice transition. It shows we are dealing with an **"or"** relationship between seriousness and the Statute. Good statement of the law and of the issue.

Note that this analysis is essentially different than the "seriousness" analysis. There we had a clear legal standard and had to apply it to an ambiguous fact pattern. Here the facts are clear and the law is ambiguous: Should the letter satisfy the Statute? The model answer uses the proper mode of analysis. Because the Statute does not tell us what it means by "notes" and "memorandums," we must define those terms in light of the **purposes and goals** of the Statute. Would they be furthered or defeated by allowing the letter to count?

> *Even if the letter could be used to satisfy the statute, I don't know how specific the letter would have to be. Must it describe the property? Must it say when delivery is to be made? I really don't know the answer.*

This is a fine example of not chickening out. Perhaps the student could have developed some notion of sufficiency of the memorandum by returning to the purposes of the Statute of Frauds. This is what the courts must do when faced with such an issue. Here we have a piece of writing that neither mentions the delivery date nor describes the property. Does it satisfy the Statute? The Statute doesn't prescribe precisely what is necessary. One can only answer the question by examining the purposes of the Statute. (Or one can look up cases that indicate how specific the memorandum must be. The way those courts determined the issue, however, was by turning to the purposes of the Statute: This is what legal reasoning is all about.)

> ***Even if*** *Bill were serious in making the offer and* ***even if*** *his letter satisfies the Statute of Frauds,* ***there is another*** *possible defense, that of illegali-*

*ty. The law is that contracts illegal on their face are unenforceable. **However**, this contract isn't illegal on its face—it is not for bookmaking, it is for the sale of a house. Assuming a seller knows that the buyer is to use what is purchased for an illegal activity, can he, must he, refuse to go ahead with the deal? I assume that contracts for illegal acts are not enforced in order to deter illegal activity. That policy would apply here and make the contract unenforceable.*

This starts well. There is a good transition. We know that even if Sam wins on the serious issue and on the Statute of Frauds point, he still may be a loser if he blows the illegality point. "Or" * * * "or" * * * "or".

Important: For you eyes only. You are to discuss *all* issues that are *fairly raised* in the problem *even though* you may think one would be determinative.

For example, even if you were convinced Bill would win his case on the Statute of Frauds point, you must still discuss seriousness and illegality because they are fairly raised in the problem. The exam tests your ability to recognize legal issues.

Returning to the answer, the discussion of illegality would be much improved had the student asked "What will the other side argue?" There are powerful arguments against Bill's position here, so powerful, in fact, that courts will likely reject the defense—although that is an issue I will leave to your Contracts course.

To summarize, I think a court would find that Bill made a serious offer but that the agreement would not be enforced because of illegality. The court could go either way on the Statute of Frauds issue.

Concluding gracefully presents difficulties. Believing that they should summarize their answer at the end, some students get into the unfortunate morass of repeating and repeating their previous analysis. Grades are not improved for mere repetition and profs find reading the same points over and over irksome.

The ideal ending summary is not a rehash, it is *further analysis*. Rather than repeating previous points, it shows how the points *relate* to one another. Well written summaries, like the one above, can be effective.

I want to end on one last point: **law is indefinite**. This doesn't sound particularly profound but it is a point that is very difficult to actually grasp and, in law practice, to live. I am working on a murder case. The defendant is a young girl who shot a man. She was 14, he was 50. Her defense is self-defense: he tried to rape me. The state's theory is that she set him up in order to rob him. The defendant has been interviewed by an expert who concluded that, given her background, it is quite likely that she shot in self-defense and quite unlikely that she would have set the man up. Is that testimony admissible? It is a matter of great mo-

ment; you would think that the issue would have
been resolved long ago.

But it hasn't.

The law is indefinite. We all hunger for certainty; but the law is indefinite, some cases suggesting the testimony will be admissible, others,
that it not will not be.

I think the people who have the most trouble in
law are those who cannot live with uncertainty.
They want answers, not a series of "on the other
hands." On exams, they close upon issues too
quickly and simply fail to explore the weaknesses
and inconsistencies in their own positions.

Relish them. They will be your daily bread.

CHAPTER 9

MORE STUFF ON TAKING EXAMS

A few years ago a national humor magazine had as its cover the cover sheet to the New York Bar Exam. It was the official one and was filled with official, scary, warnings:

Do not Open until Instructed

Do not Talk

Do not Leave this Room

Blah, Blah, Blah

Having taken one bar exam and countless law school exams, all of the anxiety, all of the uncertainty, rushed back * * * if my hands didn't tremble, they sure felt like it.

I turned the page. It was blank, except for a small note in the center of the page:

This has been a bluff.

You don't have to take this test.

You pass.

Congratulations!

Tears of joy and giggles of relief.

The possibility of this happening to you are, frankly, remote. But, then again, a lot of people play the lottery.

The Dreaded Day. After all that study, after all that struggle, one morning you will enter the room, and it's just you and your bluebook. It all comes to this. You will be given a copy of the exam, about the size of a telephone book. You sit, pending further instructions. Then, a smile face:

"You may begin."

Expect to be nervous and expect to have a hard time getting started. After the panic, however, you will likely **enjoy** the exam. It will be a fascinating intellectual puzzle. It will push you, confound you and delight you.

Exams are not awful. The prospects of exams are awful. Grades are awful. Exams themselves are adrenalin, discovery and adventure.

This chapter will give some basic advice about **spotting issues, organizing your answer and developing your analysis.** While this may sound like a three step process, things are much more fluid. While you are writing about one issue, another will suddenly **pop** into your mind.

Pop! I should also say a few words about writing style.

Given the fluid nature of the thought process, I have one very practical piece of advice and one very Zen-like.

1. Take scratch paper into the exam (if it is allowed). You will need someplace **to jot your pops**—I don't want to lose focus on explaining the need to capture your ideas by worrying about what I should say about writing style.

2. **Be with the exam. Ooommm**. My sense is that if you are thinking of things outside the exam, such as "Do's and Don't of Taking Exams," you will block the flow of your own creativity. Some students swear by "Checklists" which reduce all the learning of a course into one mnemonic device which spells out something witty ("Tippecanoe and Tyler too") or crude [Expletive deleted]. Running through a checklist will, however, get in the way of focusing on the actual question. So too the advice of second year students: "Professor Cro–Magon isn't that sophisticated; you really have to draw pictures for him" or "Professor Rehnquist is a liberal so always take the bleeding heart position."

Pop. A third point.

3. Who really knows what works? Second year students will tell you all sorts of things but **they don't know what worked for them.** Perhaps Rehnquist, deep down, loves hard headed, heartless analysis and the very thing that prevented the student from doing much better was his taking the bleeding heart position. Frankly I don't think anyone is smart

enough to "psych" out the professor and then adopt a writing and analytical style for that professor. Trying to do that will just get in the way of your being with the exam. Write the same for every one.

There are no controlled studies as to what is effective exam writing. However, some hunches are better than others. To reassure yourself as to this matter of "no controlled studies," look at the lower right hand portion of the title page of this book: make sure it doesn't say, in teeny-tiny print, Placebo Edition.

Given that there are no magic bullets in the area of exam writing, it might be good to try **teaching yourself.** After you take your first exam, to sit down and write about it. What points might you want to cover?

What did the exam teach you about the way you studied? Should you have studied differently? As to the exam, did you spend enough time analyzing the questions? Did you really carefully consider the facts and address the important facts in your discussion? Did you develop both sides on the arguments? What did you do well? What should you do differently next time?

Here are some of my ideas.

To spot issues

Reread the question and appreciate it for what it is, **a work of art**.

Don't jump right in with the first issue you see.

To organize issues

Take some time before you write to make a very rough outline of the issues you will discuss and focus on the relationship between issues (1 + 2) or (1 or 2).

Don't introduce your answer by recounting the facts of the problem. Your prof knows them. When you are ready to go, go!

To analyze the issues

Ask "So what?"   and say "Yes * * * but."

Don't take sides.

Spotting Issues

Professors are looking for your ability to see legal problems (issue spotting) and how you deal with them once you see them (analysis).

"Did you see the assumption of risk issue?" your best friend asks you after the exam. You hate this person.

Don't go into a funk. Few students, no students, get all of the issues. Usually in my classes the top exams have missed maybe two, three or more of the key issues: they developed the others with such depth and flare that these omissions are overwhelmed.

It is, of course, better to spot many issues. If you have been studying with the intensity that you should have been, issues will simply "jump" out at you. It's like going to a high school reunion. The people look strange, they look like your friends' parents, when it suddenly strikes you, "Hey, these are my old friends (or enemies); they just look a little different."

A couple of devices might help you recognize issues. It is a mistake to immediately jump at the first issue you see. Usually there are several. It will be a good idea to reread the question, looking for buried treasure. **Give us our due**.

We work hard on exam questions. They are our poetry; they are our bridges. Why is it that the defendant kicked the plaintiff's **ugly** dog? There is generally very little filler in exam questions and most everything is there for a purpose. Continue to ask yourself, as you read the question through, "Why is that fact there? Why not a cute dog? Why not a rabid dog who always wanted to be a good dog?"

Discuss all the fairly raised issues **even if** you believe that one would resolve the case.

> *Although the defendant has a very good chance of winning on the Statute of Frauds issue, there are two other defenses which should be considered.*

Don't put all your eggs in one basket.

Why did I say **"fairly raised"** issues? Some students make issues up and then go about resolving them.

Had the plaintiff assumed the risk, then that would be a defense. The doctrine was first developed in the case of * * * and today the elements of "assumption of risk" are

1. . . . .

2. . . . .

3. . . . .

4. . . . .

Of course, because the plaintiff was at home, in bed, asleep, when the defendant's car smashed through the wall, this would not be a good defense.

Law exams are to test your ability to apply the law; they are not exercises to see how much law you learned. Don't show off.

Organizing Issues

There is no set order. Probably it is best to start with the most difficult or challenging issues as those will win the most points for good analysis. **Time is always a factor** and keep track of it * * * if you run out, far better to miss the minor issues.

Don't spend time **not** making points. Long recitals of the facts and long conclusions where you essentially repeat what you have said just kill the clock. Introductions and conclusions are great in most legal writing as previews and repetitions help recall. However, the prof will be focused and hence these devices are not needed. And you will get credit for an issue only once—we have our ways.

Be clear on the relationship between the issues: to prevail, must the defendant win **both** the seriousness issue and that of the Statute of Frauds or is one enough $(1+2$ or 1 or 2)? As will be discussed in the chapter on legal writing, you can make effective use of **transitions** to show these relationships.

Let's illustrate the transition between a paragraph that discussed issue 1 and the paragraph that will discuss issue 2. Hopefully it reads better than: *Next, issue 2*.

Effective transitions tell the prof you know how things fit together and help keep you focused on where you are going.

To show a 1 + 2 relationship:

Not only must the defendant show 1 to prevail, she must show 2.

Even if the defendant shows 1, she still must show 2.

To show a 1 or 2 relationship:

Assuming that the defendant cannot show 1, she can still prevail by showing 2.

As an alternative to showing 1, the defendant can prevail by showing 2.

Be aware of these kinds of relationships. They will help you think through the problem. If you do so, **good transitions will come naturally**. Although I do not grade on style, looking back at the best papers it strikes me how well they read. Style follows understanding.

Analyzing the Issues

Opera singers bellow a few chords before going out; ball players practice their mean stares (for opponents) and their "What me?" disbeliefs (for refs). During your warm-up, repeat, and repeat, "So what?" and "Yes * * * but".

Law stuff is abstract and confusing. You must always ground it. If you are merrily discussing a legal doctrine, ask "so what?" How does it apply to the case you are discussing? If you are merrily writing of the facts, "so what?" How do they fit with the law? If you keep asking yourself this question, you will always have a good idea of where you are going and, if you tell the reader, so will she.

In the chapter on Legal Writing, I make this point again. There I call it the **need to be explicit**.

"Well, the two guys met at a bar and seemed to be joking around. Mark you that!"

So what?

*"Well, that might **mean** that maybe they weren't serious in their negotiations."*

So what?

*"If they weren't serious, that **means**, under a doctrine of contract law, that the contract is not enforceable."*

Note the progression, from bits to theory:

Data: Where they met.

Factual conclusion: They may have been joking.

Legal Conclusion: Their contract may be unenforceable.

The more explicit you are, in your analysis and in your writing, the better you will do.

Do I make myself clear?

"So what" forces you to ground your analysis. "Yes but" forces you consider the other side. As a lawyer, you can never assess the strength of your case without considering the opponent's response. And, unless you consider that response, your analysis will remain superficial.

The letter the defendant wrote should satisfy the Statute of Frauds.

Yes but *maybe it shouldn't, because it was written after the agreement.*

Yes but *maybe it should, because the purpose of the Statute is to prevent people from lying and making up a deal when none existed. Here the defendant's letter shows a deal was made.*

Yes but *maybe that isn't the purpose of the Statute. Maybe the purpose is to force people to reflect before they enter into important deals. Here, when the defendant reflected, he decided he didn't want any part of it. Then he wrote the letter. To say that it satisfies the statute is to ignore its cautionary purpose.*

Note, this back and forth forces you deeper * * * you will uncover a much richer exam question.

Occasionally you will get to a point where you simply don't know how to go further. How will the court resolve the Statute of Frauds issue? Don't **chicken out**. Some students, fearing that they cannot resolve an issue, don't even bring it up. This is a bad error.

There is an issue as to whether the defendant's letter satisfies the Statute of Frauds. Frankly I don't know how a court would resolve it.

This way you at least get points for recognizing the issue and, perhaps, some for candor.

Far better, of course, to throw yourself at the issue. **If a court got to the point where precedent didn't help, how would it resolve the issue?** It would treat it as First Case in the World and you know how they deal with them:

1. Discuss policy: Which would be a better rule in terms of justice, economic efficiency, or whatever.

2. Draw analogies to areas of the law that are known. "Are there any areas we studied that dealt with the sufficiency of a writing or the timeliness of a notice? If so, do the rules developed in those areas make sense in this area?"

3. Make up "easy cases" and draw analogies to them.

You have the tools, if not the answers. Use them.

CHAPTER 10

FEAR & LOATHING IN
THE FIRST YEAR

Why was I afraid?

Imagine, is all that I can answer.

You have a stake. You have given up a job, a career, to do this. Or you have wanted to be a lawyer all your life.

All your life you've been good in school. All your life it's been something you could count on. You know that it's a privilege to be here. You've studied hours on a case that is a half page long. You couldn't understand most of what you read at first, but you have turned the passage inside out, drawn diagrams, written briefs. You could not be more prepared.

And when you get to class that demigod who knows all the answers, finds another student to say things you never could have. Clearer statements, more precise. And worse—far worse—notions, concepts, whole constellations of ideas that never turned inside your head.

Yes, there are achievements in the past. They're nice to bandage up your wounded self-esteem. But "I graduated college magna cum laude" is not the proper answer when the professor has just posed a question and awaits your response with the 140 other persons in the class.

The feeling aroused by all of that was something near to panic, a ferocious, grasping sense of uncertainty, and it held me, and I believe most of my classmates, often during that first week and for a long while after. On many occasions I discovered that I didn't even understand what I didn't know until I was halfway through a class. Nor could I ever see how anyone else seemed to arrive at the right answer. Maybe they were all geniuses. Maybe I was the dumbest guy around.

Scott Turow, *One L*

Expect a "ferocious, grasping sense of uncertainty."

Partly, it's the arrogance, the hype. Professor Kingsfield, dreaded Contracts Professor of *Paperchase*, bellows at his first year class:

Your minds are filled with mush. You will teach yourself the law. I will teach you how to think!

Partly, it's the newness. Had you gone into other graduate programs, schools of education, philosophy, social work, you would have a fairly good idea what to expect and how you would do. Law school is, in marked contrast, a whole new game.

Partly it's the **lack of feedback**. There are no term papers or midterms. You will sit in a large class, (classes over 100 are not uncommon), awaiting the *one and only* test. Even then there is little feedback: knowing your grade doesn't really tell you what you are doing right, what you are doing wrong.

Why the lack of feedback? Economics. Legal education is graduate education on the cheap, one professor handling a class of 140! Things are getting a little better. Some schools offer at least one small section in the first semester and, in the second and third years, there will be seminars and clinical courses that have a lower student/faculty ratio and hence more feedback. With these exceptions, the general model holds: large classes followed by a single final.

In this chapter, I will look at the psychological tensions of the first year. In your darker moments, you will come to believe that "I'm the dumbest one here" and "Everyone here is viciously competitive, except me and my friends." And you will, most likely, put a wildly inappropriate meaning to first year's grades. I will also cover the almost universal fear of being called on in class. I will explain why we teach the way we do, the so-called Socratic Method, and I will urge you to help us out, by raising your hand and volunteering.

"Come on down!"

Self-Doubt and the Rejection of Others

a. I'm the Dumbest One Here!

Take heart! *Every* first year student believes this. The good news, of course, is that only one is right! The bad news is * * *.

After the first few weeks in law school, I was convinced that all my classmates were geniuses. They said such profound, insightful things, things that would never, ever, occur to me. "It's curtains for me, I'll flunk out for sure!" I did find some solace in the fact that law schools flunked out very few students. (As admission standards rose, failure rates fell. Gone the classic First Day Greeting: "Look to the person to your right, look to the person at your left * * * "). Using the rumored "flunk out rate" as a basis, I concluded that I had to be smarter than only 3 or 4 of the 120 students in my section. Not bad odds. I would come to class, looking and listening to discover someone dumber than me. Weeks would pass. I grew desperate. Finally someone would say something that seemed wildly beside the point. Mark one down. At the end of the first semester the count stood at three. It was going to be a cliffhanger. (As it developed one of the three ended up in the top 10% of the class. One of the really unnerving things about the first year is that you can't even tell who's dumb!)

As a law school teacher I now know the original of the "everyone's smarter than me" syndrome. It's that there are so many interesting and profound things to say. Student A and student B will both have interesting, insightful comments to make about a case, comments which are, however, quite different. Student A recites; student B is dumbstruck—"I would never have thought of that; there are notions, concepts, whole constellations of ideas that never turn inside my head!"

Insecurity, although understandable, leads to viciousness. Sitting, watching, counting, is one example. Another is the pathetic posturing that occurs.

"I don't study more than an hour a day and understand everything."

"My LSAT is in the 99th percentile. What's yours?"

"Why did everyone in class have such a problem with Pennoyer v. Neff? I understood it immediately."

How to cope with posturing?

An ex-professional football player, a defensive lineman, told of how his friends would rag him.

"Doesn't so-and-so play the same position as you do with the Jets?" they would begin. "And what's-his-face, he plays the same position for the Rams?"

Indeed they did.

"Well, those two guys always sack the quarterback. Why don't you?"

"They're better."

The best way to win is not to play:

"You're smarter."

Will your listener rejoice in victory? Of course not. "That just **proves** how much smarter, better looking and more balanced you are."

b. Law Students are viciously competitive

Law students are aggressive, competitive, humorless and, worst of all, they study all the time. Now, of course, *I* wasn't that way as a law student, nor were my close friends. I am sure you and your friends aren't that way either. But we can agree that everyone else is.

One of my students wrote of her first day at law school. She met another woman and thought "She's smarter than I am, better educated, better looking and, obviously, more stable." Instant hatred.

Note how this student rejected someone who might have been a good friend **simply because that person had the effrontery to come to law school**.

Note another curious fact. **You are** that smart, educated, good looking and stable person everyone is afraid of.

How about them apples?

You don't even have to play the posturing game; you have already won! What with your smarts, looks * * *.

But competitiveness and aggressiveness are not just psychological projections. They are real. Your classmates are competitive and so are you. It is important to confront and contain your aggressiveness and competitiveness. It will not do to simply deny these feelings, "Oh, I don't care what grades I get or how I do; I just want to get by!" Some students take denial to the extreme of not trying; they do a minimum amount of studying and miss class frequently. (If you refuse to try, then failure will be less painful. On the other hand, there is always the possibility of the ultimate seventh grade fantasy—an "A" in Contracts, an "F" for Effort.)

You are competitive or you wouldn't be in law school. You have achieved recognition and pleasure in competing successfully in the past. This is not shameful. Accept this part of yourself; however, do not let it consume you.

Scott Turow, the author of *One L*, describes an incident from his first year at Harvard. He and members of his study group were discussing whether they should share their class outlines with other students. Turow surprised himself by arguing that they should not:

"I want the advantage," I said. "I want the competitive advantage. I don't give a damn about anybody else. I want to do better than they."

*My tone was ugly * * ***

*It took me a while to believe I had actually said that. I told myself I was kidding * * * What had been suppressed all year was in the open now. All along there had been a tension between looking out for ourselves and helping each other; in the end, I did not expect anybody—not myself, either— to renounce a wish to prosper, to succeed. But I could not believe how extreme I had let things become, the kind of grasping creature I had been reduced to. I had not been talking about gentle-*

*manly competition * * *. I had not been talking about any innocent striving to achieve. There had been murder in my voice * * *.*

*That night I sat in my study and counseled myself * * *. It's a tough place, I told myself. Bad things are happening. Work hard. Do your best. Learn the law. But don't suffer, I thought. Don't fear. And for God's sake, don't give up your decency * * *.*

I had finally met my enemy, I figured, face to face.

Some of that is worth repeating:

*It's a tough place, I told myself. Bad things are happening. Work hard. Do your best. Learn the law. But don't suffer, I thought. Don't fear. And for God's sake, don't give up your decency * * *.*

Grades

You are not your first semester grades. Not even your first **year** grades, for that matter.

"Of course not," you laugh nervously.

Just wait.

You work real hard all semester. Suddenly, that "ferocious, grasping sense of uncertainty" come crashing down into a letter or a number. "So that's it, huh. I'm a C."

No, you are not a C. You are whoever you were before you came to law school, the same person who, as a small child, took such good care of the puppy. Only you're different: **you have a lot more knowledge and a lot more skills**. You are well on your way to becoming a competent professional.

Don't "drop out in place." Keep working hard on your studies; you will know more law and will have better lawyer skills when you really need to, when another individual puts important matters in your hands.

If you do well on your exams, more power to you. Feel good; celebrate. But don't fall victim to your own success. Don't strut, don't take everything you say seriously. I recall a movie where an elderly man is asked advice by a younger person.

> "Get to be my age, everyone thinks you know what you are talking about. But I'm the same old fool I have always been."

That's Wisdom: remember it.

Confusion and Terror in the Classroom

"Where there is light, let me sow darkness."

No. The law professors are not committed to this terrible misreading of the Prayer of Saint Francis.

As I have repeated throughout this book, you are not learning the "law", you are learning how "to do" law. In class, by tearing apart the cases, testing their coherence and rejoicing in their ambiguities, your professors are teaching you how to "do law."

"But what is the rule? What I am supposed to learn?"

We live in an intellectual milieu which downplays the ability to arrive at clear and certain answers. Psychology teaches the importance of the observer's point of view in what is observed; so too Physics. Anthropology teaches the relativism of beliefs and truth itself falls to the Sociology of Knowledge. Law has not been immune. There was a time that it was thought possible to have clear and certain laws; there was a time when the following made sense:

Certainty is the mother of repose; thus the law aims at certainty.

With a brilliant turn of phrase, Holmes captured the modern view:

Certainty is generally illusion and repose is not the destiny of man.

No wonder that law professors, committed to this view, are accused of "hiding the ball"; they don't believe there is one.

Let's talk about the fear of participating in class. I remember sitting in class, day after day, praying I wouldn't be called on. (This, of course, when I wasn't looking around the room for folks dumber than me.)

Deep down we all **know** that we really aren't all that "hot." We all **know** that our prior successes have been, at bottom, luck. Sure, we've been able to fool the others but this is law school and that "demigod" up front might prove too much. She'll expose us, once and for all, as the incompetents we are.

Relax. In all likelihood that demigod is not as tough as she looks. Indeed, she fears, deep down, that she's not that hot, that she doesn't measure up to Kingsfield!

Being called on in class: Herein the Socratic Method

You'll be in class one day, just sitting there, minding your own business, actually rather enjoying the discussion, when, without warning, you hear someone calling your name. The Professor! All eyes turn to you. There is total silence. The Professor is good enough to repeat the question:

"Quis outouc ptyo xovbiyeous oppeuawud ipptons?"

Relax! Take a deep breath, loosen your jaw. Shift your attention from "Oh no, it's happening to me!" Focus on the question. If necessary ask that it be repeated. While answering the question remember that you are probably doing a whole lot better than you think you are. Just because *you* thought of something, just because *you* understood a point, doesn't mean that it is so obvious it doesn't justify discussion. What you have to say might be terrific. Realize that you appear less nervous than you feel. When your classmates recite, they do not *appear* nervous even though they surely are. Listening to someone recite you do not hear the pounding of his heart nor feel the quiver in his lips.

Confront, finally, the dreaded fear: You make a total fool of yourself. Your classmates laugh. You bumble, meander and eventually give up. The professor moves on and asks the person behind you what has to be, and I'm not making things up here, the easiest question you have ever heard.

Shattered, you walk from class. You overhear smatterings of conversations and are greatly relieved.

*"They're **not** talking about me and what a fool I was. They're talking about the cases and lunch * * *. But wait! They don't **care** * * *."*

Play the fool and the world turns. This is a valuable lesson even if a disappointing one. The willingness to risk is absolutely essential to effective lawyering. Who was foolish enough to first assert that separate means unequal? To argue that, despite tradition and practice, police must warn defendants of their right to remain silent? To suggest that manufacturers of goods could be held "strictly liable" for injuries their products cause?

Law demands creativity; creativity demands we try new things; we must not fear playing the fool.

Think of law school as your Great Opportunity: to play the fool before a huge audience. Let them laugh as you learn you can take chances and hence free your creativity. The worse you are, the more they will love you. As you stammer and fret, there will be a collective sigh—"There's one we can mark down."

They'll see.

What happens if you *don't* fall on your face at the first question? What if you are actually able to answer it? Then expect another. Survive that, expect a third. Welcome to the *Socratic Method*. There is probably no more controversial aspect of law school than the method wherein the professor presses the student to justify his opinion, meeting answers with questions and arguments with counter-arguments. Some denounce the method as destructive of the student's self-esteem, as a device of verbal terror designed to expose the student's ignorance and to ridicule him before his fellows. Others see the ultimate irony. In law school, the argument runs, the method is not used to pursue Truth but rather to destroy Truth. The process of demanding justifications, of meeting argument with counter-argument, destroys the student's basic moral outlook. Extreme relativism reigns.

Plato saw the danger. In *The Republic* he warns against "plunging the young into philosophical discussion" as it destroys notions of honor and right learned in childhood.

> *[S]uppose he's confronted by the question, "What does 'honorable' mean?" He gives the answer he has been taught by the lawmaker, but he is argued out of his position. He is refuted again and again from many different points of view and at last is reduced to thinking that what he called honorable might just as well be called disgraceful. He comes to the same conclusion about justice, good-*

*ness, and all the things most revered * * *. [W]e
shall see him renounce all morality and become a
lawless rebel.* [Please, just not in my class.]

The *goal* of the method is not to inculcate relativism; the *goal* is not to expose student ignorance; the *goal* is not to ridicule. The goal of the method is *to force students to justify their positions, to consider other points of view and to realize that even the best of arguments, even the best of theories, suffer from "inconvenient facts."*

To illustrate take a familiar case: a tenant is suing the landlord for negligently maintaining a common stairway. The landlord sets up as defense a clause in the lease wherein the tenant agreed not to sue the landlord for negligence. Is the clause valid?

> Student: I don't think the tenant should be held to her promise not to sue if that promise was buried in the small print in the lease.
>
> Professor: Why not?
>
> Student: It just isn't fair.
>
> Professor: Why not?

Here the student may feel that she is being attacked. Still worse, the student may feel that she is being argued out of her sense of fairness. This is not the professor's goal; rather it is to force the student to get to bedrock as to why she feels the way she does, indeed, as to why her sense of justice dictates it.

Student: Well, it seems to me that one reason we enforce a person's promises
is to protect, to further, personal
autonomy. The whole notion of
contract is premised on actual
choice. Now if the tenant didn't
know what she was signing, then
the whole justification for enforcing
promises collapses.

Behind our sense of justice often lie good sound
reasons. For the professor to insist upon their
verbalization is not to attack them.

Professor: Good. But what if the evidence
showed she read the contract?
Would you still think the agreement unfair?

Student: Yes. The facts show that she was
poor and probably not that well
educated. She really didn't know
that she was giving up valuable
rights.

Professor: Good. But isn't that a little pater-
nalistic? If the law doesn't enforce
her promise because she is poor
and not well educated, aren't we
saying that she is legally incompetent? That she doesn't have that
most basic of rights, the right to
mean what she says?

The professor is not attacking the student, not
trying to trip her up and humiliate her. Nor is the
professor trying to argue her out of her position and
turn her into a mouthpiece for landlords. The

professor is attempting to force her to consider other points of view, to adopt the "yes, but" form of reasoning. "Yes, my initial reaction is valid, but there are counter considerations."

Max Weber, the great sociologist, wrote in "Science as a Vocation" that the "primary task of a useful teacher is to teach his students to recognize 'inconvenient' facts * * *. [F]or every opinion there are facts that are extremely inconvenient, for my own no less than for others."

The teacher should force students to understand what their opinions and arguments entail. Weber continues:

*If you take such and such a stand, then * * * you have to use such and such means in order to carry out your conviction. Now, these means are perhaps such that you believe you must reject them * * *. Does the end "justify" the means? Or does it not? The teacher can confront you with the necessity of this choice * * *.*

[The teacher] can force the individual, or at least we can help him, to give himself an account of the ultimate meaning of his own conduct. This appears to me as not so trifling a thing to do, even for one's own personal life. Again, I am tempted to say of a teacher who succeeds in this: he stands in the service of "moral" forces; he fulfills the duty of bringing about self-clarification and a sense of responsibility.

Having made a very compelling argument why the tenant should be excused from her promise to pay, it is discomforting to have the professor point out that the argument entails paternalism and denies tenants the very basic right to "mean what they say." Again, in Weber's analysis, the professor is not suggesting that the promise should be enforced; the professor is forcing the student to realize the important values which would be sacrificed if the promise were not enforced. *"The teacher can confront you with the necessity of choice."*

Our goal is not to hurt feelings. And, of course, we screw up. Teaching law is not easy * * * it is not lecturing. All is movement and you never know exactly what will happen next. It's like surfing in the Pacific.

Preparing for class, I see the cases raising key issues, issues important for the class to discuss. I carefully note them on my pad. I even rehearse in my mind. (It goes brilliantly.) Excited, I enter class, put a question to start the ball rolling and SMACK I hit reality. Seldom do I get the response I was planning on.

Instantaneously I must decide if the response is worth pursuing (often it is, often I find that I overlooked important legal issues in a case) and, if the point is not worth pursuing, how to gently bring the student back.

It ain't easy. Undoubtedly, I may too quickly reject what the student believes is a valid point; undoubtedly, I am too abrupt with students whom I feel meandering; and, undoubtedly, the shock and dismay I occasionally experience shows. These are but inadvertent and unfortunate slights and insults caused by the intellectually challenging and unplanned nature of Socratic discourse.

It's bumpy for us up front as well.

Volunteering in class

For a law school class to succeed **students must participate**, must share their insights, questions and experiences. You can't sit on your hands and then complain that the class is boring. A good class is as much the doing of the students as it is the professor's.

You might not believe this but it's true. Give me a good class that is on my side and is willing to take risks, I am pretty good. Give me a silent, resentful class, I stink.

A few years ago I brought up in class the hard/soft metaphor and how it played out in law study. Some courses are "soft"—family law, clinical courses, interviewing and negotiation—and some courses are "hard"—Antitrust, Federal Jurisdiction, Tax. And "hard" always trumps "soft".

Although I thought the discussion was very important because I believe that the metaphor guides a lot of our choices, I noticed a student in the back, looking bored and resentful. "Maybe this is a waste of time," I thought.

"Let's get back to offer and acceptance," I said. "Wait," the student in the back raised his hand. "Before we leave hard/soft, that is about mascu-

line/feminine. When I was a boy, growing up, I liked books and they are soft * * * and my male friends all liked sports and it was very painful for me * * * " His voice trailed off.

The discussion he facilitated, the discussion he almost shutdown, was one of the best ever.

You have a stake in your classes. **You can make them better, and you can make them worse.** Take part. Raise your hand. Ask a question. Stab at an answer.

Volunteering pays off. Even if it isn't "counted" towards your grade, volunteering gives you experience in trying out your ideas and thinking on your feet, important lawyering skills.

Don't volunteer all the time as there is a definite drawback. Volunteering requires blocking out remarks of other students while you wait until you are called on. It is difficult to listen and retain what you want to say or ask. (Try jotting down a few words and then turn attention to the class). And, if you volunteer too much, other students will resent you. (As the person doing the resenting, consider who is responsible for the "Bigmouths." The professor needs participation and is likely as sick of them as you. But if they're the only ones raising their hands * * *).

In the first few weeks of law school you are making important choices about yourself. William Blake has a marvelous phrase, "mind-forged manacles." Don't forge: "I'm just not the kind of student who raises their hand!" Volunteer at least occasionally, don't imprison yourself in a closet.

This chapter has been kind of a downer. It focused on the negatives. It started with Professor Kingsfield, who, I admit, is one of **my** heroes:

Your minds are filled with mush. I will teach you how to think.

He's right and you will come to know it. When you aren't complaining, you'll be talking law and loving it.

Too much can be made of the psychological pressures. One year at the first year orientation the topic was "Psychological Pressures on the First Year Student." Many spoke and office hours of the campus psychologists were posted. Five weeks into the semester a student came to me, aghast.

"I can't understand it. I still have friends. I'm still married. I go to occasional movies and read a few novels. What am I doing wrong?"

You are going to meet many wonderful people and no doubt make close friendships. Law students are supportive and, despite the rhetoric of Nutshell Writers, many do care:

"That was terrible what happened to you in class. That professor can sometimes be a jerk. Do you want to have lunch and talk about it?"

I want to close by stressing what you will accomplish. Too often we focus on our failures, on our hurts. Despite the bumps, you will be mastering a new and difficult discipline. At first you will be doing it wrong; you will garble facts, misstate issues, and confuse holdings. After much hard work, you will do it right.

"Hey, look at me * * * I'm walking!"

PART 3

THE LITIGATION PROCESS

In this Part, I overview the litigation process, from the initial client interview to jury deliberation. Chapter 11 deals with pretrial concerns: case planning, pleading, discovery and pretrial motions. Chapter 12 deals with trials: a general overview of what happens when, then a more detailed description of opening statements, direct and cross-examination, opinion evidence, trial objections and, what we have all been waiting for, closing argument.

My goal is to acquaint you with the overall process. It will help you to see how the rules and doctrines you study in your first year play out in the world beyond and, thus, help you better understand those rules and doctrines. Given this goal, read the chapters relatively quickly, not pausing to examine all of the intricate issues that may arise. You will have time enough during your next three years.

CHAPTER 11

THE PRETRIAL PROCESS

The Return of Ms. K

You remember Ms. K. She had tripped on a defective step in her apartment house. Recuperating, she watched a lot of T.V. Late one night, during the reruns, after the ad giving 1–900 number for Authentic Psychics (don't leave important personal matters in the hands of quacks), the lawyer C. Darrow appeared on the screen. Solemnly, indeed reluctantly, she broke the bad news:

"Insurance companies are sleaze! Physicians are murderers! Authentic Psychics are frauds. I am your only friend." Then she breaks into a warm inviting smile:

"If you have been injured, if you have been thinking about getting injured, or if you have heard about someone getting injured, come on down."

The next day, Ms. K did.

"Don't tell me what happened. Just tell me how badly you were hurt," instructed Darrow.

Ms. K. did. Her injuries were substantial.

"Do I have a good case?" She asked.

"Yes ... you ... **do**! ... Now, tell me what happened?"

Eventually, after mutual dreams of sugar plums, it gets to the unpleasant part of the interview ... fees. Rather than an **hourly fee** (used most often in business representation) or a **flat fee** (used often in criminal defense), they agree that Darrow will work on a **contingency fee** basis. If settled prior to trial, Darrow will receive 25% of the recovery, if litigated, 35%. If there is no recovery, Darrow gets nothing.

Thus Darrow was true to what she said: "And you don't pay *me* one penny unless you recover" (assuming you listened to her precise words and weren't one of those bozos who were mislead by the obvious meaning of the sentence). Personal injury plaintiffs don't pay their lawyers unless they recover, but they pay a lot of other folks. They pay **costs**: filing fees, reporter's fees for depositions, juror fees. Depending on the complexity of the case and the extent of discovery, these costs can run into, as my Norwegian relatives like to say, a "pretty penney." If Ms. K prevails on the case, however, most likely the defendant will be ordered to pay these costs. If not, she's stuck.

Two quick points about attorney fees and court costs. Usually a large amount of money can be saved by **both** parties if they settle prior to trial: litigation costs and attorney fees. In addition to uncertainty of outcome, the saving of pretrial costs is a major incentive for settlement.

Second, the tradition in this country is that each side pays their own lawyer, even if they win their case. In many European countries, loser pays for both lawyers. This rule has tremendous impact: it prevents people with small claims from getting legal representation—the cost of the lawyer will exceed the amount recovered.

Next Darrow and Ms. K sign a **retainer agreement** which spells out the fee and states the extent of Darrow's obligations. Does the fee include representation of any possible appeals? A major source of lawyer/client fights are misunderstandings as to the lawyer's commitment. (Another is the failure of the lawyer to keep the client informed as to what is happening with the case.)

Hands are shaken. Ms. K leaves. Darrow, left alone with her books, will start preparing for trial even though she knows the chances are high the case will be settled; without some trial preparation, she won't know how strong the case is and won't know what a fair settlement would be. Where does she start?

Case Planning: The Interplay of Law and Fact, Backwards

Lawyers prepare cases backwards. They begin by visualizing themselves before the jury ("My, what a dashing presence!"). What will they argue in closing? Once they know what they want to argue, they gather evidence to support it. Easy: but how will they know what they want to argue before the jury?

That's why they went to law school. What are the legal responsibilities of landlords? What is negligence? What kinds of damages can plaintiffs collect in personal injury cases? Can they get pain and suffering? Can they get punitive damages?

You will learn a vast amount of law in law school; preparing for trial, never simply rely on your memory: look up the current state of the law.

A good place to start is with **form jury instruction books** which are used in many states. If the case of Ms. K is litigated, what will the jury be told about the law of negligence, about what can be recovered, about the burden of proof? Knowing what they will be told, we can plan what we want to argue.

Visualize a warm courtroom, with jurors nodding off. The Judge begins.

Ladies and Gentlemen of the Jury. I will now tell you the rules of law which you must follow to decide this case. (1) If you find that the defendant was **not** *negligent or that the defendant's negligence did* **not** *cause plaintiff's injuries, your verdict must be for the defendant. (2) If you find that the defendant* **was** *negligent, and that his negligence* **caused** *the plaintiff's injuries, then your verdict must be for the plaintiff.*

Plaintiff claims that defendant was negligent.

Negligence is the failure to use reasonable care. Negligence may consist of action or inaction. A person is negligent if he fails to act as an ordinarily careful person would act under the circumstances.

Before you can find the defendant liable, you must find that the defendant's negligence caused the plaintiff's injury. Negligence causes an injury if it helps produce the injury, and if the injury would not have happened without the negligence.

If you decide for the plaintiff on the question of liability, you must then fix the amount of money which will reasonably and fairly compensate for any of the following damages proved by the evidence to have resulted from the defendant's negligence:

(1) The nature, extent and duration of the injury;

(2) The pain, discomfort, suffering, [disfigurement], [disability] and anxiety experienced [and (reasonably) to be experienced in the future] as a result of the injury;

(3) Reasonable expenses of necessary medical care, treatment, and services rendered [and reasonably probable to be incurred in the future]; and

(4) Earnings which were lost by the plaintiff to date, and any decrease in earning power or capacity by the plaintiff in the future.

The plaintiff has the burden of proving by a preponderance of the evidence:

(1) That the defendant was negligent;

(2) That the plaintiff was injured;

(3) That the defendant's negligence was a cause of the injury to the plaintiff; and

(4) The amount of money that will compensate the
    plaintiff for his injury.

I will now tell you the standard of proof in this case.
Preponderance of the evidence means such evidence
as, when weighed with that opposed to it, has more
convincing force and the greater probability of truth.
In the event that the evidence is evenly balanced, so
that you are unable to say that the evidence on either
side of an issue preponderates, then your finding
upon that issue must be against the party who had
the burden of proving it.

Now that's a mouth full and there is more: the
judge will also instruct about how to judge who is
telling the truth, about how to act as jurors.

Jury instructions, drawn from appellate cases and
relevant statutes, are not merely as dull as they
sound.   They reflect great political/legal battles.
The ones you have just read give the plaintiff an
uphill fight—she must prove both neglect and injuries (**burden of proof**) and she must prove it by a
"preponderance of the evidence" (**quantum of
proof**).   These are not neutral or self-evident decisions; they turn on political assessments.   Do we
want to encourage or discourage personal injury
suits? Do we want to shift losses or do we wish to
let them stay where they are?

If we wanted to help people in Ms. K's position
(to shift loss to folks who might be better able to
absorb them or prevent them) we could put the
burden of proof on the defendant to prove he wasn't

negligent. As the judge has told us, if the evidence is balanced, he who has the burden **loses**.

If we wanted to discourage people like Ms. K from bringing suit, we could increase the quantum of proof required of her, from "preponderance of the evidence" to "clear and convincing evidence" or even "beyond a reasonable doubt".

"Pain and suffering" awards are a hotly debated element of recovery. The huge jury awards one reads about (and salivates over) are mostly for "pain and suffering". Insurance companies argue that they threaten Western Civilization. Others claim that juries, knowing that the lawyer will get about a third of the recovery, use pain and suffering awards to make up the client's loss: deduct a third of what we give you and that's how much you should have gotten in the first place.

A final point on jury instructions. At some point the judge is likely to say something like:

> *Ladies and Gentlemen of the Jury, you are to decide the facts of this case. I will tell you the law.* ***It is your duty to follow the law as I give it to you even if you disagree with it.***

Again, this seems to be an unremarkable statement but, like so much of law, it reflects great debates about matters of importance. Why not tell juries "If you think the law is unjust, don't follow it"? This is known as **jury nullification** and, in the early days of our country, was a proud tradition:

local juries protecting neighbors from the unjust edicts of the King.

You might wish to consider the issue: you will find that you quickly get to issues you talked about as an undergraduate which, then, probably seemed a tad dull. Can we trust legislatures to pass just laws? If people (here juries) have power, will they run amuck? The great issues of Political Science, Philosophy and Sociology are present in law; this time they matter.

Back to the saga of Ms. K. Jury instructions set the stage. Darrow must prove that Larry Landlord was negligent and that his negligence caused Ms. K's injuries. As to this element, Landlord's lawyer will be looking to find evidence of pre-existing injuries to break the causal link. Darrow must also prove how much damage Ms. K suffered due to her fall.

As to damages, some amounts will be easy to prove. Ms. K broke her leg, hurt her back and incurred hospital and doctor's bills. She also missed 10 days of work. Darrow knows that it will be relatively easy to prove the amount of the "reasonable expenses of necessary medical care" by simply introducing the bills at trial. She can easily prove "lost earnings" by having Ms. K testify as to their amount. It will be more difficult to prove that the injuries will cause her lost income in the future and it may be hard to convince the jury to put a high monetary value on the "pain, discomfort, suffering and anxiety experienced" by Ms. K.

The real difficulty will be to prove Larry Landlord negligent. Ms. K says she fell because the step at the top of the stairs was loose. This will be easy to prove. Darrow and her photographer visit the scene and inspect the staircase. They find that the top step, made of wood, is cracked so that, when one steps on its outside edge, it gives. Neither Darrow nor her photographer can tell how long the step has been cracked. Has Larry Landlord been negligent? Has he "failed to act as an ordinarily careful person would act under the circumstances"? Does the mere existence of a cracked step prove, by a "preponderance of the evidence" that Landlord was neglectful?

Maybe Darrow could convince a jury on this evidence (she's that good). Of course, if the judge thinks the evidence is so weak that no reasonable juror could find for the plaintiff, he can take it away from the jury after the plaintiff has rested, (grant a **directed verdict**) or even after the jury comes back with a judgment in favor of the plaintiff (**enter judgment notwithstanding the verdict— "judgment n.o.v."**)

Like all good lawyers, Darrow wants more evidence. She would like to argue that Larry knew of the defective stair for months prior to Ms. K's accident, knew that many people used the stairs and was seen, beer in hand, laughing the villain's laugh, "Let them tumble!"

The odds are that Larry will deny knowing anything about the step's defective condition and will claim that he inspects them often (each week, on his way to his Temperance meeting), and that he has nothing but love for all his tenants and that his heart goes out to Ms. K but that, hey, it wasn't his fault.

Take a few moments and put yourself in Darrow's shoes. What kinds of evidence would you look for to meet these claims

———————

Unfortunately Ms. K never told Larry of the defective stair prior to her fall. She was unaware of it because she very infrequently used those stairs. (The fact that Ms. K didn't know of the defect in the stairs is helpful; otherwise Larry might argue that she was contributorily negligent in using them.) To prove Larry knew of the defect before the accident, Darrow sends an investigator to talk to other tenants. Did they ever report the condition to Larry? Were there other accidents on the stairs? Does Larry himself use the stairway, thus possibly having firsthand knowledge?

If you can't prove Larry actually knew of the condition, what about arguing that, as a reasonable landlord, he would have inspected the stairs periodically? Here Darrow has two lines of attack: legal and factual.

As to the legal side, she will research cases to see if she can find any cases saying that landlords have a duty to make reasonable inspections. If she finds them, then she can ask for a **jury instruction**:

> Ladies and Gentlemen, a landlord has a duty to make periodic inspections of common areas.

If Darrow can get this instruction, she has saved herself a lot of work: now she must prove only that Larry didn't make the inspections, not that he should have.

Assuming Darrow can't get the instruction (because she can't find any cases) then she will have to argue to the jury, as a matter of fact, that failure to inspect is negligence. Now she can simply argue that to the jury. Thinking about her case, however, she realizes that she could strengthen that argument if she could call other landlords to testify that they always make inspections and think it would be unreasonable not to do so.

Now she has something else to research: under the law of evidence, would testimony of other landlords be admissible? She will likely write a **trial memorandum** to use at trial if the issue comes up. (Note that this research can help in negotiation: "Look, I will call three landlords who will testify your client should have made inspections and that testimony is admissible.")

Darrow realizes, however, that even if she can establish a duty to inspect (either legally or factually), she still must show that the inspection would have disclosed the defect. She needs testimony that the stair was defective for a long time. She needs an **expert**. An expert need not have special degrees; an expert is simply someone who has special knowledge that will help the jury understand the facts of the case. Darrow calls a carpenter to inspect the stairs.

Let's say the evidence at trial shows this.

The step was broken but Larry did not know that it was. He knew a lot of people used the stairs but had not inspected it for six weeks prior to the accident. Casual inspection would not have disclosed the problem; the only way it would have been found would be to get on hands and knees.

Was Larry negligent?

Who knows what neglect dwells within the heart of man?

The Jury does.

The imprecision of our system is hard to live with. We want definite answers. And all we get is a shrug and a smile and a "That's a jury question."

You might be a juror. Given the jury instructions, has K met her burden?

Returning to our case, while investigations are going on, Darrow has contacted Larry Landlord's lawyer, Big Jim Owens. Her initial overtures to settle the case meet with sullen rejection:

"Larry Landlord wasn't negligent. Ms. K wasn't injured. Besides, there is a clause in the lease releasing the landlord from all liability."

If that's the way it is going to be, the only thing left to do is sue. Darrow drafts a complaint using, as a model, one in a legal form book. (A lot of legal work is simply plagiarism.)

The Initial Court Papers

IN THE SUPERIOR COURT

IN AND FOR THE COUNTY OF KERN

STATE OF CONTENTION

Ms. K

Plaintiff

vs.

Larry Landlord

Defendant

COMPLAINT FOR NEGLIGENCE AND STRICT LIABILITY

Comes now plaintiff and complains of the defendant as follows:

Count I

1. *The court has jurisdiction of this matter as all events complained of herein occurred in this county and both Ms. K and Larry Landlord are residents thereof.*

2. *At the times herein mentioned defendant owned the Owl Apartment Building, at 1112 4th Street, McFarland.*

3. *At the times herein mentioned defendant retained control in the Owl Apartment Building of the halls, lobbies and stairways used in common by all tenants of the building and others lawfully coming onto the premises.*

4. *Plaintiff was a tenant of defendant on or about November 17, XXXVCIV. [As an author, I am not about to date this book before its time. Like movie producers, I will make up a Roman Numeral and flash it so no one can read it.]*

5. *On that date, while plaintiff was proceeding down the common stairway provided by defendant for the use of all tenants, plaintiff was tripped by a defective stair on the stairway, thrown violently down the stairway, and in falling sustained injuries to her back and a broken leg.*

6. *As a result of such injuries, plaintiff sustained damages in the amount of $100,000.*

7. *Defendant knew, or with the exercise of reasonable care should have known, of the defective condition of the stairway, but negligently failed to correct, remove or repair such defective condition, and such negligence by defendant was a proximate cause of plaintiff's injuries and the damages incidental thereto.*

Count II

1. *Plaintiff realleges 1–6 of her first cause of action.*

2. *Defendant was strictly liable for defective conditions in the stairway and said defective conditions were a direct cause of plaintiff's injuries.*

WHEREFORE, plaintiff prays judgment against the defendant for $100,000, for costs of suit, and for *such other and further relief as the court deems proper.*

> C. Darrow
> Attorney for Plaintiff

———

Reread Count II. What is C. Darrow up to? Why a Count II at all? Isn't it the same as Count I? Compare #7 in Count I with #2 in Count II. Read carefully.

———

Darrow is asserting **an alternative theory of liability**. She is unsure that she can prove neglect so she is trying to simply avoid the problem by alleging strict liability. You will learn in Torts that, in some cases, people can be liable for injuries they cause **even if they were not negligent**. This is true, for example, of people who store explosives. If the explosive goes off and injure someone, that person can recover without showing that the defendant was negligence: storers of explosives are **strictly liable**.

The law is always in a state of flux; Darrow hopes to convince a judge that the doctrine should apply to landlords and dangerous stairs. She does this by alleging that basis of liability; if Larry's lawyer is on his toes, he will file a motion saying that landlords are not strictly liable and then, as we are apt to say, **the issue will be joined**.

We'll see.

Proud of her work, Darrow takes it down to the County Courthouse, pays the County Clerk the filing fee, and files the complaint. The clerk gives it a case number and we're off to the races. Darrow gives a copy of the complaint and a summons to a process server who thereupon serves it on Larry Landlord.

Now it is time for Big Jim to go scurrying to the law library. He has but 20 days to "answer."

In the Superior Court

Blah, Blah, Blah

Ms. K

Plaintiff	*Civil Action Number 1066*
vs.	*ANSWER*

Larry Landlord

Defendant

Comes now defendant to answer plaintiff's complaint as follows:

1. *Admits allegations 1–4 inclusive.*

2. *Denies allegations 5, 6 and 7.*

3. *As to count two, denies all matters not admitted to in number 1 hereof.*

AFFIRMATIVE DEFENSE

As an affirmative defense to both counts, defendant alleges

1. *That the lease between Ms. K and Larry Landlord which Ms. K signed, provides: "The Landlord shall in no event be liable for any loss or damage which may occur to the Tenant."*

2. *Said clause bars plaintiff's suit.*

WHEREFORE, defendant prays

1. *That plaintiff take nothing on her complaint.*

2. *That the court order plaintiff to pay defendant's costs of suit and order such other further relief as the court deems proper.*

> *Big Jim Owens*
> *Lawyer for Defendant*

Note that Big Jim admits certain things, that the court has jurisdiction, that the defendant owed the apartment house and controlled common areas, and that the incident occurred on November 17, XXVXXVIIIX (in case you didn't get the joke the first time).

Big Jim does deny the things he will contest at trial: the fall, the injuries, and the landlord's neglect. Ms. K, as plaintiff, will have the burden of proving them—but we already know that.

Note the **affirmative defense**. Usually a plaintiff must prove all the elements of her case; sometimes, however, the law requires the defendant to bring up certain matters and then prove them. For example, the plaintiff must prove that the defendant was negligent; if the defendant claims that the plaintiff's negligence contributed to his injuries, the defendant must allege it and prove it. Note, again, that these are political/legal decisions. One could, for example, require plaintiffs to prove, not only that the defendant was negligent, but that they, the plaintiffs, were not.

You will spend time in your Civil Procedure class on how and why courts allocate issues between things the plaintiffs must prove and things the defense must prove (affirmative defenses).

Discovery

With the Complaint and Answer filed, things are likely to sit quite some time. The lawyers will engage in *discovery*. Big Jim will *depose* Ms. K (in his office; he will offer coffee * * * he's that kind of guy). Darrow will be there and, before things start, she and Big Jim will engage in that easy banter that lawyers love and clients hate ("Why's my lawyer being nice to that sleaze?"). A court reporter will transcribe the questions and answers. Ms. K will be sworn and Big Jim will try to pin her down, both as to the cause of her accident and to the extent of her injuries. If Ms. K changes her story at trial, she can be *impeached* by these prior statements. Suppose, for example, she testifies at trial that she hurt her left arm during the fall. Big Jim has her deposition and is ready to **cross-examine**.

Cross Examination: by Big Jim Owens

Q: (by Big Jim) Ms. K, you testified on direct that you injured your arm during the fall, is that correct?

A: Yes.

Q: Do you remember coming to my office for your deposition?

A: Yes.

Q: Wasn't your attorney with you?

A: Yes.

Q: And you were sworn to tell the truth on that occasion?

A: Yes.

Q: And I told you before we began not to answer any question you didn't understand, isn't that a fact?

A: Yes, I remember. You seemed like such a nice man at the time.

Q: During the deposition I asked you to describe your injuries. You told me of your back pains and your broken leg, isn't that right?

A: Yes, my back was quite painful. And my leg was really smashed up. It was terrible.

Q: I appreciate your injuries. Please just answer my questions. Now, after you indicated your problems with your back and leg, didn't I ask you whether you were injured in any other way?

A: Yes, you asked me that.

Q: And didn't you tell me, "No, I had no other injuries." Weren't those your precise words?

A: Yes, but * * *.

Q: Thank you, nothing further.

If Ms. K has a good explanation for her inconsistency, Darrow can bring it out during redirect. In the jargon of the trial bar, this is known as *rehabilitation*.

Redirect by C. Darrow

Q: Before you were cut off by Big Jim, I believe you were about to explain your inconsistency.

A: Yes. During the deposition I was in pain and my back and leg hurt so much that I simply forgot about the injuries to my arm.

Trial lawyers will tell you that some rehabilitation is better than others.

Darrow will be engaged in her own discovery. One of the goals of discovery is to narrow and define the factual disputes for trial. Recall that Darrow alleged in her complaint that the defendant "owned the Owl Apartment Building," that the plaintiff "was a tenant of the defendant," and that the defendant maintained control over "common stairways." She alleged all these things because as a matter of substantive tort law she must prove all of them before she can recover. In all likelihood these facts will not be contested by the landlord and indeed Big Jim admitted them in his answer. But what if Big Jim was playing petty and filed as an answer what is known as a *general denial,* one which denies everything? Must then Ms. K call witnesses at trial to prove Larry Landlord owned the building? No. She can, before trial, force Big Jim's hand to see what he is really contesting. She sends the following to Big Jim:

Ms. K

Plaintiff	*Civil Action Number 1066*
vs.	*DEMAND FOR ADMISSIONS*

Larry Landlord
Defendant

You are requested to admit the truth of the following statements, pursuant to the Rules of Civil Procedure which provide that these matters will be deemed admitted unless, as to each, you serve within 30 days an answer, or an objection thereto, stating the reasons why you cannot truthfully admit or deny the matter. You may not give lack of information or knowledge as a reason for failure to admit or deny unless you state you have made reasonable inquiry and that you still lack sufficient information to admit or deny. The statements are as follows:

1. *That on November 17, and for several months previous thereto, Larry Landlord was the owner of the Owl Apartment Building.*

2. *That on November 17, and for several months previous thereto, Ms. K was a tenant of Larry Landlord.*

3. *That on November 17, and for several months previous thereto, the back staircase in the Owl*

*Apartment Building was for the common use
of the tenants of said building and was in the
control of Larry Landlord.*

Date: February 1.

C. Darrow

If Big Jim admits to these matters, then C. Darrow
can introduce the admissions at trial to prove those
aspects of her case. What happens if Big Jim
denies them? Then C. Darrow will have to prove
them at trial. So why should Big Jim admit them?
Because if C. Darrow is forced to prove them at trial
she may, under many discovery statutes, "apply to
the court for an order requiring the other party to
pay the reasonable expenses incurred in making
that proof, including reasonable attorney fees."
Best to admit what you must.

Darrow will undoubtedly depose Larry Landlord,
hoping to find that he either knew of the condition
or failed to make ordinary inspections of the stairs.
All is going per usual when suddenly Big Jim makes
a move designed *to end it all.*

DEFENDANT'S MOTION TO DISMISS COUNT 2 OF PLAINTIFF'S COMPLAINT

DEFENDANT'S MOTION FOR SUMMARY JUDGMENT

TAKE NOTICE THAT at 8:30 a.m. or as soon thereafter as the matter can be heard, on April 6 in Courtroom 4 of the Superior Court of the County of Kern, defendant will move the court to dismiss Count 2 in plaintiff's complaint as it fails to state a claim upon which relief can be granted. DEFENDANT WILL FURTHER MOVE that summary judgment be granted it as to both counts on the basis that there is no triable issue of fact in this case.

Big Jim

What's going on? Will Big Jim, Big Bad Jim, get away with it? Stay tuned. [If the matter was to be tried under the Federal Rules of Procedure, Big Jim has made a bad mistake. He should have filed his Motion to Dismiss before filing his Answer. Not to worry; you will learn all about this in Civil Procedure. Note here simply that the drafters of the Federal Rules apparently had no sense of dramatic moment.]

Pretrial Devices to Test Legal Sufficiency of Fact

Why have a lengthy and expensive trial if it is clear that one of the parties is a sure loser? Procedural law allows for various moves to abort cases without trial if there really isn't a true factual dispute. ("**Procedural law**" refers to the rules which govern the *method* by which disputes are resolved, such as rules governing which court should decide the controversy (jurisdiction), what issues may be joined in the same lawsuit, and how long one has to answer a complaint. "**Substantive law**" refers to rules which determine the *outcome* of the dispute, the rules of contract, property, and dog bite. Substantive law governs our daily lives and those of our dogs.)

The two most common procedural devices to test the legal effect and sufficiency of fact are *motions to dismiss* and *motions for a summary judgment.*

a. *Motions to dismiss a pleading as insufficient as a matter of law*

The plaintiff files a complaint, the defendant an answer, each making certain factual allegations. A motion to dismiss basically says "no soap"—what is alleged doesn't make it as a matter of substantive law.

In this case defendant is moving to dismiss plaintiff's second count. Plaintiff alleged that the defendant landlord should be liable on a theory of strict liability, that he should be liable even though the plaintiff cannot prove his negligence. Darrow wanted a fallback position in the event she could not prove negligence. Clever idea. Defendant's motion to dismiss is saying "Without showing negligence, there is no cause of action as a matter of law and hence the count should be dismissed. No need to have a trial on it."

Motions to dismiss can be used to test the legal sufficiency of answers as well as complaints. Darrow could move to dismiss the affirmative defense, the one raising the exculpatory clause, arguing that such clauses are void. If that motion was granted, then the defendant could not even introduce evidence of the clause at trial: *You can introduce evidence only in support of what you have alleged (or evidence which contradicts what your opponent has alleged).*

In olden days, days of grace and style, motions to dismiss were called "demurrers." You will find that term in some opinions you read. It is still used in our more romantic states, such as California.

b. *Motions for summary judgments*

A motion to dismiss is solely defensive in that it can only attack the sufficiency of the facts alleged by the opposition in his complaint or answer. But what if there is an important fact not alleged by the opposition that would abort the case? How can you get it before the court? By a motion for Summary Judgment. You file an affidavit setting forth additional "fact." Unless the opposing party denies it, the court deems it admitted and rules. Now, in her complaint, Ms. K did not mention the exculpatory clause (who's to blame her?). To get it before the court, Big Jim files an affidavit attesting to it. K can't deny it. The issue is joined: does the clause, does as a matter of law, bar her suit?

Come 8:30, April 6, C. Darrow and Big Jim arrive in Courtroom 4. Most likely they have previously submitted *Memorandums of Points and Authorities* arguing their respective positions. The parties will argue, quoting precedent, arguing policies, distinguishing cases, waving their arms and predicting doom. No doubt the judge will "take the matter under advisement." After a short interval the judge will enter judgment, in all likelihood striking the plaintiff's second count (nice try Darrow) and denying Big Jim's motion for summary judgment, holding exculpatory clauses unenforceable.

The matter is set for trial of plaintiff's remaining count, the one alleging negligence. Can Darrow make it out *factually?*

Trial's set for tomorrow. Knock it off for now.

CHAPTER 12

TRIALS

A Short Overview of the Trial Process

Jury trials go something like this.

1. *Jury selection.* In some jurisdictions, the lawyers question ("**voir dire**") prospective jurors. Where the lawyers don't, the judge does. It goes something like this:

Do you know any of the parties to this action?

This case involves a suit for personal injuries growing out of an automobile accident. Have you been in such an accident yourself?

The plaintiff is asking for damages for pain and suffering. The law allows for such damages. If you believed the evidence warranted damages for pain and suffering, would you award them?

This is a criminal case involving burglary. Have you been the victim of a crime? Do you have any relatives in law enforcement?

If I instruct you that you are not to put any more weight on a police officer's testimony than any other witness, would you follow that instruction? If I instruct you that you should not consider what will happen to the defendant if she is convicted, will you follow that instruction?

The purpose of voir dire is to impanel a jury which will render a fair verdict. Each side can challenge potential jurors **for cause** and each has a limited number of **preemptory challenges**—those are exercised when the lawyer feels, for whatever reason, it would be best not to have the person on the jury. However, under recent Supreme Court decisions, preemptory challenges cannot be used to systematically exclude individuals based on race or sex.

2. *Plaintiff's opening statement.* Opening statements relate what will be proven and how it will be proven. "We will then call Dr. Dread, who is not a doctor but plays one on TV. He examined the plaintiff shortly after the accident. He will testify as to her injuries and as to the great pain she was in."

3. *Defendant's opening statement.*

4. *Plaintiff's case-in-chief.* Plaintiff presents the evidence needed to make out the case. In a typical personal injury case, the following elements must be proved.

    a. That the defendant was negligent

    b. That the negligence caused plaintiff's injuries

    c. The extent of those injuries

The evidence can consist of **exhibits** (X-rays showing plaintiff's broken bones, photographs of the victim's injuries and toes, fingers and other body parts), **documents** (doctor bills) and, of course, **witnesses**, including **expert witnesses**. When the lawyer calls his witnesses, he takes the witness on **direct** examination.

Mr. Plaintiff, tell the jury of the injuries you received in the accident.

A lawyer cannot *lead* his own witness; that is, he cannot suggest the answer to him, as does the following:

Mr. Plaintiff, isn't it a fact that you received severe back injuries in the accident?

Only an extremely dumb (or honest) witness would answer "No."

On direct, you must ask **non-leading questions**:

Mr. Plaintiff, please describe the injuries you received as a result of the accident.

Leading questions are prohibited on direct because we want the witness to testify, not the lawyer.

After each witness, the defense lawyer has the opportunity to **cross-examine**.

Mr. Plaintiff, you testified on direct that you injured your back in the accident. Now isn't it a fact that you had injured your back several weeks prior to the accident?

On cross-examination the lawyer can, and usually does, lead the witness.

Cross-examination has been touted as the best known device to ferret out the truth. It usually doesn't work as well as it does on TV but it can be quite powerful. Volunteer to play the role of a witness at a trial practice court. Feel the rush of combativeness and fear when the judge says, "You may cross-examine." It's only you and the lawyer and you **must answer the questions**. Gone are your jokes, your charm, your evasions.

5. *Plaintiff rests* after presenting all the evidence supporting the claim. Quite likely, out of the jury's hearing, the defense will move for a *nonsuit* or a *directed verdict*. Although the precise name of the motion may vary from jurisdiction to jurisdiction, the basic notion is the same: "Plaintiff has failed to present enough evidence to win." In the auto accident case, for example, the defendant could make such a motion on the basis that, even though the plaintiff proved injuries, there was insufficient evidence to prove the defendant negligent. If there is enough evidence to go to the jury on *all elements* the plaintiff must prove, the judge will deny the motion. The ball is now in the defendant's court.

6. *Defendant's case-in-chief.*

7. *Defendant rests.*

8. *Plaintiff's rebuttal.* Certain things may come out during the defendant's case that plaintiff feels he can prove wrong. Rebuttal is his opportunity. Suppose defendant calls a witness who testifies he saw the accident. Plaintiff, during rebuttal, can call witnesses who will put the defendant's star witness, at the time of the accident, in Nova Scotia. (Ah, Nova Scotia! I'm writing this in Tucson and it's 110 degrees outside. Nova Scotia, Nova Scotia, the very name speaks of cold * * *).

9. *Defendant's rebuttal.* Quite infrequent. Perhaps witnesses could testify that plaintiff's rebuttal witnesses don't even know where Nova Scotia, Nova Scotia, is.

10. *Plaintiff's closing argument.* Here the task is to marshal the evidence and convince the jury.

11. *Defendant's closing argument.* The job is to expose plaintiff's errors.

12. *Plaintiff's rebuttal argument.* This is to answer *only* points raised in defendant's closing. It is not to bring up new arguments. The defendant had a chance to respond to plaintiff's closing argument and it is only fair to allow the plaintiff to respond to the defendant's closing argument.

In criminal cases, the prosecution is the plaintiff and hence gets last shot at the jury.

13. *Jury instructions,* finally.

14. *Jury Deliberation and Verdict.*

15. *The Joy of Victory, The Agony of Defeat!*

A Long Overview of the Trial Process

Here I will highlight some of the great moments in trial to wet your appetite or to send you back to the Registrar to get your money back.

One thing I want to illustrate is that *objections to evidence* often fulfill the same role as motions to dismiss (demurrers without poetry) and motions for summary judgment: They force a legal determination of the legal status of fact. Again we will see the interplay of law and fact. After that, a quick look at closing argument because, well, because it is the most artistic of the lawyer's craft.

Darrow, for the plaintiff, has the burden of proof and goes first. She plans to call Ms. K to testify to her fall and injuries. She plans to call Dr. Dread to establish the extent of those injuries. To establish Larry Landlord's negligence, she will call Joseph Ham, an ex-tenant of the apartment house who will testify that he complained of the loose stairs to Larry Landlord two weeks before the unfortunate accident. Darrow will also call a carpenter, with the unlikely name of Woody Nails, who inspected the stairs shortly after the accident and concluded that they had been in a dangerous condition for at least two months.

The defense, at the pretrial hearing, indicated to the judge that it would call only two witnesses, Larry Landlord and Chuck Pile, a tenant who will testify that weekly he takes out the garbage by way of the back stairs and has not once tumbled. He may even do a little jig.

Darrow can call her witnesses in any order she pleases. Knowing that the first and last positions are key, she decides to put Ms. K on first and to put on Dr. Dread last. She wants to leave the jury with a powerful presentation of her client's suffering. The weak part of her case, that of Larry's negligence, she plans to sandwich in between high points, the fall and the suffering.

As to each witness, Darrow knows she can develop the testimony in any order she selects. With Ms.

K, for example, she plans to develop four main points. First she plans to use Ms. K to prove up medical bills and loss of earnings. These matters are not controversial and lack emotional impact; they should go in the middle of the testimony. Second, Darrow wants Ms. K to testify she was being careful at the time of her fall. Although defense did not, in its pleadings, raise the issue of contributory negligence, Darrow is concerned that some juror during deliberations might remark "If she had been looking where she was going, this would never have happened." Third, Ms. K will testify as to the accident itself and, fourth, to the pain and suffering she experienced. Darrow decides on the following order:

1. Introduction and personalization of Ms. K.

    Ms. K may appear nervous in testifying, what with what happened to her brother when he went to court. Or is he the one who turned into a cockroach? Either way, the jurors should be sympathetic to her.
2. Description of the accident and its terror.
3. Testimony showing Ms. K was not negligent.
4. The amount of medical bills and loss of earnings.
5. The pain and suffering; the fear she would never walk again.

Note, again, lawyers sculpt their cases to make them powerful. Let's pick up the testimony at point three:

Q: (by C. Darrow). Now, Ms. K, you weren't at fault in this, were you?

Q: (by Big Jim). Objection. Leading. You can't lead on direct. You know better!

Q: (by C. Darrow). Of course I do. This is an instructional book and the author keeps making me do things I know better than. I am not my own person. In fact, I am made up!

Q: (by Big Jim). Oh ... does that mean that I too am a fictional character? I'm crushed ... I got such a great parking spot in front of the courthouse ....

Cut and back to fiction:

Q: (by Ms. Darrow) Prior to the accident, did you know the step was loose?

A: No, I seldom use the back stairs. I hadn't used them before my fall for at least two months.

Q: Now as you approached the top of the stairs, were you distracted in any way?

A: No, I was looking where I was going.

Q: Then why did you step on a step that was loose?

A: Well, when you walk you look ahead, not at your feet. I had no idea that the step was going to give way like it did.

Note how Darrow develops the facts. It is far more effective to develop a conclusion than it is to simply come to it: "Were you careful?" * * * "Yes."

Q: After the accident, did you have occasion to inspect the top step?

A: Yes.

Q: Is it your opinion that Larry Landlord was negligent?

Q: (by Big Jim) Objection! That question is clearly improper as it calls for an opinion of a lay witness. Darrow knows better than that.

Court: Sustained.

Darrow does know better than that. She knows that the question is improper. She also knows that it is **unethical** to ask an improper question to sneak impermissible material before the jury. You can't ask "When did you stop beating your dog?" unless you have a good faith belief that the witness did at one time beat his dog.

But before you get too upset with Darrow's questionable behavior, let me come to her defense. I, as puppeteer extraordinaire, urged her to ask that question. (But to you, Dear Reader, Darrow is more real than I am. Perhaps I am someone else, maybe the same guy who really wrote Shakespeare. Maybe I don't exist ... in which case I should stop complaining about the heat.)

Cut.

I wanted to introduce a very important rule of evidence, the **opinion evidence rule**. One statement of the rule is found in the Federal Rules of Evidence:

Opinion Testimony By Lay Witnesses

If the witness is not testifying as an expert, his testimony in the form of opinions or inferences is limited to those opinions or inferences which are (a) rationally based on the perception of the witness and (b) helpful to a clear understanding of his testimony or the determination of a fact in issue.

The rule forces witnesses to testify about the raw data of experience, what they saw, heard, smelled, tasted and felt, not what they concluded from those experiences. Drawing conclusions is the job of the jury. A witness cannot testify "Landlord was negligent." That opinion is neither "rationally based on perception"—the witness didn't *see* the landlord being negligent—nor is it helpful to a "clear understanding of his testimony." A witness can testify:

I stepped on the stair and *felt* it give. I *looked* at the stair and found a crack about 6 inches long and a quarter of an inch wide. I told landlord about it and *heard* him say "That sounds dangerous. I will fix it immediately." A week later I *looked* at the stair and *saw* nothing had been done.

From the facts perceived by witnesses, the jury concludes whether the landlord was negligent.

Some witnesses can testify as to their opinions: experts. For example, the Federal Rules provide:

Testimony by Experts

If scientific, technical, or other specialized knowledge will assist the trier of fact to understand the evidence or to determine a fact in issue, a witness qualified as an expert by knowledge, skill, experience, training, or education, may testify thereto in the form of an opinion or otherwise.

Darrow plans to call two experts. Dr. Dread, based on his training in medical school and his experiences as a physician, will testify as to the extent of Ms. K's injuries and as to her prognosis. [Ed. note: Dr. Dread has been previously described as not being a doctor but as playing one on TV. While critics might put this glaring inconsistency down as an instance of sloppy editing, I like to think of it as an important learning device: never take your opponent's experts' qualifications for granted.]

Woody Nails, carpenter, will be the other expert. He will testify about the condition of the stairs. Let's pick up the trial with him.

Court: Call your next witness.
Darrow: Plaintiff calls Woody Nails.

Witness is sworn.

Q: (by C. Darrow) State your name and address for the record.

A: Woody Nails. 5010 Randlett Drive.

Q: What is your occupation?

A: Carpenter. I have been a carpenter for thirty years.

Q: Have you ever built staircases?

A: More than I can count.

Q: Do you ever have occasion to inspect staircases for safety?

A: Quite often. Several insurance agents ask me to inspect buildings before they insure them. I pay particular attention to stairways because if they're not proper folks can get hurt real bad.

Q: What happens if you find a staircase that is dangerous?

Q: (by Big Jim) I object, Your Honor. This line of questioning isn't relevant to the issues of this case. What happens when this witness inspects other staircases is besides the point.

Q: (by C. Darrow) Your Honor, this line of questioning is relevant to show this man's expertise. That insurance agents rely on him is evidence that he knows what he is talking about.

Court: Objection overruled.

Q: Again, what happens when you find a staircase that you think is unsafe?

A: I'll tell the owner or the agent. They have me repair it.

Q: Do they ever go ahead and insure the building without insisting on having the stairs repaired?

A: Not that I know of. It would be real dumb.

Q: Did you have occasion to inspect the back staircase at the Owl Apartments?

A: Yes. I went over there about two days after Ms. K fell.

Q: What was the result of your inspection?

A: The top stair was unsafe. It was loose and gave when you stepped on it. The problem was that it had a big crack in it, about 6 inches long and a quarter of an inch wide.

Q: Could you determine how long the crack had been there?

Q: (by Big Jim) Objection, Your Honor. There is nothing about this witness that would make him an expert in this matter. I let his testimony about "unsafe" pass but not this. Without some showing that this witness has some expertise in knowing how long conditions have existed, I object to the testimony.

Court: I'm going to allow the question. I think carpenters can make these decisions. You can cross-examine Mr. Nails about how he came to his conclusion. How much weight to give his testimony will be up to the jury but I will let it in.

Q: (by C. Darrow) How long would you say the stair had been in that condition?

A: Well from the dirt and grime embedded in the crack, I'd say a fairly long time.

Q: Could you be more specific?

A: At least a couple of months.

Q: Thank you, no further questions. You may cross-examine.

Cross–Examination.

Q: (by Big Jim) Now isn't it a fact that life's a stage and we're but actors?

A: (nervously) Well ... er ... I guess you can say that.

Q: And isn't it true that your testimony has been sound and fury, signifying nothing?

A: (looking desperately at C. Darrow) I ... I ... don't know.

Q: Well you know this, **Mr.** Woody Nails. That isn't even your real name is it! ? And not even a very clever one at that! ?

(Note leading questions are **not** questions. They are statements of fact followed by question marks.)

A: (beginning to sob) I ... I don't have a real name.

Q: Of course you don't. That's because you're made up. Your Honor, I move to strike his entire testimony! Your Honor ...? Where's the judge? What's happening?

Fade to black.

Note, as to the admission of evidence. It is a two step process. The judge decides whether or not to *admit* the evidence; once it is admitted, the jury decides whether or not to *believe* it. Admission of evidence is a question of law and you will see it at issue in several of the cases you read. The **exclusionary rule**, for example, makes certain evidence inadmissible: The jury will never hear it. On the other hand, just because evidence is admitted does not mean the jury must believe it. Even if a criminal defendant's confession is admitted in his trial, he can still testify to his innocence and attempt to convince the jury that his confession was not true because the police tricked him, beat him or whatever.

To illustrate something of cross, let's take the testimony of Joe Ham who, on direct, stated that two weeks before the accident he had told Larry Landlord of the bad condition of the stair and that Larry had said "That sounds dangerous. I will get it fixed immediately." Larry has told his lawyer, Big Jim, that the conversation never happened. As this is not something Joe could merely be mistaken about (like an eyewitness identification), it must be that Joe is lying (or Larry is). The purpose of cross examination in such cases is to suggest possible motives for perjury. Note, however, that Big Jim realizes that even hostile witnesses can be used to make needed points. Note too that the questions on cross are leading.

Cross Examination of Joe Ham

Q: (by Big Jim) It's true that you used those stairs on several occasions both before and after Ms. K's fall.

A: Yes.

Q: And you never noticed the defective condition before the time you reported it to Larry Landlord.

A: That's right.

Q: So as far as you know, the condition was of fairly recent origin, isn't that right.

A: Well, I didn't notice it before.

Q: So as far as you know, the stairway was not cracked before the time you reported it?

A: Yes.

Q: And that was two weeks before Ms. K's fall, and not a couple of months.

A: Yes.

Q: Thank you. Now you never fell on those stairs, did you?

A: No.

Q: And you never heard of anyone else tripping on those stairs, isn't that right.

Q: (by C. Darrow) Objection, Your Honor. The question is not relevant.

Q: (by Big Jim) Your Honor, the lack of other accidents is relevant to the issue of whether the stairs were safe.

Court: Objection overruled. You may answer the question.

Note: This might be an error on part of the judge. If Ms. K loses, she can **appeal** and base her appeal on judicial error. But good luck if this is all she has, even if the judge was wrong. Appellate courts don't like to reverse cases and make the parties start all over again. They reverse only when the judge below really screws up. (That's a legal term.)

A: No, I never heard of anyone else falling.

Q: Thank you. Now you are a very good friend of Ms. K's, isn't that right.

A: Yes.

Q: And you want her to win this lawsuit, don't you?

A: I think she should.

Q: Please answer the question. Do you want her to win this lawsuit or don't you?

A: I guess I do.

Q: Do you guess or do you?

A: I do.

Note how Big Jim pursues the witness. Most witnesses will try to deflect the lawyer's questions; you must become something of a bulldog.

Q: And isn't it a fact that you don't like Larry Landlord?

A: Well, maybe not.

Q: Maybe not? Isn't it a fact that he evicted you two months ago?

A: Yes.

Q: And didn't you tell him at the time you would get even?

A: No, I didn't say that.

Again, to ask that question, Big Jim must have a good faith belief that Joe said it. You just can't make up dirt.

Q: Weren't you upset at being evicted?

A: Of course.

Q: And angry at Larry.

A: Yes.

Q: Nothing further.

During trial lawyers make points to use in closing argument. Big Jim's closing argument, as it relates to Joe, will run something like this:

Ladies and Gentlemen, there is one glaring contradiction in this case. You remember Joe, the tenant who had been evicted by Larry. He testified that he told Larry of the faulty condition of the stairs a good two weeks before the accident. Not only did he tell him, but he told you Larry said "That sounds dangerous. I'll get it fixed immediately."

Now that's quite convenient Larry said that. Note how well it fits into the plaintiff's theory. It shows not only Larry knew of the condition but also knew it was quite dangerous. What better evidence could you ask for?

Larry testified he never had that conversation with Joe. You must decide who to believe. Someone is lying to you. How can you decide who is telling the truth? His Honor will instruct you that you can consider the "character and quality of the testimony" and the existence of any bias or interest.

Does Joe's testimony make sense? To believe that that conversation actually took place you must believe that Larry knew that there was a very dangerous condition on the stairway but simply failed to do anything about it. Joe would have you believe that Larry was content to wait until someone tripped and fell, to wait until someone sued. Joe's story doesn't make sense. Further, he continued to use the stairs. Does it make sense to go on using a staircase after you have reported its dangerous condition to the landlord?

Joe's story just doesn't hold together. Had he told Larry of the condition, it is reasonable to assume Larry would have acted, not only to prevent someone's injury but also to avoid a lawsuit. Does Joe have a motive to make up his testimony? A motive to lie to you? You bet. He is a good friend of the plaintiff. He admitted that he wants her to win this case and obviously he knows his testimony is essential for her victory. And he dislikes Larry. Larry evicted him. Joe even admitted his anger.

No, Joe is not to be believed. He was simply lying about his conversation with Larry. Larry told you it never happened because it never did.

Closing Argument: Weaving Law and Fact

Effective closing argument relies on the primary lawyering skill, the ability to bring law and fact together. Here it is done in public.

The witnesses who have testified and the documents and exhibits which have been introduced have put before the jury bits of information: that Joe was evicted by Larry, that the carpenter believes that the stairs had been in a state of bad repair for a long time, that Ms. K fell. At closing the lawyer *marshals these bits of information into factual conclusions that have legal relevance.* To illustrate this let's pick up part of Darrow's closing argument.

Closing Argument: C. Darrow:

From the fact that Joe told Larry of the condition of the stairs and from the fact that they had been in disrepair for a long time, we can conclude that Larry knew or should of known that the stair was dangerous.

Next Darrow shows the jury what these factual conclusions mean in terms of law.

That Larry Landlord knew of the dangerous condition and yet did nothing about it means that he was not acting as would an ordinarily careful person under the circumstances. An ordinarily careful person would have done something to prevent the accident. As the judge will instruct, if you find that Larry did not do as would an ordinarily careful person, you are to find him negligent.

This mode of analysis will become quite familiar. It is the *very same process you will use to analyze exam questions.* The bits of information in the question are turned into factual conclusions which are then turned into legal conclusions. More of this later in the book.

Closing arguments are, however, more, much more, than logic. They are emotion and power. In the hands of a good criminal defense lawyer, "reasonable doubt" becomes the finest and most delicate flower of Western Civilization, a flower about to be ground under the shiny black boot of the State. Listening to a good personal injury lawyer you experience the victim's anguish as he lies sleepless in a hospital bed thinking of what might have been.

When it comes your time to make a closing argument, there are few experiences so intense and immediate. When you start, there will be distractions. You will be nervous, you will be aware of the spectators, of the judge and of your trembling hands.

Soon, however, you soar. Forgotten are your notes and gone is the judge; for awhile it is just you, your argument, and the jurors.

Just once makes three years of law school worthwhile.

PART 4

BASIC LAWYERING SKILLS

Here we cover the basic lawyering skills; research, writing, argument. All rest upon your ability to do legal analysis; expect "Yes, but" and "So what?" and a plethora of "on the other hands".

Moot Court is the grand first year tradition, your opportunity to dress up and dazzle judges with the depth of your knowledge and the sparkle of your wit. You will learn techniques to avoid passing out (or what to do when you wake up and confront the delicate issue of carrying on as if nothing had happened); you will learn of the central importance of fact (and how to tell a compelling story), how to meet and defeat the dreaded "slippery slope" argument and, finally, what your role as appellate advocate should be.

As to legal research, I stress essentials that are often overlooked in the rush to the library: planning research and avoiding pitfalls along the way, particularly those of computer assisted research.

"Legal Writing" stresses clarity, not only to improve your writing, but also to improve your analytical abilities. I will give you some models to consider and will conclude with an editorial checklist which you can use to check your own writing.

These chapters are best read, not "in advance," but rather in conjunction with your Research and Writing class and as you prepare for Moot Court.

Of course, you could read them now just, to make sure.

CHAPTER 13

LEGAL ARGUMENT
(MOOT COURT)

Just when you get comfortable, they spring Moot Court.

It will be your first introduction to Chaos Theory ... live.

For Moot Court, you will be assigned to represent one side of an appeal. You will have to write an argumentative brief as to why your side should prevail and then, as your opponent sits there calmly taking notes, you will have to make a twenty to thirty minute oral argument before, quite likely, a panel of three judges.

Chaos theory, which predicts you can't, kicks in during oral argument. You prepare; you plan; you practice. Finally it's Opening Night. Then, as you stand before the Court, something happens. Everything falls apart.

It may happen right up front. "May it please the Court? My name is ..." and one of the judges, the kindly one with the glasses, blind-sides you with a question from Hell. My case, as chaos theory would predict, was different.

I was well into my argument and was making a telling, well-rehearsed, point, when one of the judges bent to pick up his pencil and his chair flipped, landing him, plop, on the floor and one of my old high school friends, who was sitting in the first row behind me, erupted with infectious giggles ... it was funny (as long as you weren't the one standing there) ... it was all so grown-up, with robes and serious talk about matters of great moment, and this guy goes and slips on a banana peel! And so there I was, alone at the podium, all by myself, the center of attention, indeed, the focal point of the universe, my knees shook and I fought off the giggles, while one of the two remaining judges (ignoring his fallen colleague) asked me, again and again, with his voice rising with each again, "Is negligence a question of law or of fact?" and I all I could think of was "A question of what?" and I knew I was lost and that my brilliant career was over and I was about to shout "Neither!" when I heard Jimmy lose it again and so, my friends, did I.

Relax. The worst thing in the world cannot happen to you; it has already happened to me.

Prepare. Plan. Practice. But don't be surprised if things go differently. Chaos is fun (at least thinking back). And the truth of the matter is that we are all better when we are spontaneous, when we get away from the script that went so well in front of the bathroom mirror.

To begin our discussion of legal argument, I will draw on an incident from **your** childhood, proving, once and for all, that Socrates was right, that you already know this stuff.

> *No, Mommy, please don't put me in time-out. I didn't mean to spill it * * * it just slipped. When Ben knocked over his soup, he didn't have to go to time-out. Put me in time-out only if I'm really bad.*

There you have it—the big three, instinctively. Arguing spilt milk in the kitchen or *Gideon* in the Supreme Court, all you have are *facts*, *precedent*, and *policy*. The rest is technique and avoiding passing out.

This chapter presents a theory of legal argument; the next focuses on technique of argument and what you can teach yourself after your Moot Court experience.

How do judges come to their decisions? They will likely be concerned with three things: (1) doing justice between the parties and this usually turns on questions of **fact**; (2) correctly applying existing law (**precedent**); and (3) creating good law (**policy**). Let's take a look at each.

Doing justice: The importance of facts

It is critical, both in your written brief and in your oral argument, to present the facts in such a way as to lead the court to view the controversy from the viewpoint of your client. The statement of facts is "not merely part of the argument, it is more often than not the argument itself. A case well stated is **far more than half argued**."

Those are the words of John W. Davis, a leading appellate lawyer of his day.

I cannot overemphasize the importance of factual perceptions on legal decisions.

Take the case of *Alaska Packers*. During a fishing voyage, the ship's captain agreed to raise the salaries of the fishermen. After the voyage, he refused to pay the higher salary and the crew brought suit. Should the captain be compelled to pay the raise?

The judge who decided the case recounted the facts along these lines.

> "High at sea, Captain Goodship was confronted by his mutinous crew which angrily demanded more money. His only choice was to agree or to return to shore, thus losing his entire investment."

Seeing the lone captain surrounded by ruffians as the ship tossed dangerously on stormy seas, the answer is easy: of course the captain should not be made to pay. But is this an accurate picture? What would the fishermen say? Would they sheepishly acknowledge their guilt?

> *"Egads! Foiled again! Yes, we are all devils. 'Twas the devil's rum that convinced us that we could take unconscionable advantage of dear ol' Cap, even though the man has been like a father to us."*

Only in the movies.

In real life, this is basically what they said:

"We are honest fisherman. We risk our lives to support our families. The Captain promised us a set salary plus a percentage of the catch. That would have put food on the table. However, when we got to sea, we discovered that the nets were in very bad shape; we realized that the catch would be much less than we had thought and hence our families would go hungry. We approached the captain, hats in hand, explained our plight and he graciously agreed to raise our set salary. If he hadn't, we would have asked him to return to shore so that we could have taken other jobs; Tiny Tim is dying."

In litigation, both sides have lived the same basic events. From those events, however, they come to radically different conclusions. This is because they start with the basic human premise, "I'm right," and then go about viewing the world in a way that supports that premise. The two sides will emphasize different events and will draw different inferences.

In your statement of facts, your goal is to try to get the court to *see the events as did your client.*

Edward Charles Davis was arrested for shoplifting but charges against him were eventually dropped. Thereafter, however, his picture appeared on a flyer, showing "active shoplifters," which was distributed by police to local merchants. Davis was not amused; he filed a civil rights action against the police. The United States Supreme Court introduced the case as follows:

*Petitioner Paul is the Chief of Police of Louisville, Ky. * * * while petitioner McDaniel occupies the same position in the Jefferson County.   * * * They agreed to combine their efforts for the purpose of alerting local area merchants to possible shoplifters who might be operating during the Christmas season. In early December petitioners distributed to approximately 800 merchants in the Louisville metropolitan area a "flyer," * * * [of active shoplifters.]*

*The flyer consisted of five pages of "mug shot" photos, arranged alphabetically. * * * In approximately the center of page 2 there appeared photos and the name of the respondent, Edward Charles Davis III.*

Paul v. Davis, 424 U.S. 693.

Guess who won? The case could have been introduced differently, as it was in a law review:

*[P]laintiff Edward Charles Davis, a photographer for the Louisville Courier–Journal and Times, was arrested in Louisville, Kentucky on a charge of shoplifting. He plead not guilty. [T]he charge was "filed away with leave [to reinstate]," but he was never called upon to face that charge in court. With the onset of the Christmas season * * * defendants McDaniel and Paul, the chiefs of police for Jefferson County and Louisville, jointly prepared a five-page flyer containing the names and mug-shots of "Active Shoplifters." Copies of this bulletin were distributed to merchants warning them of possible shoplifters. In fact, the flyer*

was composed not only of persons actually convict-
ed of shoplifting, but included persons who had
been merely arrested.　* * * Plaintiff's name and
mug-shot were included in flyer.　* * *

Note how this statement makes one more sympathetic to Davis. How do these two statements, covering much of the same ground, create different impressions? Reread them.

The Supreme Court version begins with a focus on the defendants, both "Chiefs of Police," who were combining efforts to alert local merchants of possible shoplifters. It was, after all, Christmas. The law review version begins with the Plaintiff, and we immediately learn some sympathetic facts about him: he has an actual job and, although arrested, was never convicted. The law review version stresses that the list included folks arrested but not convicted. On the other hand, while the law review points out that Davis' name and "mug-shot" were included in the flyer, the Supreme Court points out they were buried—in the center of page two—and the photos were described by the Court as "photos," not as "mug shots."

This might be a good format to follow in your own statement of facts. Begin with a discussion of how your client fits into the case and bring up favorable material early on. We tend to be most sympathetic with the first person we meet and their viewpoint is apt to become ours. Latecomers usually have an uphill battle in convincing us that we are wrong.

Law follows vision. In the *Davis* case, Law Review Writer "saw" an innocent man getting hurt; it is clear how he or she would have decided the case. Conversely, the majority of the Supreme Court primarily "saw" two government officials doing their jobs in a creative way. In *Alaska Packers*, the judge saw "stickup" while I saw *A Christmas Carol*.

There is a famous gestalt drawing which includes the images of both a young woman and an elderly woman. Some see one, some see the other; *both are there.*

Along these lines, realize that you have some flexibility in stating the issue to be decided. A case involving a possible consumer fraud by a local ghetto store can be characterized narrowly or broadly: as an instance of a particular customer being taken advantage of by a particular salesperson; as an instance of a storewide practice of gouging poor customers; or as an instance of the rich exploiting the poor (forget the last, no one's a Marxist any more).

A warning. Be honest. The other side will have its say. If you misstate facts or omit important information because it is damaging, the court's sense of sympathy will turn to one of betrayal. If the court trusts you, you are halfway home; if you lose that trust by playing fast and loose with the facts, you might as well stay home.

Dealing with unfavorable material. In a student negotiation role play, one of the "secret" facts we give to the plaintiff's lawyers is that their client, who is claiming substantial personal injuries, has begun to play tennis. Law students, bless them, lie: "My client is still badly injured." Later, in critique, "That wasn't a lie, I didn't say she wasn't playing tennis." Or if they **did** say she wasn't playing tennis, they argue, "That wasn't a lie; what I meant was that she wasn't playing tennis **right then**."

We had two experienced litigators demonstrate the negotiation. The longtime P.I. lawyer opened:

> *Let me tell you something about my client. She is so anxious to overcome the harm inflicted on her by your client that she is even trying to play tennis.*

In evaluating a case, think long and hard of the facts and of the law that hurt you. If you cannot somehow turn the facts or distinguish the law, you shouldn't be pursuing the case. The facts and the law won't go away.

I don't mean to suggest that your statement of facts should be one long apology. It is perfectly fine to put positive spins on negative facts, such as was done above. And you can omit some negative facts simply on the basis that you cannot include everything. The *test for omission* that I employ: when my opponent brings up the fact, will the court feel a sense of betrayal? Is the fact of such significance that its omission is misleading? Had the Supreme Court never mentioned Davis was not convicted or had the law review writer never mentioned the motivation of police, I think they would have told essentially misleading stories. Had I heard the original story without being told those facts, I would feel betrayed when I learned them.

One final warning about statements of facts. *Write facts, don't howl for justice.* If justice is really on your side, your proclaiming it in grand sweeping manner won't convince the court but your reciting facts might. Again look at the two statements in *Davis*—neither statement resorted to adjectives or pleas and yet each convinced the reader of very different positions.

A compelling factual statement motivates the court to rule in your favor; now you must establish a rationale that permits it to do so. You must discuss both the past (precedent) and the future (policy).

Following the law: Arguing precedent

Courts must follow the rules of law announced in prior controlling decisions unless (1) those decisions are distinguishable or (2) the court is willing to overrule those prior decisions, a thing courts are loath to do.

The first part of this book describes how one goes about distinguishing cases.

Given the operation of *stare decisis*, a "morning line" on appellate arguments is possible.

1. *If precedent is with you, you're favored.* Convince the court the prior cases are indistinguishable and you win—unless, of course, the

court is willing to overrule those cases. Against the overruling of precedent you have several powerful stock arguments:

a. Overruling in **this** instance is a bad idea because people relied on the rule announced in prior decisions.

b. Overruling in *any* instance is a bad idea because it rejects the wisdom of the past and creates uncertainty in the legal order. The more decisions that are reversed, the less any can be relied upon.

2. *If precedent is against you, try harder.* Even if you convince the court that the prior cases are distinguishable, you still are not a winner. All that you have done is show the court it *need not* apply the rule to your case. Now you must, citing reasons of policy, convince the court that it *should not*.

Creating good law: Arguing policy

Never forget **justice**. Even where precedent is on your side, don't just cite it and then sit down:

"The rule is X and I win, nannie, nannie, nannie."

You should **motivate the court** to follow rule X; tell the court why rule X is a just rule and why it advances sound public policy.

For example, if you are raising a Statute of Frauds defense to a oral contract, don't just point to the statute, tell the court that it must refuse to enforce the agreement and then, raising your arms, begin your victory lap around the playground. Tell the court why refusing to enforce the oral contract is a good idea; tell the court how the Statute of Frauds protects important social interests. Otherwise, who knows? There are exceptions to the Statute of Frauds, and a judge, unsympathetic to your technical argument, might just find one. Nannie, nannie, nannie.

When you are arguing public policy, try to ground it in some official pronouncement. Courts don't like to be accused on "doing their own thing" and of making up public policy as they go along. They weren't elected. How do we know it is "public policy" rather than simply "their policy"?

Let's return to the argument that a clause in a lease, releasing the landlord from negligence liability, should not be enforced as it is against "public policy"?

How do we know it is against public policy? How do we know it isn't just a matter of personal whim?

"Well, Your Honor, first there are Building Codes requiring that certain safety steps be taken in all construction, thus showing a societal interest in protecting against physical injury, and a recent special report of the Governor's Commission on housing discussed in great detail the lack of bargaining power on the part of tenants due to the housing storage. Then there are various governmental welfare programs providing medical care for indigents and surely there is a public interest that negligence landlords not be allowed to shift those costs to those governmental programs."

Cast about in the attempt to find any official pronouncements that tend to validate your assertion of public policy. Almost anything will do, although obviously some pronouncements are more equal than others. Your goal is to convince the judge that you simply haven't made up the "public policy" and hence, if she adopts it, she will not be accused of "judicial legislation."

In terms of arguing policy, note that *stare decisis* cuts both ways. The decision that the court in your case makes will guide future judges. Be prepared to answer the court's concerns:

Will the "rule" you ask for always produce justice or will it lead to ridiculous results?

Is the "rule" operational in the sense that juries can understand it, lawyers work with it, other legal functionaries administer it?

There are two kinds of policy argument that need to be addressed: *Slippery Slopes* and *Flood Gates*. These are not the names of race horses but they have been ridden enough.

If we invalidate this lease clause which exculpates the landlord from liability for negligence, the next thing you know we'll have all kinds of tenants in here demanding that we rewrite their leases, even the amount of rent.

There are *three* responses to all slippery slope arguments. Write them out—they will be on the final. (Yeah, but hey, if they are on the final, will everything be on the final?)

1. **All slippery slope arguments are reversible.** Knowing this, you can at least make an offensive feint.

   If you refuse to invalidate this clause, then the next thing you'll have all kinds of landlords in here wanting to enforce the most repugnant of clauses—"They agreed to forfeit their firstborn in event of late payment; it says so in clause 43(F)(iv) and this court doesn't rewrite leases!" (If this point isn't on the final, will anything be on the final?)

2. **Most slopes have dumps**, things to grab on to. Here you show how future judges can distinguish the madness you are asking the court to pursue.

   Your Honor, this exculpatory clause is unique in that it relieves the landlord from liability for personal injury. There is a strong policy to encourage landowners to take reasonable steps to avoid such injury. No such policy is involved in other lease terms, surely not the amount of rent.

3. **Or you can take the slide all the way down.**

   Your Honor, now that you mention it, that would not be such a bad idea.

Floodgates is a particularly virulent and repugnant form of slippery slope.

If we do justice to your client, why then all kinds of ragamuffins will be coming in here to demand justice!

You now know how to cope.

"Your honors, if you refuse to do justice to my client, you will never do justice to anyone." (Reversing the slippery slope although a tad "in your face.")

"Your honors, doing justice for ragamuffins might not be a bad idea." (Taking the slide all the way down although a tad unrealistic.)

Probably here the best approach is option three: finding a dump to grab.

"Your honors, not to worry. Only rich folks know where you are."

———

To review, your goals in Moot Court are modest: convince the court that fairness between the parties means your client wins, fidelity to precedent means your client wins, and writing great law and making the casebook means your client wins. Simple enough. But how to get there? That is the subject of the next chapter.

CHAPTER 14

MECHANICS OF ORAL ARGUMENT

In the last chapter I discussed the overall substance of legal arguments. Here I discuss the mechanics of oral argument: what to say first, how to make a graceful exit, and how to remain cool and calm while those around you panic. I will end with some advice with will help you make the most of your Moot Court experience.

Before reading further, put yourself in the position of a judge facing a difficult decision. What would you want from the lawyers arguing the case?

I. The Right Attitude

Making an oral argument, should you be brilliant? Witty? And what do you do with your hands?

Surprisingly enough, the right attitude is one of service: you are there to **help the court** make what is no doubt a difficult decision. In helping the court, you will direct your remarks to the key issues in case, probably no more than two or three, and will be interested in answering the court's questions rather than sticking to your script.

If you are clear in your intention, that your job is to help the Court, your hands will take care of themselves.

A. Be helpful

The most important thing for an appellate lawyer to have is "a sincere and single desire to be helpful to the Court." This is from John W. Davis, one of the best.

Be helpful to the Court? How can this be? Isn't your job to win? Perhaps Davis winked ... fain "help" as a clever technique but, by all means, close the sale.

In preparing your case, you will have spent a long time sorting out the facts, wrestling with the law, considering the policies at stake. Because you have done so from the perspective of your client, you will come to believe that a careful consideration of those factors should lead the court to rule in your favor. (If you don't believe that, with one exception I will discuss momentarily, you shouldn't—at least in real life—be pursuing the case).

Your job is not to force the court to come to your conclusion but to help it see how you came to it. Any case worth its salt will be close. In real life, the Court wants to come to the correct decision and needs your help in sorting out the law and facts. The judges need your guidance through the thickets.

Judges don't need dazzle, mirrors or bullying.

Attitude tells, not technique. But when one is committed to helping the court, one is likely to:

1. Concede the valid points the opponent raises. "Yes, my opponent is correct, the case did hold that. However, we believe that it is distinguishable."

2. Listen to the Court's concerns and respond to them rather than simply deny them. "Yes, if you were to hold for my client, certain expectations may be upset. However, we believe that they may not be as extensive as feared because of the following limiting features."

3. Acknowledge the closeness of the contest. "I wish the cases were more clear in this area but they are not. A fair reading of them, I submit, supports my position because * * *."

4. Cite and discuss cases and statutes that tend to go against your position, even if the opponent hasn't. The Rules of Professional Conduct require citation of adverse "controlling authority." To help the court, you should go further: you don't want the court to render a judgment upon ignorance—that's not helpful. If you don't have good arguments to get around the contrary rulings, *you shouldn't be there*.

A caveat on criminal defense. In order to protect the rights of the accused, criminal defense lawyers are allowed much more room to advance arguments that stink. "Your Honor, the statute says 'obtaining money by false pretenses.' I move for a directed verdict as the state has only proved one pretense." Enough said.

When one has the wrong attitude, when one is *not* committed to helping the court, when one is selling used cars, one is likely to:

1. Take no prisoners. Deny every point the opposition makes.

2. Attack one's opponent. Personal attacks ("If my worthy opponent bothered to read the cases") are seldom justified.

Should you argue points you don't believe? No! But I used to be more sure. Argue a point you don't believe in and likely your lack of belief comes across and undermines your overall credibility ("This lawyer doesn't want to help me; this lawyer wants to make a fool of me.") Further, you don't have much time and it is probably best to stick with your winners. If you can't convince yourself, it is doubtful that you will convince others. On the other hand, I have seen courts buy arguments that I think were foolish (but, then again, I wasn't the one arguing them).

B.   *Focus on two or three points*

Beginners want to cover everything they did in their written brief. "That point in footnote twenty-three sparkles."

John W. Davis pointed out that most appeals turn on two or three main points, some on one. Focus on them; don't clutter your argument and waste your time by trying to get in everything you said in your brief. Note the major difference between written and oral advocacy. Briefs should cover all the points while oral presentations should focus on those that matter.

Davis, to describe this point, used the phrase "go for the jugular." He was writing in a time when people ate meat. Today, while our lives may be enriched with vegetables, they are impoverished by the lack of vivid metaphors.

C.   Address the Court's concerns, not yours

A football coach once said of the forward pass that, of the three possibilities, two are bad. Ditto oral argument.

Keeping your head down, you are earnestly arguing a particular point. The possibilities are:

1.   The judges are not convinced of your position and never will be; thus you are wasting your time.

2.   The judges are already convinced of your position; thus you are wasting your time.

3.   The judges are undecided about your point and need further guidance.

How can you find out it is 3, not 1 or 2? Formal argument is highly stylized; as much as one would like, one can't stop and ask: "Well, Your Honors, have I convinced you on that one yet? If not, do I have a prayer on it?"

Some judges will pepper you with questions. Others are reticent, too shy to interrupt, too unsure to voice their concerns. So, how do you draw them out?

Invite intervention.

"I'll discuss the following three issues.   * * * Is there any order in which the Court would like me to proceed?"

————

"That finishes my discussion of the collateral estoppel issue. Are there any questions before I go on?"

————

"This area is extremely difficult and I probably haven't been as clear as I should. Are there any areas that I need to clear up?"

Never tell the judge to shut up.

"Your Honor, I will answer that question in a few minutes. Right now I would like to spend a few minutes throwing interceptions." Always answer a judge's question when it is asked.

Encourage questions.

Watch oral arguments. Lawyers are almost always better when they are responding to questions than when they are giving their speeches. There is movement, creation, engagement. The only time this is not so is when the lawyer hasn't anticipated the question and doesn't have a clue. *Rehearse questions.* You should be able to anticipate many of them: "Your opponent, in his brief, argues that * * * and I find that's an interesting point. How do you respond?"

Maintain eye contact.

Sure, the flag does look nice but only by looking at the judges will you sense what points are important. *Never read* your argument. Have a list of three or four major points and perhaps some citations you want to get right. You should probably write out your entire argument but then distill it to its essentials to use as a crib sheet.

Forget footnote twenty-three.

Give up on the notion that you will get in everything. In real life, there is dispute as to the value of oral argument. Perhaps most cases are won or lost long before, "May it please the Court." But even if oral argument matters, no judge has changed her mind simply because counsel was able to squeeze in one last point, a point which, of course, has already been argued in the brief.

II.   The Structure of Appellate Argument

1. *Introduce yourself and the one you represent.*

   "May it please the court, my name is C. Darrow and I represent Allprovidence Insurance, the defendant in the action below and petitioner here."

2. *State the nature of the case* (contract, tort criminal) *and briefly describe its procedural history*.

   "This is a suit on a life insurance policy on the life of Mr. Humpty Dumpty, brought by his widow. Our defense was that suit was barred by a suicide clause. At trial, it was our contention that Humpty did not have a great fall but rather that he took a great leap. After a jury trial, judgment was for the plaintiff. We appeal on the basis that the judge improperly applied the 'plain meaning rule' and improperly instructed the jury."

3. *State the facts of the case*.   Remember they are extremely important.

   "In order to protect the widows and orphans, the true owners of Allprovidence, and in order to discourage suicide, the Allprovidence Insurance Company routinely includes a suicide clause in its policy, something akin to 'snooze, you lose'."

Often the court will cut you off with, "We are familiar with the facts, proceed with argument." Dashed, the hope of killing the first several minutes on safe turf!

4. ***State the legal issues and overview the points you intend to argue***. A clear introduction to your legal argument is critical. Otherwise the judges may not follow it.

"It is our contention that the court below erred in applying the Plain Meaning Rule to Nursery Rhymes, thus preventing our argument that 'had a great fall' can be read as meaning 'took a great leap.' Unfortunately, the Yokel below is unfamiliar with Critical Legal Studies and trendy French Literary Criticism which suggests that texts can be read any way one wants.

*"Further, and as an **independent justification for reversal**, we assert the court below improperly instructed as to the burden of proof. Which issue do you wish me to address first?"*

5. ***Argue the case***. As with your written work, your oral argument will be improved by the effective use of transitions.

Not: *"The next issue concerns the jury instructions."*

But: *"That concludes my discussion of the Plain Meaning Rule. Unless there are any questions, I would like to now address the matter of the jury instructions. **Even if** this court decides that the court properly applied the Plain Meaning Rule, **it must reverse** this case if it finds that the jury instructions were improper."*

As more fully described in the chapter on legal writing, *RILS* transitions are best: they *R*elate the new topic to the last; *I*ntroduce it, and show its *L*egal *S*ignificance.

Note that the **relationship** between legal points can be either "and" or "or." That is, the relationship between the plain meaning point and the jury instruction point could either be that insurance company has to prevail on both to win or, as is the case, on either one. The phrase "even if" captures that relationship in the above example. It is critical, given the law's complexity, to make these relations clear.

Note that you should make clear the **legal significance** of the topic you are introducing. Here you are introducing the matter of the jury instructions and, if you are correct as to this point, the court **must reverse** the lower court. This is so much stronger than just introducing the subject.

The more *explicit* your argument, the more you *tie law and fact* together, and the more *concrete examples* you use, the clearer your argument will be. Consult the chapter of legal writing for further explanation of these hallmarks of clarity.

6. ***Rejoice*** if the court asks you questions.
7. ***Conclude and sit down***. In many appellate courts, you are allotted a certain amount of time. There is no requirement, however, that you use it all. If you are done, sit down. To avoid mindless meandering, have a concise and powerful conclusion in mind. Tell the court exactly what you want it to do and state your best reason for why it should.

Appellate arguments require clear introductions, clear transitions and clear summaries. These will mean some repetition but repetition is necessary. As listeners, we can't go back to see how the arguments fit together. Often our minds wander. Repetition is needed. Realize too that the judges, no matter how prepared, will not have the same familiarity with the law as you do. Give them a break and don't jump to the heart of your argument which may turn on a rather fine point of law. Put that argument in context. As with legal writing, *begin with the basics*: "The Plain Meaning Rule basically provides that * * * "rather than "The Plain Meaning Rule shouldn't apply here because * * * ." The latter construction forces the judges to go back and think "What is the Plain Meaning Rule?" and there is simply no need to do this. By the way, what is the "latter" construction?

III. A Few Pointers on Delivery and on Not Passing Out

1. Don't read long quotes to the court. If you must quote specific language from a statute or opinion, refer to the page in your brief where you quote the language so that the judges can sing along.

2. If you are citing a case it is usually best to describe briefly the facts of that case. Rules of law are always announced in specific factual contexts; abstract statements of law are always suspect.

3. Avoid monotone. Vary your volume, speed and pitch. Not everything you have to say is of equal status. Pauses can highlight. There is *no* need for you to be making noise *all* the time. When asked a question, *don't* immediately reply. Think about your answer. What may seem like a long intolerable silence to you will seem a very short period to your listeners. Occasionally, "That's a very good question which I hadn't considered. Let me think a few moments."

4. Don't assume all questions are hostile. Judges can ask questions because they need help or *because they want to help you out*. Seldom is their goal to humiliate you.

Coping with nervousness. While sitting there, stop thinking, "Oh no, I'm next!" One way to cope with nervousness is to get your mind off yourself. Concentrate on your opponent's argument while he argues. Listen to what the judges ask him and watch the judges when he responds. You may want to change your argument in light of what you hear and see. While you argue, concentrate on the argument, not on how you are doing.

Remember to breathe. Nervousness often leads to shallow breathing which leads to oxygen deficiency which leads to more nervousness. Take deep breaths; relax your jaw and the back of your neck.

You appear much less nervous than you feel. As for your smug opponent and mighty judges—they are jelly.

Defining and stating your intention. Ultimately the problem of nervousness stems from confusion as to what you are about. In oral argument your goal is not really "don't be the fool" nor is it even to "appear brilliant." Your goal, your intention, should be to convince specific people, the judges, of specific factual or legal conclusions. State your intention to yourself just before you get up there.

My intention is to help Binder, Boland and Bergman understand why the lower court didn't understand the Plain Meaning Rule.

If you are clear on your intention then your demeanor, gestures and words will tend to reinforce that intention without conscious effort on your part. Thus you won't have to worry about what you should do with your hands nor about talking too softly.

At least that is true if you are playing a lawyer on television and you are following the advice of the great Russian drama director, Stanislavski. The importance of defining and stating intention comes from his work but it makes sense in ours. See McGraw, *Acting is Believing*.

V. On Teaching Yourself

Anytime you actually do something is a great opportunity for learning. Most of us don't take advantage; we simply go on to our next chore. In the old days, when giants staggered the earth, we would go out for a drink.

After Moot Court sit down and ask yourself what you have learned from the experience. What have you learned about oral argument? What have you learned about preparation and delivery? What have you learned about getting judges to ask you questions? What have you learned about the adversary process and the law? What have you learned about yourself? And, of course, what have you learned about chaos theory?

A variation on this theme is to list, before your argument, the criteria by which you will evaluate yourself. This will force you to do some serious thinking about the process of argument rather than the substance of your argument.

This is general advice. We all talk about teaching ourselves, but we seldom do anything about it. After your first law school exam, after your first client interview, after your first Supreme Court argument, after sweeping every state but Maine, sit down and ask yourself: "What went well and why?" "What went badly and why?"

Now, what have I learned from writing this chapter?

CHAPTER 15

LEGAL RESEARCH

HIGH DRAMA IN DULL PLACES

Legal research can be fun. More than fun: it can be breathtaking.

... Well ... maybe not in law school.

Learning the techniques is like learning to play the piano, a tad boring. ("Can I go out and play now?").

Ah, my foes, and oh, my friends, visualize Carnegie Hall!

Using the techniques "for real," lifeless volumes shake as you open them to read **just what might be** the "controlling case," and words, merely underlined as a student, now put a dagger in your heart.

"But wait ... the case is distinguishable!"

You die a thousand deaths; you pick yourself up a thousand times. In the quiet of the law library, great battles rage.

Let's jump to next year. You are clerking for a law firm and your supervising attorney calls you into his office and tells you that a client, Ms. Hopper, wants to get out of a contract. She agreed to sell land to Mr. Mattei, a land developer who is thinking about building a Mall.

"Here's the contract. Give me your best thinking."

Supervising attorneys are cryptic.

Covering your panic with your bright (hire me next year) smile, you slink back to your cubby. Your read the contract, several times. Nothing. Nada.

"Well, I won't bill for this time; in fact, I better not bill for any time since I have been here. They're never going to hire me anyway. What's the use?"

You reread the contract. Something strikes you as funny.

> *Subject to Coldwell Banker & Company obtaining leases satisfactory to the purchaser.*

"That's funny," you think.

There have been great moments in intellectual history. In 1928, Alexander Fleming saw a strange green growth on his dirty Petri dish and remarked:

"That's funny."

Fleming was about to discover penicillin. Frank Ryan, in *The Forgotten Plague*, quotes a colleague of Fleming's:

> *What struck me was that he didn't confine himself to observing, he took action at once. Lots of people observe a phenomenon, feeling that it*

may be important, but they don't get beyond being surprised—after which, they forget.

Lesson one: **pursue your puzzles.**

From the deep, dark, recesses of your mind, from first year Contracts, first a name, then a flickering thought.

> *"Lucy, Lady Duff Gordon. Wasn't there something about if one side isn't bound, neither is the other? Didn't she want to get out of her contract because her agent wasn't bound to do anything? Maybe, just maybe, because the purchaser can get out of the contract if he isn't satisfied with the leases, then maybe Ms. Hopper isn't bound either."*

You too take action. You rush to the law library.

There you will have several magical retrieval methods at your disposal: WESTLAW and LEXIS, Digests, Treatises, and so on and so forth. How to use these retrieval systems is the focus of Legal Research classes and far be it from me (thank heavens!) to steal their thunder. But remember this: **legal research is more than the mechanics of retrieving applicable law; legal research is also legal analysis.** We will see.

A few words of general advice:

1. **Don't start researching too quickly.** Think about the problem before you jump in. Characterize it in as many different ways as possible and play **"sounds like."**

Lawyers argue by analogy. "Like cases" may be found, not only in the same area of law as the case you are working on, here Contract, but in other areas of law where courts have faced the same kinds of problems. In the case of Ms. Hopper, the problem raised by the "satisfaction clause" is that one side is bound while the other might not be. Are there any other areas of law where courts have faced similar kinds of problems?

I can't think of an example. What sounds like "writer's block"? How about "batting slump"? Sports psychologists may be helpful to writers.

In the area of "Contract," courts (and legislatures) characterize this problem in several different ways: "No consideration," "Lack of Mutuality," or "Illusory Promise." And the problem may arise in several different contexts: when one side must be "satisfied", or when one side must "approve" or when one side has the right to "cancel."

All retrieval systems (computers, digests, statutory indexes), are triggered by your characterization of the problem. If you restrict your search for cases involving "satisfaction clauses," and "illusory promises," you may draw a blank. There may be winners "filed" under "approval clauses," or "lack of mutuality."

This is a very basic point: premature characterization of a problem may prevent you from coming up with the best solution or from solving it at all. The sad truth is that, once we characterize a problem, we tend to overlook other characterizations and hence other solutions.

Take Ms. Hopper. Her **basic** problem is **not** that the contract is one-sided and her **basic** problem is **not** even that she wants to get out of it. Her **basic** problem is whatever leads her to want to get out of the contract. **Why** does she want to get out of the contract? We, of course, don't know—we are just law clerks. But if we knew, we may find that her problem could be best solved by a method other than getting her out of the contract or, indeed, if we concluded that getting her out of the contract was the best solution, perhaps the "lack of mutuality" defense is not the best way of going about that.

To hammer home my point, I take an example from medicine. Rene Dubos, a medical researcher who helped develop wonder drugs to fight tuberculosis, wrote in *Mirage of Health*,

> *The incidence of malaria in a community can be reduced by drugs that attack the parasite, by procedures that prevent mosquitoes from biting man, by insecticides that poison mosquitoes, or by agricultural practices that interfere with their breeding.*

Some solutions are easier than others. **Don't** simply run to the books or turn on the computer. In your rush to "get started," you may have stumbled upon the most difficult path of all.

And once you are on your way, take time to smell the roses.

2. **Mosey around some.** Your quest, at least in the beginning, should not be to find "controlling authority." Your first job is to educate yourself as to the general area of law, what are the problems, what are the solutions? Moseying around helps.

Modern research techniques are like smart bombs: they can take you directly to authority "on point," such as cases in your state dealing with "land contracts involving satisfaction clauses." Smart bombs can be dumb bombs; to change the metaphor, unless you are already fairly familiar with the area of the law, "Always pass GO". **Begin with a treatise or secondary source.** They will provide a general overview of the area and will suggest other issues that may be involved.

When your research takes you to a statute, back up and look at the Table of Contents to see how the statute fits with others. Other statutes in that section might give you additional ideas and might help you interpret the one before you. Also after the text of a statute, there will be references to other statutes that might prove relevant. Pursue them.

Finally, when your research takes you to Headnote 14 of a case, don't just read the headnote (it can be wrong) and don't just read the text under Headnote 14. Read, or at least skim, the entire case. If you read only the "key" paragraphs, you will have no context in which to place them. The **major point** which I have repeated again and again: you cannot really understand or correctly apply statements of legal principles without knowing their context.

Moseying around places rules in context and will suggest other approaches to your problem. Worst case, you learn some law.

3. **Don't overlook statutes**. In law school, mostly you deal with cases; in practice, mostly you deal with statutes.

A state Supreme Court Justice told me of a lawyer who stood before his court, arguing that his client should have a particular right as a matter of Constitutional law.

"Have you checked the state statute?"

"No, your Honor."

"Well, you should have. Your client already has that right."

As my colleague Ron Cherry says, "Never assume the absence of legislation."

4. **If it matters, go to the primary source.** A case (or legal treatise) may discuss another case (or statute) and characterize it in a fashion that helps (or hurts) you. If the case (or statute) seems important, **read it**: don't rely on someone else's characterization.

Never accept your opponent's characterization of a case; always read the cases they cite against you. I am not suggesting all lawyers distort cases; I am suggesting that "seeing what one hopes" is inherent in the adversary system (and that goes for you, too).

5. **Shepardize, Shepardize, Shepardize; let no case escape your eyes.** (Tom Lehr has a song on the virtues of plagiarism: "Plagiarize, plagiarize, plagiarize; let no one's work escape your eyes." Good advice Tom, I'll steal it). If you don't know what "Shepardize" means, you will have a good question to ask your Legal Research and Writing Instructor or Law Librarian.

As a general matter, while you should always Shepardize, you should never cry wolf (but you probably already knew that).

6. Finally, **pushing buttons is not legal research.** In the old days, before computers, when we found a case or statute that we thought might be important, we had to take notes. Taking notes is a pain. We would make sure, by close reading, whether the material was in fact important. And, by copying out key language, we would actually focus on it.

Computers facilitate sloth. "Oh, yes, that case looks like it might apply so I will push a button, print in out and then go fishing."

That's not legal research; that's Video Arcade.

The same is true of photocopying case after case. Do the analysis now; don't take home half the library to "do it later."

With all of this in mind, we return to the case of Ms. Hopper.

Using whatever retrieval method you choose, you discover a case name: *Lawrence Block v. Palston*.

It is from an intermediate appellate court in your jurisdiction and appears to address an "approval clause" in land sale contract and whether it makes the contract illusory. It is potentially **a controlling case**. What does it say? Will it kill you or save you?

Your heart pounds as if you were in a Poe short story. Trembling, you access the case. There it is: *Lawrence Block v. Palston*. You blink away the sweat and read the language that was at issue:

> "Subject to buyer's inspection and approval of all apartments."

It is almost **identical** to the language in Ms. Hopper's contract. What did the court decide?

Illusory! No contract!

You let out a yell and take a victory lap around the perimeter of the library.

"I'm brilliant! * * * My picture will be on the cover of *The Rolling Stone*!"

But wait! Have you Shepardized the case?

"Oh, no. Please may it not be overruled."

You rush back to your seat. Your heart pounds as if you were in a cheap movie of a Poe short story. You Shepardize. Finally great joy. Unbelievable news! *Block* hasn't been overruled; in fact, **it has been followed**. In the case *Pruitt v. Fontana*, a land sale contract was thrown out as illusory because it provided that the sale was subject to the covenants and easements being "approved by the buyers." Again, almost identical language to that in the contract of Ms. Hopper.

"Do they ever make second year students partners?"

The supervising lawyer pats you on the head and calls Ms. Hopper. "The contract isn't enforceable. Walk on by."

Let's see what happens.

MATTEI v. HOPPER

Supreme Court of California, 1958.

51 Cal.2d 119, 330 P.2d 625.

Plaintiff brought this action for damages after defendant allegedly breached a contract by failing to convey her real property. After a trial without a jury, the court concluded that the agreement was "illusory" and lacking in "mutuality." From the judgement accordingly entered in favor of defendant, plaintiff appeals.

*Plaintiff was a real estate developer. He was planning to construct a shopping center on a tract adjacent to defendant's land * * *.*

Under the parties' written agreement, plaintiff had 120 days to consummate the purchase and pay the agreed price. The concluding paragraph of the agreement provided "Subject to Coldwell Banker & Company obtaining leases satisfactory to the purchaser." This clause and the 120–day period were desired by plaintiff as a means for arranging satisfactory leases of the shopping center buildings prior to the time he was finally committed to pay the balance of the purchase price and to take title to defendant's property.

While he was in the process of securing the leases and before the 120 days had elapsed, defendant's attorney notified plaintiff that defendant would not sell her land under the terms contained in the agreement. Thereafter, defendant was informed that satisfactory leases had been obtained and that plaintiff had offered to pay the balance of the purchase price. Defendant failed to tender the deed.

For the contract to bind either party, both must have assumed some legal obligations. Without this mutuality of obligation, the agreement lacks consideration and no enforceable contract has been created. If one of the parties is free to perform or to withdraw at his own unrestricted pleasure, the promise is deemed illusory and it provides no consideration.

While contracts making the duty of performance of one of the parties conditional upon his satisfaction would seem to give him wide latitude in avoiding any obligation and thus present serious consideration problems, such "satisfaction" clauses have been given effect. They have been divided into two primary categories. First, in those contracts where the condition calls for satisfaction as to commercial value, operative fitness, or mechanical utility and the standard of a reasonable person is used in determining whether satisfaction has been received * * *. However, it would seem that the factors involved in determining whether a lease is satisfactory to the lessor are too numerous and varied to permit *the application of a reasonable man standard as envisioned by this line of cases. Illustrative of some of the factors which would have to the considered in this case are the duration of the leases, their provisions for renewal options, if any, their covenants and restrictions, the amounts of the rentals, the financial responsibility of the lessees, and the character of the lessees' businesses.*

This multiplicity of factors which must be considered in evaluating a lease shows that this case more appropriately falls within the second line of authorities dealing with "satisfaction" clauses, being those involving fancy, taste, or judgment. Where the question is one of judgment, the promisor's determination that he is not satisfied, when made in good faith, has been held to be a defense to an action on the contract. Although these decisions do not expressly discuss the issues of mutuality of obligation or illusory promises, they necessarily imply that the promisor's duty to exercise his judgment in good faith is an adequate consideration to support the contract. None of these cases voided the contracts on the ground that they were illusory or lacking in mutuality of obligation * * *.

If the foregoing cases and other authorities were the only ones relevant, there would be little doubt that the agreement here should not be deemed illusory or lacking in mutuality of obligation because it contained the "satisfaction" clause. However, language in two recent cases lead the trial court to contrary conclusion. The first case, **Lawrence Block C. v. Palston***, stated that the following* condition made the resulting contract illusory: "Subject to buyer's inspection and approval of all apartments." This was said to give the purchaser "unrestricted discretion" in deciding whether he would be bound to the contract.

The other case, **Pruitt v. Fontana**, presented a similar situation. The court concluded that the written instrument with a provision making the sale of land subject to the covenants and easements being "approved by the buyers" was illusory. It employed both the reasoning and language of **Block**.

Both courts were concerned with finding an objective standard by which they could compel performance. This view apparently stems from the statement in Lawrence Block Co. that "the standard 'as to the satisfaction of a reasonable person' does not apply where the performance involves a matter dependent on judgment." By making this assertion without any qualification, the court necessarily implied that there is no other standard available. Of course, this entirely disregards those cases which have upheld "satisfaction" clauses dependent on the exercise of judgment. In such cases, the criterion becomes one of good faith. Insofar as the language in Lawrence Block Co., and Pruitt represented a departure from the established rules governing "satisfaction" clauses, they are hereby disapproved.

We conclude that the contract here was neither illusory nor lacking in mutuality of obligation because the parties inserted a provision in their contract making plaintiff's performance dependent on *his satisfaction with the leases to be obtained by him.*

The judgment is reversed. [Editor's note: this case has been somewhat rewritten—the original prose was even worse.]

Now you know the rest of the story.

Your research convinced you that Ms. Hopper would win. She lost. What went wrong?

Well, first you probably overlooked the fact that both *Block* and *Pruitt* were intermediate appellate court decisions and were not binding on the state's Supreme Court. That's why the Supreme Court could "disapprove them." This is not a terrible error, however, as most often appellate court decisions correctly state the law.

Probably what got you into trouble (to say nothing of the trouble Ms. Hopper got into) was "smart bomb research": finding cases involving "satisfaction" and "mutuality". Note what the California Supreme Court says of the cases it used against you: none were voided "on the ground that they were illusory or lacking in mutuality of obligation." Quite likely, those cases **did not use those words**. The smart bomb flew right on by.

Had you started with a treatise, no doubt you would have picked up the notion that satisfaction clauses can be interpreted to require "good faith" efforts. **That's probably where your opponent picked it up.**

Deep down, however, **you forgot to think.** In your giddy search for controlling language, you forgot the need to analyze cases and you forgot *Lucy*. Remember her? She tried to get out of her promise on the basis that the other side had no obligations under the contract. This is exactly Ms. Hopper's claim.

Lucy lost! Had you reread that case, you might have noticed that there the state's highest court **reversed** an intermediate appellate court which held that Lucy was not bound due to the illusive nature of her agent's promises. So much for intermediate authority. You might have also noticed that the Court did this by implying some duties on the part of the agent. The Hopper court could simply imply "good faith." Finally, you might have come away with the feeling that courts are not sympathetic to folks like Lucy and Ms. Hopper, folks who wish to walk away from their absolute promise on the grounds that, in theory, the other side, which now wants to perform, could have walked away.

Let me close by helping you pick yourself back up. You were not alone in overlooking the "established rules governing 'satisfaction' clauses." Indeed, the lawyers in *Block* and in *Pruitt* did too. Given this, and the fact that the California court cited no cases directly on point, one is lead to suspect that perhaps the "established rule" wasn't all that well established at the time.

The Court relies upon cases in which it was held that **good faith was a defense** and then tells us that they "necessarily implied" that "good faith is an adequate consideration to support the contract." In case the reader gets suspicious of this leap in logic, the Court quickly adds, by way of "Well, at least * * * ":

> *None of these cases voided the contracts on the ground that they were illusory or lacking in mutuality of obligation.*

Perhaps that was because the issue was never raised.

Why am I beating up the Court? To illustrate a important point.

Judicial opinions are winner's history. No doubt, had you read *Mattei v. Hopper* in a casebook, the result would have seemed obvious. "Why did the defendant even bother to litigate the issue? The judges in *Block* and *Pruitt* must be dopes."

Remember this. Almost always, the losers thought they would win. In reading cases, don't assume they were dopes. Ask why they thought they would win.

A writing lesson lurks in this discussion. Note how the *Mattei* Court leads you to this sense of certainty. It first tells you that everyone knows that "satisfaction" can be measured by either "reasonableness" or "good faith." Only then does it tell you that apparently not everyone knows this. **This is an illustration of primacy—the tenden-**

cy to believe the side of the story you hear first.

Consider an opinion which began by stating that the lower court correctly applied the "well-established rule" that satisfaction clauses are "illusory" and then cited *Block* and *Pruitt*. The opinion would continue:

> *But we have a better idea; that these clauses can be saved by implying "good faith" and in fact we have some authority for that proposition * * * well, OK, not direct authority, but authority that necessarily implies it.*

Had the Court written its opinion that way, you would have been more suspicious: "good faith" would be the stranger and *Block* and *Pruitt* would no longer seem like comic relief.

I need to close this chapter by returning to the subject of legal research. I could probably write a couple of paragraphs which would conceal the fact that I had written myself into a corner. I won't. I'll just abruptly get back to my point.

Bottom line (nice touch), technology and research tricks help; but *they can't think critically.*

CHAPTER 16

LEGAL WRITING

There are two things wrong with al-
most all legal writing. One is style.
The other is content. That, I think,
covers the ground.

Fred Rodell, "Goodbye to Law Reviews" 23 Va.L.Rev. 38 (1936)

Style affects content. We *think and act* badly in
part because we *write* badly. That is the thesis of
George Orwell's brilliant essay, "Politics and the
English Language."

Modern English becomes ugly and inaccurate
because our thoughts are foolish, but the sloven-
liness of our language makes it easier for us to
have foolish thoughts. Modern English is full
*of bad habits * * * If one gets rid of these*
*habits one can think more clearly * * ***

To illustrate modern English, Orwell rewrites a
well-known verse from Ecclesiastes:

Objective consideration of contemporary phe-
nomena compels the conclusion that success or
failure in competitive activities exhibits no ten-
dency to be commensurate with innate capacity,
but that a considerable element of the unpredict-
*able must be taken into account * * ***

What's wrong with that? It reads well enough, has a certain flow and smacks of intelligence. We read it, perhaps underline it, and then we move on. But have we understood it? Have we considered the devastating implication? What of our plans? What of our hard work?

> *I returned and saw under the sun that the race is not to the swift, nor the battle to the strong, neither yet bread to the wise, nor yet riches to men of understanding, nor yet favor to men of skill; but time and chance happeneth to them all * * ***

Unless writing is grounded in specifics, both writer and reader skim along, confident but not engaged. When the phrase "a considerable element of the unpredictable" crashes into "the race is not to the swift," both writer and reader can *understand what is being written.* If the race is not to the swift, how come you are studying so hard? Dealing in specifics both writer and reader can *test what is being written.* Is this a true description of life as you have lived it?

Orwell's list of bad writing habits are those that allow a writer to compose without actually seeing or thinking about what is being written:

Abstractions, where the "concrete melts into the abstract" and a "mass of * * * words falls upon the facts like soft snow, blurring the outlines and covering up all details" and where "murder" becomes "pacification," which then allows for more murder;

Stock phrases, pasted together like sections of "prefabricated henhouses," and

Stale metaphors, where both writer and reader read the words but do not see the image, the cat and the disgusting, twisted, bloody thing it dragged in.

Ground your legal writing; see what you are writing. Lawyers tend toward the abstract. Grounding legal prose consists of using specific examples, beginning legal discussions with basic (and easy) propositions of law, and taking great care to show how each legal and factual point fits into one's overall analysis. *Grounding your writing will help others understand it; more important, it will force you to understand it and test it as you go along.*

If you read a legal brief that you cannot understand, dollars to doughnuts it is because the writer doesn't understand it either.

Time to lighten the fare with a story, not as profound as Orwell's essay, but funnier.

The teen-age daughter of a lawyer announced, "Dad, you can't write." Dad disagreed and a test was decided upon. Daughter took one of Dad's briefs to her creative writing teacher for critique.

"I was right, Dad. My teacher says you can't write! He says your sentences are too short, your paragraphs are too short, and besides, anyone can understand what you have written."

We lawyers do not flatter ourselves that our prose will bog down countless generations of undergraduates. Speaking of one of his poems, Robert Browning remarked:

> *God and I both knew what it meant once.*
> *Now God alone knows.*

According to Archibald MacLeish:

> *A poem should not mean but be.*

Lawyers mean. Write poetry on your own time.

I. The Quest for Clarity

Explicitness, hard-working transitions, copying the statutes and beginning with basics

I'll stress the following:

1. Conclusions up front. There should be no surprise endings.

2. Hard-working   transitions.   Not   just, "Next, I will discuss * * * "

3. Explicit ties between law and fact. As to each fact you discuss, as to each legal point you make, ask, "So what?"

We will begin our discussion by reviewing a typical office memorandum. The case is that of *Mills v. Wyman*. The memo follows one of many acceptable formats:

1. Caption

2. Facts

3. Issue

4. Conclusion

5. Statement of controlling law (when in statutory or Restatement form)

6. Analysis

OFFICE MEMORANDUM

To: *Senior Partner*

From: *Humble Associate*

Re: *Contract Claim of Charles Mills*

Facts

Levi Wyman, 25–year-old son of the defendant, fell sick upon his return from a sea voyage. The plaintiff cared for the young man for several weeks. Unfortunately the young man died.

Upon hearing of the kindness plaintiff bestowed on his son, the defendant wrote plaintiff, promising to pay the expenses he incurred in boarding and nursing his son. The defendant now refuses to pay on his promise.

Traditionally, legal writing begins with a statement of facts. But give up on the notion of a radical split between "fact" and "law". There is a chicken and egg problem: without knowing something of the legal issue to be decided, the reader will not know the significance of the facts you are reciting. Consider a brief statement of the legal question before you begin your factual statement:

Facts

The defendant made a promise to pay plaintiff for the expenses the plaintiff incurred caring for

*the defendant's son.   The promise was made after
the services were given.   The question is whether
the promise is enforceable.   Levi Wyman, the 25–
year-old son of the defendant * * * [Continuing
with facts].*

To return now to the memo:

Issue

*Is Mr. Wyman's promise, made in recognition of
services rendered to Wyman's son, enforceable under
Section 89a of the Restatement of Contracts?*

Conclusion

*I think the promise is enforceable under the Re-
statement.*

Statement of Law

*Statement of Law: Restatement Section 89a pro-
vides*

*(1) A promise made in recognition of a benefit
previously received by the promisor is binding
* * ***

(2) A promise is not binding under Subsection (1)

*(a) if the promise conferred the benefit as a gift
* * *; or*

*(b) to the extent that its value is disproportion-
ate to the benefit.*

Let's begin our analysis with the *Statement of
Law*. First, the nice stuff. It copies out, verbatim,
the Restatement Section. This puts the reader in

immediate contact with the source material; there is no need to rely upon first-level interpretation. Compare:

> *The Restatement would enforce a promise if it was made after the person making it receives some benefit and provided that the other person wasn't making a gift.*

The reader is forced to take the writer's word for it. Not so if the controlling language appears.

Copying out statutes and Restatements also helps you fully concentrate. When you read a statute, even when you read it carefully, you may read it incorrectly. Writing slows the mind, and little words like "not" tend to jump out.

In copying out controlling language, some provisions may not apply. Edit them out, showing their omission with " * * * "

Make good use of quotes throughout your legal writing:

> *Was the promise "made in recognition of a benefit previously received"?*

By using quotes the reader is brought face to face with the legal requirements and need not rely on a paraphrase.

The only problem I see with the Statement of Law is the failure to *begin with the basics*. Reading the memo you may have been concerned about why the promise wasn't simply enforceable. Most prom-

ises are. Why do we need a special Restatement
Section?

Statement of Law

Under common law, promises need consider-
ation be to enforceable. A promise made in recog-
nition of some prior benefit is not enforceable
because there is no current consideration: the
benefit came before the promise. The Restatement
allows for the enforceability of some such promises
*today. Section 89a provides * * * [continuing as*
previously written].

Law is complicated stuff. Always help the reader
get up to speed by beginning with basic propositions
of law before moving to the more complicated. Can
police search inside dental fillings? Start with the
Fourth Amendment.

What about the *conclusion*?

Lawyers don't write to pass the time of day.
They write to analyze problems, to advise clients, to
convince judges. They write to do. The conclusion
is central. It links the world of analysis to the
world of action. It tells us what to do next—our
only real concern.

Put it up front, before the analysis as to how it
was reached. Knowing where you are going, the
reader can test your analysis step-by-step. Surprise
endings are out.

The conclusion in the memo "I think the promise
is enforceable" is not as helpful as it might be.
Compare:

Conclusion

The Restatement enforces promises made "in recognition of a benefit" previously received. If the benefit must be a direct material one, then the father's promise is not enforceable as the services were rendered to the son. However, if the court interprets "benefit" to include the benefit of knowing one's child died in peace, then the promise is enforceable as the other requirements of the Restatement seem satisfied.

This conclusion does more work. It flags the key issues to be discussed. The reader will have a much easier time understanding and testing your analysis.

Let's return to the analysis section of the memo, which I will give in skeleton form, highlighting the transitions.

Analysis

*The first requirement under that Restatement is that a promise must have been made. Was a promise made? A promise is defined as * * * Applying that definition to the facts of this case, it seems a promise has been made.*

***Next**, was the promise "made in recognition of a benefit previously received"? That depends upon how the court would interpret "benefit." (The analysis continues).*

***But did the promises confer that benefit as a gift?** Mills was acting voluntarily but that may* *not make his act a gift. How should the court interpret "gift"? (Analysis continues).*

The next question *is whether the value of the promise is "disproportionate to the benefit"?* * * *

Next, transitions. First, "Next, transitions" isn't much of one. Transitions can, and generally should, do more than introduce the new topic. They can *tie that topic* to the previous material and can *explicitly state the legal significance* of that topic. To see how this works:

Compare: *Next, was the promise "made in recognition of a benefit previously received"?*

With: **Even if** *there is a promise,* **it will not be** *enforced unless it was made in "recognition of a benefit previously received." Was there a benefit here?*

Compare: *But did the promise confer the benefit as a gift?*

With: **If the court interprets** *"benefit" to include the kind of benefit the father received, the next issue is whether the benefit was conferred by the Good Samaritan as a gift. If it was, then the father's* **promise is not enforceable***.*

Compare:　*The next question is whether the value of the promise is "disproportionate to the benefit."*

With:　**Assuming the court finds** *the requisite benefit and that it was not conferred by the Good Samaritan as a gift, the father's* **promise appears enforceable** *as the value of the promise (to pay expenses) does not seem "disproportionate to the benefit."*

A transition can accomplish three goals: it can *relate* the new issue to the one discussed previously; it can *introduce* the issue, and it can show the *legal significance* of the issue: does resolution of the issue resolve the entire case or is it simply a building block? A mnemonic device might help you check your own work: RILS transitions.

*R*elate

*I*ntroduce

*L*egal *S*ignificance

It is one thing to understand something ("Oh, I see that!") and it is quite another to execute something. Take a few minutes to practice writing RILS transitions. Take the following three elements:

— Promise

— Benefit

— Gift

Write out a transition introducing the "benefit" issue, showing its legal significance, and relating it to a prior discussion of the "promise" issue.

Now introduce "gift," transitioning from a discussion of "benefit."

In editing your own work, always check your transitions. Flag those that are not *RILS* transitions. Should they be? Will your writing be improved?

I will now discuss three other matters. (A RILS transition isn't needed here.) These matters help achieve clarity: explicitness, concreteness and candor in citing cases.

Make explicit the relationship between law and fact. Compare the following:

1. *The Good Samaritan cared for the son voluntarily.*

2. *The Good Samaritan cared for the son voluntarily and thus it may be said that his action was a gift.*

3. *The Good Samaritan cared for the son voluntarily and thus it may be said that his action was a gift. If so, then under the Restatement of Contracts, the father's promise to pay for the services would not be enforceable.*

The first statement simply identifies a fact. It fails to tell the reader why that fact is legally important. The second statement is more explicit. It tells the reader that from the identified fact it may be concluded that the action was a gift. The third statement is even more explicit. It tells the reader the legal significance of that conclusion, that the promise would not be enforceable.

Not only is explicitness essential in helping your reader understand, it is essential in helping you analyze the law. Simply stating that the Good Samaritan acted voluntarily and then going onto other matters, you will not consider the key legal issue. Are all voluntary acts "gifts"? By forcing yourself to tie your factual conclusions to principles of law, you immediately face the essential legal questions. How should the word "gift" be interpreted?

Another way of thinking about this is the need to *ground your analysis*, be it factual or legal. Traditionally you start with a statement of law, and then analyze the facts under it. Well and good. However, when you finish your factual analysis ground it in the law, that is, come back to the legal standard:

*Fact, fact, fact * * * Therefore the action was a gift and hence the promise is not enforceable.*

Similarly, legal analysis should be grounded in the facts of the case you are discussing.

*Law, law, law * * * Therefore, given the facts of this case, the result is * * * .*

When you are writing, your little voice should be chanting, "*So what? So what?*" When you are discussing facts, "*So what?*" will force you to be explicit as to how those facts relate to the law, and, when you are discussing propositions of law, "*So what?* " will force you to articulate just how and in what ways that law relates the facts of the case you are discussing.

A spiffy slogan might help: "Law and fact, never leave home without both of them." So too a short poem:

Of every fact you write,

Of every law you cite,

Ask **"So what?"**

A poem need not rhyme as long as it *means*. So what?

Avoid abstractions, even those that don't seem to be

Abstractions "fall upon the facts like soft snow, blurring the outlines and covering up all details." Law is difficult, and without concrete and specific markers, it is easy to get lost. *Use examples.* Don't just write about the "intangible benefit the father received"; identify the benefit. "He now knows his son died in peace." Think in terms of specific events. One might define a gift, in the abstract, as "something done voluntarily without expectation of return." That sounds pretty good. But visualize Mills standing beside the bed of young Wyman, wiping his brow and administering to his needs. If someone asked you to describe the scene, would you describe it as someone making a gift? Most likely not. Checking the abstraction against a specific event suggests that the abstraction is wrong. "Gift" must mean something else, perhaps as in "birthday."

Other kinds of abstractions confuse:

"The promisee will argue that he did not confer the benefit as a gift."

Don't compel your reader to ask, "Who is the promisee here, Mills or Wyman?" Instead, tell him.

"The promisee, Mr. Mills, will argue * * *"

Still your reader must ask, is Mills the father or the guy who helped the son?

The promisee, Mr. Mills, the man who aided the son, will argue that he did not confer the benefit as a gift.

Good. But what is the benefit we are talking about?

The promisee, Mr. Mills, the man who aided the son, will argue that he did not confer the benefit, here caring for the son, as a gift.

Write in concrete terms so that the reader will know immediately and without thought whom and what you are talking about.

The plaintiff, the woman injured, * * *

The respondent, the doctor who filed the false return * * *

Avoid constructions like

As to the former argument, the plaintiff would argue * * *

> *Under Subsection 2a of the Restatement, the promise would not be enforceable.*

These constructions *stop* the reader. "Which was the *former* argument?" "What did Subsection 2a provide?" These interruptions are irksome and can be easily avoided. You need not repeat the entire *former* argument, you can usually identify it in two or three words. The same is true in identifying particular subsections.

> *Under Subsection 2a of the Restatement, dealing with benefits conferred as gifts, the promise would not be enforceable.*

Indicate the factual context of legal rules

Legal rules have meaning only in the context of facts. To illustrate, take the case of Speedy Delivery Pizza.

> *Defendant ordered a pizza. Upon learning that Speedy Delivery broke the speed limit in delivering the pizza, the defendant refused to pay. Defendant has a good defense as it has been held that "no one will be allowed to profit from his own crime." Riggs v. Palmer, 115 N.Y. 506, 22 N.E. 188 (1889). Speeding is a crime and Speedy shouldn't be allowed to profit from it.*

This sounds good. The language from *Riggs* seems to be "on all fours." But are we sure that the rule of *Riggs v. Palmer* should apply? Compare the following:

> *Speedy Delivery should not be able to recover because "no one will be allowed to profit from his own crime." Riggs v. Palmer (preventing a murderer from inheriting from his victim.)*

Unless one takes his pizza very seriously, the cases are clearly distinguishable.

In citing key cases, briefly indicate their facts. Otherwise the reader will not know whether the rule should apply. Abstract statements of law are *always suspect*. It is not always necessary, however, to indicate the facts of a case, for example when you are citing a case for an unremarkable proposition of law.

II. Tips on Editing

Lincoln, on the train to Gettysburg, edits his Address.

> *A long time ago, almost ninety years ago in fact, our forefathers * * ***

> *Eight decades and seven years ago, more or less, our forefathers * * ***

Revise, revise, revise. Shorten, shorten, shorten.

> *Four score and seven years ago, our forefathers * * ***

The most important editing device is the passage of time. Wait a couple of days to return to your draft. You will spot areas of confusion (now God alone knows) and you will spot words, sentences and perhaps paragraphs ready for the chopping block. Of course, they will scream, "No, not me,

I'm the crux of the whole thing; look at that paragraph over there, why, it's nothing but fluff. Cut it. Leave me. In fact, *expand me!*"

Remember, the reader never knows what you cut out, only what you left in.

Other editing ideas follow. All of this, by the way, will be reduced to an editing checklist at the end of the chapter; read now for ideas.

A. *Edit needless words*

The less cluttered your work, the more forceful it will be. "Omit needless words," advise Strunk and White, the authors of the classic *Elements of Style*. Omitting needless words does not mean omitting detail and treating subjects only in outline form. It means that *each word must tell*.

There are several ways to reduce clutter, and *small savings add up quickly*. If you cut a couple of words per sentence, by the end of twenty pages, you will have saved your reader three pages of garbage. If I had done that, you would have been at the movies by now.

When editing, watch *verbs*. Prefer the present tense, the active voice and grunts. Your writing will become engaging, forceful, sharper.

Present tense. It is possible to recount past events in the present tense. Compare:

> *Plaintiff's car crashed into the tree. A fire broke out and the plaintiff ran from the car.*

> *Plaintiff's car crashes into a tree. A fire erupts and the plaintiff runs from the car.*

Current events are more engrossing. Remember what Groucho said: "We're past tense. We live in bungalows now."

Active voice. An easy way to delete words is to find sentences written in the passive voice and rewrite them in the active. Compare:

> *The case was reversed by the Supreme Court.* Passive voice, eight words.

> *The Supreme Court reversed the case.* Active voice, six words.

Grunts. Language began with grunts—short, powerful and very much to the point. With civilization came decadence and, still worse, verb derivatives—people not longer *act*, they *take action*; they no longer *decide*, they *make decisions*; they no longer *steal*, they *obtain money through false pretense*. Verb derivatives are weak, wordy and sinful. Write in grunts.

Likewise some words are strong, others weak. Choose the strong. When editing, look at the word you used. Is there a more forceful one? Note that they are almost always shorter.

Strong	**Weak**
copy	duplicate
burn	incinerate
make	produce
lie	fabrication
trap	enmesh

Strong	**Weak**
hoax	deception
give	contribute
need	necessity
write	compose
fight	altercation

Excess verbs.   Any sentence with *more than one verb* is a target.   Clauses (a group of words with a verb) can often become phrases (a group of words without a verb).

"When the lawyer *was conducting* her cross-examination, the witness got up and left."   14 words.

"During cross-examination, the witness got up and left."   9 words.

"The lawyer asked the witness what he had for lunch, a question *which had been designed* to embarrass him."   19 words.

"The lawyer asked the witness what he had for lunch, a question *designed* to embarrass him."   16 words.

When editing, watch *inflated style*.

At the present time	now
In the event of	if
In the majority of instances	usually
With the exception that	except
For the reason that	because
In my considered opinion	I think

With countless ready-made phrases we build our hen-houses.   The temptation is great.   As Orwell points out, they sound good and have a certain flow. They seem intelligent. We hope to shore up our simple ideas with respectability; instead we bury them in pomposity.

When editing, watch *puffing*. Facts, not volume, convince. The overuse of *intensifiers, adjectives* and *adverbs* is puffing.

The lecture was very boring.

The author is asking us to take her word for it. If the matter is important, she should tell us what *facts* lead to her conclusion. Then we can come to our own conclusion.

During the lecture I went to sleep.

Verbs and nouns tell. Adjectives opine. H.L. Mencken, on writing headlines—

Not: *McGuinnis Lacks Ethical Sense*
Rather: *McGuinnis Steals $1,257,876.25*

B.   Edit sentence length

We read and understand in segments. When we get to a period, the mind assembles the words into a communication. If a sentence is too long, if too many words separate verb and noun, people will lose it. It's like holding your breath. It's possible, but why? Richard Wydick, author of *Plain English for Lawyers*, advises that most sentences should contain only one main thought and, on the average, should be less than twenty-five words.

Vary the length of your sentences.

Short ones spell relief.

C. Edit for order

First and last are the most important positions in sentences, paragraphs and arguments. Put important points either first or last; points in the middle tend to be overlooked and forgotten.

Compare:

According to Fred Rodell, the style and content of legal writing are its only two defects.

With:

Legal writing, according to Fred Rodell, has two defects, style and content.

The second has more punch. It puts the key words, "legal writing" and "style and content" in the most forceful positions, first and last. This is a powerful concept.

1. At trial, put on your star witnesses first and last. The plumber goes in the middle.

2. In editing your work, does your paragraph order reflect this maxim? Do the sentences?

3. Don't begin with a citation (the lawyer's sin). Lawyers always begin: "In the case of *Cat v. Dog*, 42 P.2d 443, 182 Cal.Rptr. 123 (1992) rehearing denied, 43 P.2d 18, 184 Cal.Rptr. 456 (1993), the Court barked * * * "

Why do lawyers do this? Do they hate us?

4. Don't start sentences with long qualifiers or parts of the hen-house:

> *It is very important to note that* the order of thoughts in a sentence is important.

> The order of thoughts in a sentence is important.

D. Edit to make the copy visually inviting

Alice, of Wonderland, once remarked, "What's the good of a book without pictures?" Unfortunately, in our business, forget about using pictures to break up the type.

Make frequent use of paragraphs and vary their length. I am not suggesting arbitrary paragraphing, just frequent paragraphing. There is nothing worse than a page full of print and nothing better than an occasional paragraph of one or two sentences.

So there.

IV. Editing Checklist

The two-day edit:

Wait a couple of days and edit for clarity and for excess baggage. Problem areas will jump out. After editing the draft as a whole, I would go back twice, once doing a legal edit and once doing an excess word edit.

Legal edit: The quest for clarity:

— Do you begin with basic propositions?

— Do you use strong transitions? Consider going through your draft, highlighting your transitions and reading only them. Does your draft hold together? Remember RILS transitions.

— Do you quote the actual language of Restatements and statutes? Do you put cases in context by briefly indicating their facts?

— Do you avoid the lawyer sins of beginning sentences with citations and of using flow-stopping abstractions like "promisee," "respondent," "Section 301a" and "the former"? Are you being reader-friendly?

Word edit: The quest for brevity:

Verbs. Take a look at each of the verbs. Prefer the active voice, the present tense (where possible) and grunts. Sentences with two verbs can likely be shortened.

Adjectives, adverbs and intensifiers. They are the usual suspects. If you want something other than smoke and mirrors, use facts.

Structure edit: The quest for impact and spiff:

Do you lead and end with your strong points? Do you make your copy visually spiffy by an occasional short paragraph, indented quote or tabulation? Do you use strange words to engage your reader, like "spiff"?

Finally, *end forcefully*. But everyone knows that.

One last tip about breaking up type: quotes help.

"Yeah, but no one ever talks in legal writing."

"Oh."

*

PART 5

THE GREAT HEREAFTER

In this part we look beyond the first year. Chapter 17 discusses your second and third years, what to take, whether you should clerk and other matters of great moment. It also has some interesting tidbits about the history of legal education.

Again, these are matters of great moment, but not right now. Save this chapter until the end of your first year, when you are making your plans.

The next chapter is on career choices. I describe the options and suggest things you can do now to help you better decide on what you want to do when the time comes. Although these matters might seem a long way off, I think it is important to begin thinking about them sometime in your first year.

For the last chapter, I have asked lawyer friends to write about what they do. These lawyers do different kinds of law; some write about a typical day, others about joys and frustrations. The chapter makes for excellent browsing.

I hope you have enjoyed the book. I have.

CHAPTER 17

THE SECOND AND THIRD YEARS

The rush and intensity of the first year become the calm, some say the boredom, indeed, the stupor, of the second and third. The first year is a tough act to follow and we don't do a very good job of it. Still, it's worth a chapter.

Many enter the second year wounded. They did not do as well as they had hoped, they are worried about getting a job and real lawyers, downtown, have told them that theoretical legal education is bunk. "They don't even tell you how to get to the courthouse!"

The first thing you need is a pep talk. Then I will discuss course selection, clerking and other fun activities. Along the way, there will be some interesting things about the history of legal education, pro bono, and the dullness of most legal prose.

I will begin with a war story.

On Theoretical Legal Education

When I was a law student, in the days of the Civil Rights Movement, I spent a summer working for C.B. King of Albany, Georgia, one of the two black lawyers in the state. Early that summer an election for Justice of the Peace was to be held in the small town of Americus. It was to be a great occasion: black voters, for the first time since Reconstruction, were going to be able to vote. In fact, a black woman had decided to run for the office herself.

On the momentous day, when she arrived at the voting place, there were two lines, one marked "Colored." She stood in the other line. The deputy sheriff who arrested her was later incredulous at being asked why he had done so. He testified, "I ain't completely color blind, you know." I'll never forget that; sitting in the courtroom, I remembered reading a Supreme Court Justice saying "Our Constitution is color blind."

C.B. wanted me to research the law to see if we could get a court to throw out the election and make them do it over; make them do it right. I looked up the cases on election irregularities and election fraud (mostly from Chicago).

"C.B., we've had it. You can't challenge the election. The law is clear. Unless the illegalities affected the result, it stands. Given the fact that the incumbent got 83 of the 95 votes, we can't allege that."

C.B. simply sat and stared. Didn't say a word.

I went back to my desk and went into a funk. "Why had I gone to law school? A monkey could have looked up those cases and reported the bad news to C.B. Why had I sat in class for two years, struggling, if I couldn't even try to force the law to do justice?''

I went back to the cases. Maybe they could be distinguished. Indeed, maybe there would be language in those cases suggesting that if the controversy wasn't simply about dead people voting, the rule might be different.

I sat and thought and read and reread. Yes, those cases where distinguishable and, yes, there was even language to support our position.

I went back to C.B. This time he smiled. About a year later, under federal court order, the small town of Americus, Georgia had another election. The same guy won, but this time they did it right: one line.

————————————

There will be other outrages, down the road. Work hard at your studies. Don't tune out those "nice" theoretical discussions in law school. They won't be easy and you won't understand them all. I know I didn't. But stay awake. Your time will come.

Enough preaching. What are your choices in the second and third years? I will begin with Law Review, not because it is most significant, but because its mere presence says something curious about the law (and because it allows me to take a few shots at the dullness of most legal writing).

Law Review and Bad Writing

Law reviews present a mind boggling affront. Law students write and publish articles criticizing appellate court judges.

Where else does this happen? Do second year medical students routinely castigate leading surgeons? Routinely congratulate heart specialists with "All things considered, nice job!" ?

Holmes wrote:

The life of the law is not logic, it is experience.

Au contraire, the life of the law, at least as attested to by the law reviews, is not wisdom; it is wit.

That beginners can play on the same field as veterans is one of the curious facts about the law. It's refreshing in a "Question Authority" kind of way.

In any event, this routine dissing of the judiciary by the likes of you plays an important institutional role. It helps keep appellate judges accountable for the quality and justice of their opinions.

Law reviews provide an outlet for scholarly work (by academics, judges and practitioners) as well as a place for student members to publish. Reviews are run almost exclusively by students with very little help or interference by the faculty.

"Law review" is hard work. Do it if you can. You will be involved in the law's development. Lawyers read student notes and, who knows, you might even get cited! Student editors can make a major impact; law reviews have focused national attention on otherwise neglected areas of the law, such as the law of the poor, the law of mental health, the law of the elderly.

Your work will be extensively edited and you will come away with a feeling of how hard it is (and how satisfying) to produce good work. And, of course, having written for the review helps come interview time.

Now a few words on law review writing. Yale Law Professor Fred Rodell wrote the classic critique of law reviews and of legal writing. I know good stuff when I see it.

> *There are two things wrong with almost all legal writing. One is style. The other is content.*

> *[I]t seems to be a cardinal principle of law review writing and editing that nothing may be said forcefully and nothing may be said amusingly. This, I take it, is in the interest of something called dignity. It does not matter that most people—and even lawyers come into this category—read either to be convinced or to be entertained. It does not matter that even in the comparatively rare instances when people read to be informed, they like a dash of pepper or a dash of salt along with their information. The won't get any seasoning if the law reviews can help it. The law reviews would rather be dignified and ignored.*

> "Goodbye to Law Review," 23 *Virginia Law Review* 38 (1936).

Rodell's ultimate point goes, however, to content. And in this he is quite serious. Society faces real and pressing problems. Law may be our only hope.

It seems never to have occurred to most of the studious gents who diddle around in the law reviews that * * * they might be diddling while Rome burns.

I do not wish to labor the point but perhaps it had best be stated once in dead earnest. With law as the only alternative to force as a means of solving the myriad problems of the world, it seems to me that the articulate among the clan of lawyers might, in their writings, be more pointedly aware of those problems, might recognize that the use of law to help toward their solution is the only excuse for the law's existence, instead of blithely continuing to make mountain after mountain out of tiresome technical molehills.

Don't make too much about law review. If you don't make it, most famous lawyers didn't either. At a UCLA alumni party in a beautiful Malibu home overlooking the Pacific, the owner walked over to his old Torts Professor, "Good to see you Prof. This is what a "D" in Torts gets you."

You can get many of the benefits of law review elsewhere. Take a course which requires extensive research and writing. Second and third year Moot Court Programs also offer writing and editorial experience.   As to being involved in the life of the law, you can represent clients in clinical courses, volunteer at Legal Aid, or help kids learn how to read.   More of this when we get to pro bono activities.

Course Selection

a. What Not to Do

Some students are scared; they take bar courses. Some are lazy; they take ten o'clocks.   Some are despicable: they choose courses in order to protect their high class standing.

Don't trivialize your life.

There is no need to take every course that the bar examiners may test you on.   Following law school graduation there are bar review courses.   Many subject areas can be learned sufficiently for exam purposes in several hours of study.   So why waste a semester?

It is also a mistake, I think, to focus exclusively on courses you "know" you will need in practice.   If you think you know what kind of law you want to practice, surely take some courses in the field in order to test whether you like it.   However it is foolish to over-specialize in law school.   Career interests can and often do change.

b. What to Do

Take professors.

Select interesting and provocative professors, not just those you agree with or feel comfortable with.

Quite likely your faculty is composed of many types: those who see criminal law through the eyes of a cop and those who see it through the eyes of the accused; those who stick closely to the "law" and those who spin off into the realms of philosophy, economics and social theory; those whose classes are like boot camp and those whose classes are like an encounter group.

Sitting there you are learning more than "Federal Jurisdiction" or "UCC". You learn how one lawyer approaches and solves problems, uses and communicates knowledge, treats and reacts to people. Think back to the "great" teachers you have had. Images and incidents return, sometimes the jokes, but mostly things that were said off the cuff, things that weren't really about the course at all, whatever it was.

Take writing courses.

It is essential to take at least one course requiring *extensive research and writing* even if (particularly if) you dread it. While it is true that some law practices do not frequently require these skills, without them you are a sheriff without a gun, a traveler without Travel Checks (a small promotional fee was paid).

Your credibility as a trial lawyer, for example, will soon vanish if it becomes known that you never appeal; trial judges will impose on you, secure in the knowledge that their decisions will not be reviewed. Being afraid of going to court hurts you as a practitioner; so too the fear of going to the library.

Take perspective courses.

Often what we learn we take as inevitable. It is only by getting outside of status quo, can we realize its contingent and political nature. In comparative law courses, in legal history courses, you are not learning about the law of Brazil or the law of the Colonial Period; you are learning about our law, today.

Without contrasts we can't see.

Here I will go on a lengthy digression, not because it really fits, but because it is really important (and involves a great story—I'm not ashamed to add a dash of pepper).

Legal education presents a distorted view of human nature.

In my first year Contracts class I wished to review. I put a hypothetical. Seller is continually late in making his deliveries. Buyer, after pleas and much patience, finally cancels the contract. After stating the problem, I asked:

"If you were Seller, what would you say?"

I was looking for a discussion of the various common law theories which throw Buyer into breach for canceling the contract, legal arguments which would allow Seller to crush Buyer.

I looked around the room. As is so often the case with first year students, they were all writing in their notebooks or inspecting their shoes. There was, however, one eager face, that of an eight-year-old son of one of my students. He had been biding his time, drawing pictures. Suddenly he raised his hand. Such behavior, even from an eight-year old, must be rewarded.

"Okay," I said, "What would you say if you were Seller?"

"I'd say 'I'm sorry'."

———————

Assuming the worst of everyone is a great teaching ploy. It forces the student to come up with all of the arguments, pro and con. Indeed, Holmes himself once wrote that we should approach law as would the "bad man", the one who cares nothing about morality. The bad man only asks, "If I do X, what will the law do to me?"

This question forces close analysis.

However, *don't confuse a teaching ploy with life*. I know I did. When I was fresh out of law school, a seller would tell me, "Well, you know, this dispute is really my fault. Why don't you call the buyer and work things out."

"Work things out? !!!" I would scream. "I have five separate theories which make buyer the breacher! We can sue him! Bankrupt him. I've stayed up late working on this case. Work things out? You can't do that to me!"

In law school, Seller doesn't even have a name, much less a life history. As to what we build, as to what we cherish, those things become "widgets."

Can justice be a matter of the manipulation of abstract rules or must it be the matter of concrete and specific individuals and events?

Writes law Professor John Noonan, in *Persons and Masks of the Law:*

> *As a law student, I saw, or thought I saw, the great advantage of legal education over the philosophical education I had just received—it dealt with cases. Working with cases, I supposed, was a way of exercising and developing a sense of justice—a sense of what was due to particular individuals in a concrete situation. Law students and a fortiori lawyers, I imagined, had a better sense of justice than philosophers or, say, sociologists. Unlike such dealers in abstractions, the lawyers could never forget that their actions affected persons.*

> *After twenty years' experience, I see that I was wrong. The cases are not concrete enough. The characters in them, turning into A or B, P or D, lose personal identity.*

As a young lawyer, I don't think I really understood tort law until I had to tell a father, whose seven-year-old son had lost an eye during school recess, that "there was nothing to be done." And I don't think I really understood criminal law until one of my clients, a young mother, was sentenced to two years in the state prison. The bailiff stepped behind "the defendant," put his hand on her shoulder, and pointed to the door at the back of the courtroom, the door that led, eventually, to prison.

She turned and handed me her baby.

This stuff is real.

Take clinical courses

"Why should I take trial practice? I never intent to litigate?"

There is no better reason. Maybe you will love it and, if you don't, then you can be sure.

I think everyone should take at least one clinical course, if for no other reason that grounding your legal studies in lawyering tasks. You get a better feel for the law once you have a hands on sense of how it plays out in trial, in negotiation and, indeed, in client interviewing.

Approach a simulated skills course with reckless abandon. *Don't Be Yourself.* As Mark Twain once said, "Be yourself" is the worst advice you can give some people.

Do you really know who you are? Who you can be? In skills courses, take a chance and be someone else. If you are shy, yell and pound your shoe on the table. Break out. You never know.

If you are working in the field, doing actual cases, approach it as would an anthropologist working with the natives. During the day, do your job, work the pots. At night, sneak off to your tent and get out your pencil.

1. Are the lawyers you see happy?

2. Are they bitterly adverse to each other or is the practice of law something of a country club affair?

3. Why do some witnesses seem more believable than others? What arguments seem to impress judges?

4. Does the system produce justice? Does it work they way your professors told you it would?

5. What are the most important skills for a lawyer to have?

Once you graduate and go into practice, the doing overwhelms the questioning; gone is the time for cool reflection and the challenging of assumptions.

Clerking

a. A Short History of American Legal Education

In the old days, there was only clerking; there were no law schools and the LSAT hadn't even been thought of. See, generally, Milton, *Paradise Lost.*

After working several years as an apprentice, the novice took the bar and that was that. Originally law schools **supplemented** apprenticeship; apprentices gathered to hear lectures on legal principles. Slowly law schools took over new turf: they became *alternatives* to apprenticeship, novices becoming eligible to take the bar by either route.

The key year is 1870 when Christopher Columbus Langdell became the first dean of the Harvard Law School. At the time, a lot of people thought (and, indeed, some still do) that law school should not belong in a University. It was a trade school, devoted to practical knowledge, preparing people to make a living. Yuk!

Langdell made a grand end run. He proclaimed law study to be a science and the law library to be our laboratory.

> *[L]aw is a science [and] all the available materials of that science are contained in books * * *. [T]he library is the proper workshop of professors and students alike; * * * it is to us all that the laboratories of the university are to the chemists and physicists, all that the museum of natural history is to the geologists, all that the botanical garden is to the botanists.*

Who could keep us out now?

While this got us in the door, the anti-practical, the anti-professional aspect of the move has soured legal education since. For a long time law professors kept to their libraries, making "mountain after mountain out of tiresome technical molehills."

But even botanists go on field trips.

Things are getting better; how much so I leave to you.

A few more points about Langdell. He remained Dean for 25 years and the contours of modern legal education emerged. Thanks to Langdell, it's three years. The "case method" replaced lectures. Langdell himself wrote the very first casebook. (There had to be one and now you know who wrote it).

Interestingly, the case method originally had "nothing whatever to do with getting students to think for themselves." At least that is the conclusion of Grant Gilmore, who actually sat down and read Langdell's book. It was, on the contrary, "a method of indoctrination through brainwashing."

The justification may change but the method hangs on. It is so much fun.

The Harvard model swept the field; all university law schools aped it. But still, all was not well. People could still become lawyers by tending garden. From the library, that just didn't seem right.

The struggle between law school education and apprenticeship education was a long one. We won! Today in most states you can't even take the bar unless you have graduated from an A.B.A. approved law school.

Of course, there was a downside to this victory. We didn't want just **any** gardener showing up. We began to "raise standards." At first, we required "some college," then "college graduation," and finally, as you well know, good grades and high LSAT.

Consider the result. Without good academic credentials, you can't attend law school; without graduating from law school, you can't take the bar. The circle closes.

All of this was, of course, in the "public good". Law school trained lawyers will provide better representation than those merely doing an apprenticeship; and the more "qualified" the law student, the more able the lawyer.

Cynics smile at all this, seeing simply the imperatives of expansionism in the conquest of the apprenticeship system and the ugly impulse of elitism in "raising standards".

Who knows? But know this: the status quo is not a lump of clay: it is the product of fierce battles and the status quo is not inevitable. Things can change. (In the 1840s, the Popular Health Movement, rebelling against the medical experts of the day—and their reliance on bleeding—was able to convince several state legislatures to repeal all licensing requirements for doctors.)

If you are interested in learning more about the fascinating history of the institution you are inhabiting, see Stevens, "Two cheers for 1870: The American Law School" *Law in American History* 425 (D. Fleming and B. Bailyn, eds., 1971). For the cynical account, see Auerbach, *Unequal Justice* (1976).

b. Should you clerk?

The history lesson was to introduce the debate about whether law students should clerk. Some professors would take "no prisoners." Clerking competes with classwork and diminishes the quality of life in the school. With many law students involved in clerking, there is less energy for law review, interest clubs, speaker programs and school plays.

Christopher Columbus Langdell would not approve.

Times change. Many students need the money. And a good clerkship, just like a good clinical experience, can be quite educational. If you do clerk, try to make sure it is a good experience. Some clerking jobs are a joke.

"Tell me Prof, I have a clerking assignment. Can husbands be forced to testify against their wives?"

"What are the facts?"

"Facts? The lawyer didn't tell me. Just gave me the question and told me to research it."

Treat your lawyer as your client. Learn to interview your boss, to gently prod the necessary information. As my colleague Kay Kavanagh advises her students, "Insist on at least **one** fact."

I know you don't like to make waves. But most lawyers like spunk and probably are simply unaware at how vague they have been.

Negotiate a meaningful clerking experience. The ideal is where you are closely supervised, where you get feedback, and where the tasks are varied: not **always** arcane memos, sometimes interviewing witnesses, sometimes observing trials and, why not, sometimes going to the zoo.

Finally, I think it is a *very bad idea* to clerk in the first year. (There is a little Christopher Columbus Langdell in us all.)

Underground Activities

Sometimes, it's true, we get so carried away with trying to figure out what to do with the decedent's stuff that we forget the question of life's meaning.

"That's OK. We covered that as undergraduates."

The problem I see with undergraduate education is that it has no point of view and is simply a giant smorgasbord of great ideas. "Should I take the Hamlet or the Social Psychology?" Once you have a year of law school, you will have a point of view: everything, all of those great ideas, are relevant to what you have studied and to what you will become.

After the first year in law school, it would be great to go back and redo your liberal arts requirements. Second best is to get together with friends to discuss great ideas. You will need a catalyst; otherwise everyone will die of embarrassment. That's where good books and good films come in.

The group can be as informal or formal as you wish. You can ask professors—even those from other disciplines—to sit in (they come and go, talking of Michangelo) and you can invite lawyers and judges to take part. I have run both Law and Literature Groups and have put on Film Forums. If you wish, I can send you details. Here, simply some ideas of the books we have read and films we have seen:

Books:

Bolt, A Man for All Seasons

Bugliosi, Till Death Us Do Part

Camus, The Stranger

Cozzens, The Just and the Unjust

Doctorow, Book of Daniel

Dostoevski, Crime and Punishment

Kafka, The Trial

Kanton, Andersonville

Melville, Billy Budd

Miller, The Crucible

Nichols, The Milagro Beanfield War

Phillips, No Heroes, No Villains

Pirsig, Zen and the Art of Motorcycle Maintenance

Shakespeare, Hamlet, The Merchant of Venice, MacBeth

Solzhenitsyn, One Day in the Life of Ivan Denisovich

Sophocles, Antigone

Stewart, Earth Abides

Tolstoy, Resurrection

Wambaugh, The Onion Field

Wolfe, Bonfire of Vanities

Wright, Native Son

As long as I am about recommending books, if you have kids, take a look at Bennett's *Book of Virtues*. Although a tad preachy, it has a wide variety of provocative writings, from East to West, from nursery rhymes to Tolstoy and Lady MacBeth. Finally, something intelligent to read with your children.

It is filled with such marvelous things,

We should all be as happy as Kings.

Films:

A Man for All Seasons

Paths of Glory

Twelve Angry Men

Breaker Morant

I Never Sang for My Father

The Informer

Lord of the Flies

Inherit the Wind

To Kill a Mockingbird

The Stranger

Billy Budd

Anatomy of a Murder

Salt of the Earth

Pro Bono Activities

Face it. You were born smart. And a lot of people have helped you along the way. Time to start paying back.

In Washington D.C. law students help prisoners learn to read ... by tutoring them as they read story books to their children.

Elsewhere law students tutor elementary students as part of "Lawyer for Literacy" Programs. Others do law work at Legal Aid, Women's Shelters, AIDS clinics, Homeless Programs and Public Interest Firms.

Law school classes can be organized so as to provide a community service. In my AIDS and the Law class, we wrote "A Guide to the Law of HIV and Agencies that Help." Designed for people living with AIDS and those who help them, it covers the basic law in the areas that we thought they would need most: discrimination, access to medical care, living wills, children, dealing with collection agencies and, of course, landlord/tenant: Alphagraphics duplicated the booklet gratis and we distributed it to the community. Similar booklets could be written for battered women, the elderly and for folks on welfare. They would have to focus on local agencies and on state law but I'd be happy to send you what we did if it will get you started.

Some law schools have **High School Teaching Programs**. They are easy to organize and are great fun. We've had one for years. To give you some feel for the program, law students, who receive one unit of academic credit, are assigned to specific high school classes—usually senior American Problems classes—where they teach one hour per week for a period of seven to ten weeks. (Some have presented the Program at other levels, including Junior High). We have prepared materials which mostly raise hypos in various areas of the law and give discussion questions. Students are free to make up their own lessons and roleplays.

Our goal is not to teach law (after all, we want to be invited back). We want to introduce high school students to legal decision making. We want to introduce them to "yes, but" reasoning; using the hypos, we attempt to force them to think long and hard before reaching a decision.

High school teachers love us, one less class to prepare; the high school students love us, a new face and issues that affect their lives; and law students love us, and for the law student, a chance to be in charge, a chance to create their own thing.

There are rewarding and moving occurrences.

> Once the law student noticed one of the high school students never said a word. With a stroke of genius, she made her the judge in the trial unit. The girl was transformed; she broke out of her painful self-conscious shell and became an active participant in the class.

> Two students once presented the program in a custodial institution for juvenile delinquents. At first the law students were greeted with "Pigs!" They stayed with it. Ten weeks later, I got letters from the "inmates": "I always

thought all the police and lawyers were pigs, out to get me. Now I know that some might actually understand me and help me."

One great aspect of such programs is that you get to discuss law with people other than law students, law teachers and bored and resentful companions at cocktail parties. What do they think of laws prohibiting discrimination? Of the fact that juveniles don't get juries? Of the fact that lawyers defend the guilty?

To start a program, best to get someone on the faculty involved. They have the keys to the academic chest. As for materials, West has a book which is widely used, *Street Law.* I'll be very happy to send along the materials we use at the University of Arizona, *Tough Decisions,* for the cost of duplication.

We have also developed three videos, all running about 15 minutes.

Choices. The theme is that life isn't about big decisions but about little ones ... whether to stay home and study or go out and get high. We interview a young man, Manny, who made wrong decisions and ended up committing murder at the age of 15. We interview others, folks with similar backgrounds but difference end points: how did they get through the pressures and temptations of high school? The video begins with a murder scene and ends with joyous kids tossing their caps at a high school graduation.

The Sentencing of Bill Thomas. A fleeing teenager is arrested by police. He is taken to Juvenile Hall and, after he pleads guilty to drug possession, lawyers argue his fate: jail or probation. The video stops and the students must decide. We talk about the juvenile justice system, the impact of drugs, responsibility, and obligations to one another. **Bill Thomas** is narrated by one of his friends, who knew Bill was getting into trouble and wanted to say something but "didn't want to get involved."

You, the Jury. The students see a trial and then, as would a jury, decide guilt or innocence. This sets up a discussion about Constitutional Rights (right to jury trial, right to lawyer, right to confront witnesses against you) which the students saw illustrated in the video.

Although we can use these videos as part of our regular high school program, we have also started an Outreach Program which targets eight and ninth "at risk" students. It is a two day program. We show *Bill Thomas* the first day, *Choices* the second. We have teaching materials for the law students. We do the program during semester break when our students are off. Usually we have about 40 students covering about 80 classes.

I would be happy to send you further information about our programs and the videos. The information is free, but the videos aren't.

I know that even thinking about getting up in front of a high school class makes you nervous.

Students tell me, however, that it is one of the best things they have done in law school. Once you get up there, it will be hard to get you offstage. Indeed, some of us have been dodging the hook for a long time.

Another program we are trying to get started is a Big Brother/Big Sister Program. Law students would act as Big Sibs three to four hours a week during their second and third years. We would have a seminar for the law students. "Children at Risk: Legal Issues," which would explore general topics. This is in the planning stages—it should work out. Write and I will let you know.

So ends my discussion of possible pro bono activities. If your school does not have a program, for shame.

But don't curse the darkness; light a candle.

A Final Word on the Second and Third Years. Space allocations in this chapter may prove misleading. Much space is devoted to clinical practice, clerking, and high school teaching. The space is devoted to these subjects because I think there is more that needs to be said of them, not because I believe that they should be your main diet during your last two years. An overwhelming majority of your time will be, and should be, devoted to traditional courses. Again, the "right attitude" is to learn law even if some is boring, even if some is painful.

In your future lurks the boss's long, cold, stare: "Don't tell me that."

CHAPTER 18

CAREER CHOICES

Once upon a time, one of my students asked for a reference. His quest: the large, prestigious law firm of Blah, Blah and Blah in Gotham City. Making small talk, I asked, "Looking forward to Gotham?"

"No, I hate it there. I would rather go back home, to Hicksville."

"Well," I laughed nervously, "it must be that you like the kind of law they practice at Blah and Blah."

"I'd rather work with kids," he said. "That's what I did before law school and that's why I came to law school. I worked at Blah last summer and I hated it. As I told another summer intern, 'Terence, this is stupid stuff, yet you do your research fast enough.' "

"Then why apply to the firm?"

"Because everyone tells me it's a very good job."

John Lennon, at the time of his murder, had pretty much given up music; he was too busy managing his money.

—————

A friend of was talking about those books which urge us to slow down and "smell the roses."

"You know, when I read those books, I feel guilty. I vow, right then and there, to take some time off and go fishing. Then it strikes me. Those authors aren't fishing; they're working on their next book."

—————

Get a job you enjoy more than smelling roses. Get a job which draws you in each morning, because you like the people you work with, because you are enthralled with a task, because you are doing good and important work.

Get a job that puts a spring in your step!

> *70% of the lawyers in this country are in private practice, the vast majority in firms of five or less or on their own. Only 5% are in large firms. (By way of comparison, 8.3% of Hollywood actors play big firm lawyers on T.V.)*

5% of lawyers defend and prosecute criminals. Most lawyers change jobs after law school; many start at a government agency, go to a large firm and finally settle in a small one. Others start off in trial work and move to an office practice. Others leave law altogether, to govern nations, to make revolutions, or to broadcast the Dallas Cowboys.

50% of lawyers, more or less, were in the bottom half of their class.

But why, in a book designed for first year students, am I addressing the issue of legal careers? Shouldn't you be frolicking on first year fields, along with Hadley and Baxendale? Shouldn't you be green and golden, singing in your chains like the sea?

A few years ago the Dean of a Very Prestigious Law School had finished his Inspiring First Year Welcome. Those in the front rows thought they saw tears; all would agree that his voice had cracked when he spoke of the law's glorious tradition and of the opportunity to be of service.

"Dean, Dean," yelled one first year student, wildly waving his hand, "In terms of making partner in national firm, is it best to start at the home office or in one of the regional offices?"

Alas. Childhood is over so soon. Even if you get by the first day, reality will soon raise its ugly head. Law firms come to law schools to interview students. The students dress up. "Dress up" is an old tradition, like Halloween. Halloween is fun; "dress up" is stupid. I mean who is fooling who? Do interviewers actually believe that applicants want to look pompous middle age? That not one of them will rage against the dying of the light?

"Dress up" is in the first semester. Only second and third year students are invited but first years notice. Rumors fly, as do anxieties. Not everyone is dressing up! "I am doomed. Very few people even get interviews ... I will never get a job."

Again, only 5% of lawyers are in large firms, and by and large, *only large firms interview on campus*. Most firms, most government agencies interview after graduation; sometimes, after the Bar Exam.

95% of lawyers got their jobs without humiliating themselves at law school.

You should begin thinking about career alternatives early. There are things you can do now which will help later. This chapter attempts to identify some of those things. It is not a guide to specific jobs and how to get them (although being enthusiastic, convincing the employer you **want** the job, is the best I can offer). No doubt your law school has excellent placement office that will help you when the time comes. Drop by now just to get acquainted.

My goals are modest.

First, I hope to cheer you up and broaden your vision. Employment opportunities are rich, varied and exciting. There are good jobs that you probably haven't even thought of; you are limited only by imagination and gumption.

Second, I want to suggest a few things you can do now, and during the next three years, that might help you find a job ... not just any job, but one that will put a spring in your step. These things have more to do with exploring yourself than with exploring the market.

Before those two matters, I want to discuss two others: first, our fear of success and, second, how the law school experience can lead us astray.

We fear success ... perhaps even more than we do failure. Abraham Maslow calls it "fear of one's own greatness" or "running away from one's own best talents." He asks his students:

> "Which of you in this class hopes to write the great American novel, or to be a Senator, or Governor, or President? Or a great composer? Or a saint?"

His students giggle, blush, and squirm, until he asks, "If not you, then who else?"

This is not to say that you should crave fame or fortune; it is to suggest that you should not run away from your dreams because you fear boldness, because you fear your own best talents.

"Mind-forged manacles" ... the words of William Blake. "I could *never* do trial work." "I could *never* get a job in Washington." "I could *never* make a living in Hicksville representing kids." How do you know?

> *"I'm going to sit right down and*
> *write myself a letter."*

That was a lyric from song from my childhood.

Indulge me. Do it.

Put this book down and write yourself a letter, a letter to be opened in a year or so. This will provide a catalyst to begin some serious thought about what you want to do with the rest of your life.

You might want to start with "mind-forged manacles": are there things you "know" you can't do? What you really want to do after law school (or, perhaps, *instead* of law school)? What fears hold you back? What did you enjoy doing before law school? Maybe there is a job out there that allows for similar tasks and accomplishments.

Trust me: write the letter now or forget it. It simply isn't one of those things to do when you get around to it. If you can't devote 45 minutes to the rest of your life now, surely you will be too busy tomorrow.

Once you get in touch with your goals, don't let law school distort them. It happens.

A lot of students (maybe you) come to law school for idealistic reasons: to work with business in improving the environment, to work with abused children or to return to their community to help those less fortunate. Many get diverted and end up with Blah, Blah, and Blah, fighting traffic in Gotham City.

How come?

Many change career goals in law school for good reasons: learning more about themselves and more about the choices, they realize that they will be happier doing something they hadn't previously considered. Some of my best friends work for Blah, Blah, and Blah and love it. More power to them.

However, some change goals because they get caught up in law school hype.

Tom Wolfe, in *The Right Stuff*, writes that America's astronauts were not motivated by money, fame or challenge; they just wanted to prove they were the "right stuff".

There is nothing wrong with this, as long as the "right stuff" is where you want to be.

In law school the "right stuff" is working with ideas rather than with people. This is the implicit lesson. Law school goodies are passed out on the basis of academic performance; compassion, common sense and, alas, humor, can't be graded and hence don't count for much.

To prove that they are the "right stuff," the "best" students go to large firms (where the "interesting" legal work is done). The rest of the class goes into "regular" practice; only the academic losers would consider the grunt work of legal aid.

This bent is wrong. First, many of the "smartest" work in small firms, governmental agencies and public interest firms. The two smartest lawyers I know both work for Legal Aid. Second, some of the most legally exciting work is done at that level (while those lucky enough to be hired by Blah, Blah, and Blah, chase their opponents around the table, waving unanswered interrogatories). Third, much of the practice of law is not intellectually demanding or intellectually satisfying. Even the most exotic specialty becomes routine and, quite frankly, you can impress yourself with your own brilliance only so many times.

"The intellectual side of law, even the rush of combat, gets stale. But if you like people, you'll love practicing law." This from an old-timer, a man who had "made law" in his day, including one significant United States Supreme Court victory.

Whatever you end up doing, make sure it is what you want to do rather than what others have told you to do.

One final "big point" about choosing a career. Getting a job is so much more than getting a job; so much more than resumes, dressing up and remaining calm during the interview.

In choosing a job, you are choosing yourself.

George Orwell once wrote of how we all wear masks and, over time, how our faces grow to fit the mask.

I went to school in Berkeley when everyone was a radical. One of my friends was hired by a commercial firm in Santa Barbara. They told him he would be a Republican in a year. I saw him about six months later.

"They were wrong. I became a Republican after three months. But I haven't changed at all, not one bit. It's the *radicals* who have changed!"

After twenty years prosecuting criminals, what world view will you have? After a career of advising business, defending insurance companies, or teaching law, who will you know? What books will you read? Who will you be?

> *In this life we prepare for things, for moments and events and situations * * *. We worry about things, think about injustices, read what Tolstoy has to say * * *. Then, all of a sudden, the issue is not whether we agree with what we have heard and read and studied * * *. This issue is **us**, and what we have become.*

Robert Coles

I guess the point of these meanderings is this. There is a lot of job dissatisfaction out there; there is a lot of alcoholism and there is a lot of drug abuse. I don't know how many lawyers hate their jobs but a significant number do. Perhaps, just perhaps, they didn't choose correctly.

Sure, everyone "knows" that career selections are of utmost significance, but, perhaps fearing the enormousness of it all, most focus on questions dealing with resume preparation and whether they should start in the home or a regional office. Many students "take a job" just because it's there, just because they are afraid they won't get another one, just because they have a lot of loans to be repaid, or just because "everyone tells them it is a good job."

Bottom line: don't take time to pick the roses; take time to pick your compulsion.

The Good News: Jobs are Plentiful

*When you get in practice, it's how hard you work, how honest you are, and whether you have common sense that counts ... no one, hardly ever, asks you where you went to school or how well you did. (Of course, if you had been President of the United States and had sat on the United States Supreme Court for several years, and then had decided to go into law teaching, **we would ask!**)*

Like other markets, the demand for lawyers fluctuates. Sometimes it may be difficult to get a traditional job. But there is good news here as well. You can punt (decide not to seek long term employment immediately) or you can quit the field entirely and look for employment elsewhere.

Punt

It is OK to be indecisive. At least I think it is. After law school, you can take a job that lasts, by definition, only a year or two. This is a good option. These jobs are usually exciting and are of a "once in a lifetime" variety. They can provide valuable training for your future employment. Mostly, however, they do wonders in getting folks off your back: "And what will you do next year?"

Judicial clerkships are a good choice. Most appellate judges and many trial court judges hire recent graduates as clerks. Additionally, there are numerous **internships** offered by governmental agencies, public interest groups, and even some law schools.

Clerkships are highly competitive and the race starts second year. See your Placement Director.

As you already well know, another way to avoid growing up is to **stay in school**. Perhaps you will decide on a career which will be aided with more schooling. Some law schools offer advanced law degrees in such things as tax. Or you may wish to get another degree in a field which you plan to use in conjunction with law, such as business, finance, real estate, counseling, ventriloquism.

The hardest part of this option, and one which might prove insurmountable, is telling your family.

Your placement office has information on all of these choices. As some require applications during the second year, best to touch base now.

Non-Legal Careers

Kafka went to law school. He hated it. In fact, it has recently come to light that the first line of his classic, the *Metamorphosis*, has been incorrectly translated. The inaccurate translation reads:

> Gregor Samsa woke up one morning and found that he had turned into a gigantic cockroach.

The corrected translation reads:

> Gregor Samsa woke up one morning and found that he had turned into a rather large lawyer.

A surprising number of disgruntled lawyers become novelists (and, no doubt, disgruntled novelists swell our ranks). Others go into business (Kafka wouldn't have liked that either), teaching, politics, and the media. A good friend of mine went into "development" (fund-raising) using his legal knowledge of wills and tax law. Another wanted to get into producing movies. She went to Hollywood, rented an apartment, hung out at the studios, finally, after several months, got a law job and now, after several years, is producing her own movies.

Karen Waterman, a law school placement specialist, advises that routine want-ads can be rich sources of ideas. "Would this job involve the use of legal skills?" Many jobs involve legal skills (such as risk management and compliance work) but have traditionally filled with non-lawyers.

Show up and surprise everyone.

Of course, it is easier to get a traditional law job, particularly if it comes to you in the law school. However, maybe the rest of your life is worth a little effort, a little imagination, a little gumption.

Traditional Law Jobs

There is a lot more than big firms versus small firms, prosecuting versus defending.

Public Interest Law

Legal Aid

Law Reporting for print or TV

Law Teaching (in law schools or colleges or community colleges)

Risk Management; contract compliance

    In house legal counsel

    Legislative counsel

    Government work (from Washington to Hickville)

    Law publishing (writing ALR articles)

    Law Enforcement (FBI)

    Military Justice

Your Placement Office will have tons and tons of information as to these and many others. Here I want to give you some ideas about how you might go about evaluating your options: what factors might you want to consider?

Ideas versus people. Some people prefer working with ideas, others with people. Some law practices involve almost exclusively legal research and drafting. These jobs offer "nice" theoretical problems, the luxury of extended research and reflection, and the satisfaction that comes in drafting a well written and thorough legal document, be it a brief or contract. Large firms traditionally offer this kind of employment but so too do many smaller "specialized" law firms, "law reform units" of legal aid offices, and "appellate departments" of the public defender and of the district attorney.

At the other end of the continuum are those law jobs which involve working closely with people. Great satisfaction can come in helping people solve real life problems: helping work out a sensible child custody arrangement, helping two friends set up a partnership, helping a client understand a bureaucratic maze. As a general matter, smaller firms and some government agencies offer greater opportunities to work with people.

This is not to say that "people practices" are intellectually bankrupt. Far from it. Routine cases can raise critical issues of legal theory. *Miranda* was, after all, just another kidnap case. Further, there are no routine cases at the level of fact. Doing trial work, I slept with a pad and pencil next to my bed to jot down the flashes that would come in the night. Doing appellate work, I slept soundly.

Responsibility. The larger the firm or agency, the less responsibility you likely will have. Your work will be constantly reviewed. You will work on parts of elephants.

At the other end of the continuum are jobs that throw you directly into the heat of battle. In some small firms and legal aid offices, you interview clients the first day; in some district attorney and defender offices, you try cases your first week.

Responsibility can be exhilarating; after all those years of studying about the real world, you are suddenly part of it. Your decisions count.

Responsibility can be terrifying. Law is quite complex and, as a beginner, you know so little. Add to that the elusive criteria of good practice: "Have I worked hard enough?" "Have I raised all the points?" "Has my client been well represented?"

Training. It is **essential** to develop your professional skills. Larger firms and agencies generally offer good training. Your work is almost always reviewed. This is the other side of "lack of responsibility". Generally you will be given time to "do it right" and the standards of practice are quite high.

Many smaller firms and smaller public agencies also insist on the highest professional standards. **The worst thing you can do is to take a job that allows for sloppy work habits.**

An aside on solo practice. Some "hang out there shingle" upon graduation. But times, since Lincoln, have changed.

Without someone to show you the ropes, without someone to discuss your cases, you will teeter on the edge of malpractice. The most common cause of legal malpractice is missing deadlines. Once you get three or four cases, it gets very difficult to keep track of things ... working with an established firm or lawyer, you will learn the various retrieval systems. Going out on your own, you may not.

Two pieces of advice, assuming you ignore the implicit advice in the last paragraph. Keep your overhead low. Second, don't take "dog cases". In every community, there are folks who were drugged by the CIA and brainwashed. They flutter, like moths, around new shingles. Don't take these cases, just to put bread on the table. They never go away.

Aggressiveness. Many law jobs do not require aggressiveness. Estate planning is one example, business planning another.

"Alternative Dispute Resolution" is a movement to substitute more kinder and gentler methods into our adversary system. Perhaps mediation can replace litigation and problem-solving the zero-sum game (those in which what one side wins, the other must lose). Brave lawyers are entering traditional combative fields with these goals. If you are repelled by the adversary system, consider this route. Even in traditionally combative law jobs, it may be possible to do something other than "chase each other around the table," where the "good" solution leaves both sides sullen but not mutinous.

Income and security. Larger firms start associates at higher salaries than do other law employers; partners in large firms do exceedingly, embarrassingly, well. Some lawyers in smaller firms undoubtedly overtake their fat-cat brethren and occasionally make "megabucks" by getting into business ventures with their clients. Personal injury lawyers can almost retire if they get "the big one" (but, what with TV advertizing, the chances of getting "the big one" are about the same a winning POWER BALL).

Lawyers making a career in governmental agencies often do quite nicely. Gone, of course, the dream of vast wealth, but many government lawyers earn salaries higher than many lawyers in their area, with better benefits and job security.

Travel, Adventure. It's possible.

Esprit de corps. Some law jobs involve a strong sense of shared purpose. One of the things I most value about my own days in practice was my relationship with the other lawyers in the office. We knew about each others' cases, we talked about them, argued about them and shared the moments of joy and despair.

I found this sense of shared purpose and involvement in legal aid and in public defending. I am sure it exists in most prosecuting offices, in most government jobs, and, I am told, in most small law offices. The larger the firm or agency, the less likely the feeling. This lack of *esprit de corps* will not bother some, those who prefer to work alone (perhaps writing Nutshells) and those who simply want a job and look for a sense of community elsewhere.

What to do in Law School

First, a little off the wall advice. I teach Sports Law. An agent, who had played pro basketball, spoke of how difficult it was for many players to readjust after their playing days were over.

"I tell them to keep a diary when they are still playing. What do they enjoy doing in their off hours? What are they good at? That way, when the time comes, they will have some idea of what kind of job they may like."

Law school isn't practice ... but it is life. Keep track of, or at least become aware of, what you like and what you do well. A diary might help.

Do you enjoy the conflict of Moot Court or Trial Practice? Do you find the verbal encounter in the classroom exciting? Do you love research? Do you rush to your computer to get your thoughts on paper? Do you like close supervision? Do you like working with classmates? Do you prefer to work by yourself?

Many lawyers don't like their jobs. Probably a large number of these folks didn't like law school, didn't like studying law. Once you have given law school a fair run, at least a year, and you find you don't like the law, find it too nitpicky, too confining, too boring, consider getting out. Although law practice is different than law study, a lot of it is the same, reading cases, making arguments. If this is not for you, cut your loses. Kafka went on to achieve modest success.

Another source of lawyer unhappiness is a mismatch between personality and the job. While I don't want to make too much of this distinction, of those who love the law, some love it for its ability to do justice while others love it for its intellectual puzzles. If there's fire in your belly, don't take a job which offers only tricky cross-words.

Again. Keeping a diary in law school may help you sort out who you might be.

Course Selection

If you are considering a specialty, obviously take the courses that relate to it. Similarly there may be courses in other departments of the university which will expose you to the "nuts and bolts" of a particular career. For example, if you are considering something in the media, check the catalogue of the Journalism Department. Better yet, go over and chat with the people there. Another obvious example is Business School. However, *as career goals often change*, it is a mistake to focus too exclusively in the area of law you think you'll practice.

If you think you know what field you want to practice in, by all means, take courses in it. If you find you hate the subject matter, you probably won't like practicing it. Conversely, if you take a course and love it, think about the career possibilities.

A warning, however, about "subject matter" career selection. Sure, we all love Contracts, but to "practice" contract law may not be as exciting as it is to "study" contract law. Lucy, Lady Duff Gordon, Hadley and Baxendale, Ship Peerless, gone, all gone. Without them, where's the salt?

Most law schools offer courses in **trial practice** and in **clinical practice**, which involve representing real clients either in a law school clinic or in a field placement. I feel that these courses are very important, particularly if you are shying away from them. It may be a matter of breaking out of "mind-forged manacles." You may find that you enjoy the hurly-burly of trial and that you find deep satisfaction in helping people solve real life problems. Or you may conclude "Never again." Either way, you win.

Clinical courses are needed by those students planning to work for small firms or on their own. There is the danger of developing sloppy work habits. Law school courses will instill a sense of excellence in practice.

Work for lawyers

A good way to experience practice is to work for a lawyer. Law firms and agencies often hire second and third year students to do legal research. Doing the research, hanging out at the office, talking to attorneys and staff can give you a good feel for that particular kind of law practice.

Many law professors advise against clerking, arguing that students will learn more by sticking to the books. I disagree and believe that clerking can be, if approached from the proper perspective, a valuable learning experience, both in terms of legal doctrine and in terms of career choice.

If you are to work for a lawyer, what kind of lawyer? Should you take a job with the kind of firm or agency you "think" you would like to eventually work for? Or should you take a job with one of those "I-could-never-work-with-them" firms? There are pros and cons for each. Some students find permanent employment through their clerking. On the other hand, much can be said for testing as many alternatives as possible. Even if you confirm your suspicion that you could never do insurance defense, having clerked with such a firm will make you a better personal injury lawyer.

Ask lawyers and professors

Most of us like to give advice (me, apparently, more than others). If you are considering prosecuting, why not go to the prosecutor's office and ask to see one of the attorneys?

I'm not here looking for a job. I'm here because I want some advice. I am thinking about prosecuting when I graduate but I really don't know much about it. Perhaps you can tell me about it, perhaps I could sit in and watch what you do.

Note: This can be turned into a very clever job getting ploy.

Now, Ms. Banker, I'm not looking for a job working in your legal department. I realize you are probably full. What I would like is some advice on how to go about getting a job in the legal department of a bank.

Of course *I* would never be bold enough to simply show up at a law office, unannounced. The problem is meeting lawyers. One possibility is to get together with some classmates, ask a friendly professor for some names of recent graduates, and throw a party.

We're first year students and we want to meet some lawyers so we can get some feel for what it's like. Want to come to a party?

You can also infiltrate sections of your local Bar association; many have student memberships. Another way to meet lawyers is to attend Continuing

Legal Education programs (CLE) and go to Bar conventions.

Try to get your professor talking about her practice experiences. Most likely they will be more interesting than the Rule in Shelley's Case. I sincerely hope so, for her more than yours.

Go to court

It takes absolutely no courage to quietly walk into the back of a courtroom and sit through a trial. Again this experience is probably most needed by those who will "never" step into a courtroom—who knows, perhaps they'll never leave.

Reading books

There are several books about practice. I recommend, as openers:

The Associates, Jay Osborne (author of *Paper Chase*), deals with life in a Wall Street firm.

Trial and Error, D. Michael Tomkins, story of a young lawyer starting off in solo practice.

Confessions of a Criminal Lawyer, Seymour Wishman, a criminal defense lawyer reflects on several years of practice.

These books are relatively short, quite candid, and at places, humorous. They are excellent introductions to various kinds of practice.

A final word on careers

I have written another Nutshell, **Trial and Practice Skills**. It covers about everything you will ever need to know: client interviewing, legal problem solving, case planning, discovery, negotiation, client counseling, and, of course, trial skills from opening statement to closing argument. I have shown great restraint in not plugging the book before. In any event, I end the book with some general remarks about the joys of law practice. I quote Holmes:

It is possible to live greatly within the law.

I believe that and so should you.

I close with some thoughts about ambition. I like the closing so much, I'll end this one the same way.

———————

Perhaps you will argue cases that shape your times, or perhaps you will be the trusted advisor of powerful groups, huge corporations or even Presidents. Or perhaps you will never make the front page and will be simply another lawyer in the yellow pages, helping people with everyday problems. There is greatness in that as well.

We make too much of our ambition. In John Bolt's play, *A Man for All Seasons*, Sir Thomas More is discussing careers with the politically ambitious Richard Rich.

> More: Why not be a teacher? You'd be a fine teacher. Perhaps even a great one.
>
> Rich: And if I was, who would know of it?
>
> More: You, your pupils, your friends, God. Not a bad public that * * *

That's such a comforting thought.   I'll call it a day.

CHAPTER 19

LAWYERS TALK ABOUT
THEIR JOBS

My thinking about this chapter has changed. The original intent was to have lawyers write about what they do in order to provide career information. Reading what they have written it strikes me that the real value of the chapter lies elsewhere, in combating cynicism concerning the practice of law. My sense is that law students quickly lose idealism and enthusiasm for their chosen profession. I think this happens because in law school, law practice is presented as something abstract and lifeless, as intellectual game-playing without emotional or ethical content. My hope is that, in reading what these lawyers do, you will realize that yours was a wise decision. The practice of law is neither abstract nor amoral; it is alive, fulfilling, and caring.

The lawyers who write on the following pages are friends, not statistical abstracts. I selected them because they are reflective and insightful. Although I selected lawyers doing different kinds of law jobs, no attempt was made for "balance", either in terms of "type" of practice, age of practitioner, or geography. In describing to them their task I again rejected the goal of balance. I prescribed no format. I simply told them that I was writing a

343

book for first-year law students, students who likely knew little about various legal careers and who likely knew little about what lawyers actually do. Write, I advised, what you think might prove useful.

Some focused on questions of career: how they made their own career decisions, the pros and cons of various kinds of practices, things you might do as a law student to help you prepare. Others focused on what they do as lawyers, describing either a typical day or a typical task. A quick disclaimer. These are *individual statements*. I told the lawyers that they were not writing as "representatives" of their kind of practice and not to worry if what they wrote might be atypical. People experience things differently.

This then is not an encyclopedia of the types of law practice. It is rather a collage of what some lawyers thought important to share with you. I have learned from them; so will you.

DAN COOPER

Public Defender

The most satisfying part of being a public defender is representing people who are despised by the public, the press and the prosecutors. Most cases remain obscure and create no reaction. On occasion, however, a defendant comes along who stirs the conscience of the community into moral outrage. It is defending this person that makes me proud to be a lawyer.

I recently represented a man who, along with his wife, was charged with child abuse. The facts were grisly. When I first met my client I was somewhat taken aback by his absolute and total lack of guilt. I try not to prejudge my cases. I was, however, aware when I received this case that the evidence was overwhelming against my client. I was perplexed at his total lack of emotion. Throughout the duration of the case he remained stoic in the face of constant hostility. The prosecutor called my client "a monster." The newspapers covered the case extensively and without objectivity. Even some close friends of mine asked how I could represent this man. The trial lasted nearly two weeks and, although I could not honestly say that I had fun, it was an experience I would not trade. The victim in the case, a nine-year-old girl, was found hog-tied in a motel room. She weighed thirty-two pounds and had been beaten. She had a chipped front tooth, bruises on her face and at least twenty scars on the top of her head which, the State alleged, came from a blunt object. A psychiatrist testified that she had never seen a worse case of psychological and emotional child abuse. A pediatrician testified that the child had been systematically starved for at least four years. A radiologist testified that the child's growth would, in all likelihood, be permanently stunted. And the most damaging witness of all was the little girl,—tiny, charming, precocious. She broke down in tears as she turned to look at her mother and stepfather. My client stared at her impassively.

Against the advice of some very skilled trial lawyers, I put my client on the stand. The other
lawyers felt that my client's testimony would only
enrage an already upset jury. But I wanted the
jury to see how narrow and rigid was my client's
view of the world. His testimony was stilted, rigid,
unsmiling and, I felt, demonstrated a myopic, inade-
quate personality perfectly capable of being unaware that his nine-year-old stepdaughter had been
systematically starved and abused. Certainly his
testimony would not prove his innocence. But
there was an outside chance that the jury would
convict of the lesser, non-intentional child abuse
charge if they felt my client was rigid, myopic and
pathetic. It was a slim chance in an unpopular,
highly publicized case. My closing argument to the
jury was emotional. I had convinced myself, if no
one else, that the lesser offense would be the appropriate verdict. That the jury convicted my client of
the greater offense has not changed my mind. But
perhaps my feelings today about that child abuse
case typify the nature of this job. I am proud that,
in the face of overwhelming adverse publicity,
against insurmountable evidence, while not able to
convince a jury of my client's innocence, that jury
knew that the defendant had a lawyer who believed
in him.

RANDY STEVENS

Prosecutor

It took just a little more than a year after my
graduation from law school for me to realize that

private practice wasn't for me—at least not at that time in my life. I wanted more variety, more action, more excitement. I also wanted to be handling cases that had greater significance than just importance to the client. Having watched several excellent trial attorneys perform in court, I knew that courtroom practice was something I had to try, but I also realized it would take years to get any meaningful experience if I stayed in private practice. Telling the people I worked with that I'd be back in a year or two, I left and joined the local prosecutor's office. That was fourteen years ago.

From my perspective, the *total* experience available in prosecution cannot be duplicated elsewhere, especially for an attorney in the first four or five years. It isn't just the legal experience; it is the broader awareness of life, people and society, awareness of aspects of our society that most of us never dreamed existed. While at the same time, prosecution is an accelerated course in all aspects of trial practice.

Prosecution is the perfect opportunity for you to find out if you really want to be a trial attorney. Almost every young attorney experiences some degree of trial resistance—a hesitancy to try a case in front of a jury. There is a fear of making mistakes, of embarrassing oneself, of "freezing up" and not knowing what to do next. In a busy prosecutor's office, this resistance is usually overcome simply because there isn't time to dwell upon it. A heavy caseload doesn't allow for it. It isn't unusual for new prosecutors to find themselves trying several cases a week. If he or she begins to enjoy what they are doing, and are comfortable in court, it is only a matter of time before they want to begin trying more complicated and more serious cases. But not all attorneys experience this. After six months to a year, and sometimes even sooner, some realize that they aren't enjoying courtroom work, that they don't like the pressure and the demands of trial work, something no one can really know before they've given it a try. Most prosecutor's offices expect this to happen with a percentage of the young attorneys they hire.

It is usually during the fourth and fifth years when trial skills begin to reach a plateau, which means the attorney can try any type of criminal case with a high level of competency. Most trial attorneys will agree: if a person can competently prosecute a lengthy, difficult criminal case, that person can probably try most any type of civil case. Law firms recruit heavily from prosecuting offices.

Most attorneys who prosecute do so for five to ten years, then they move on to something else. Looking back, asking myself why I've stayed so long in prosecution, the answer really isn't that hard to determine: I've thoroughly enjoyed myself. I've actually looked forward to going to work each morning. The constant flow of different types of cases, the interchange with victims and witnesses; working with every level of law enforcement; all go together to constitute a level of excitement that makes the job more than just enjoyable. It's experiencing life three or four times more than the average person. Along with this is the additional feeling that in some small way, you are doing something positive for society.

GRACE McILVAIN

Mid–Size Firm

When I decided to become a lawyer, it was not because I thought the law would be exciting. I thought it would be boring. I did not expect to like the law, let alone love it the way one is supposed to. I wanted a job that would give me responsibility, a chance to use my brain, a good salary, and a chance to advance, none of which I had as a secretary. Those were my sole reasons for applying to law school.

It is amusing to recall what I expected the practice of law to be like when I was in law school. I expected it to be boring and tedious, so tedious that the hours in the office would drag by. Nothing could be further from the truth. I enjoy at least 90% of the things I must do. Filling out time sheets and preparing bills to send to clients are no fun at all, but litigation is very interesting. I think about my cases all my waking hours and often most of the night. I even dream about them.

The responsibilities and time pressures are, however, very stressful. The matters one handles are extremely important to the clients, and they place a great deal of trust in you. Because of that, and for many other more selfish reasons, there is great pressure to achieve an excellent result in every single case which is, of course, impossible. There is never enough time to be as thoroughly prepared as you would like to be. No matter how well organized and self-disciplined you are, every day is a struggle against time. There are never enough hours in the day. In that respect, law school is good preparation for the practice. But the time pressures in practicing law are much greater than time pressures in law school.

There is so much emphasis on legal theories in law school that you begin to believe that legal knowledge and analytical skill are all you need to be a good attorney. Law school doesn't prepare you for the psychological aspects of practicing law. You must build a good relationship with your client and make him or her have confidence in you. You must make the opposing attorney at least respect you, and it is to your advantage to convince him that you are tough, that you know the law, and that you will persevere no matter what. It is to your advantage to make him afraid of you. Yet sometimes you need his cooperation, so you must know when to be nice to him and when to apply pressure. (I use "him" when referring to the opposing attorney because, in litigation, nine times out of ten your opponent is male. If you are a woman, the difficulties of dealing with him are multiplied because even before he meets you, he has probably decided that you are either a pushover or a bitch, and that whichever you are, you are not a good lawyer.)

You need to convince the judges before whom you appear that you know the law, that there is a good reason behind every statement you make, and that you would never ever mislead them. You must convince juries that you are credible and that deserves their verdict.

There is always room to grow. There are always ways you could have handled a case better, which is one of the reasons you are never bored.

RICHARD DAVIS

Private Practice, Mid–Size Firm

I arrive in my office at 7:30 a.m. I look at my calendar and realize that I have to travel to a hospital which our firm represents to meet with the Administrator and Risk Manager. Others will be present. A few days ago a 20–day-old premature baby died at the hospital while on a ventilator. The original account suggests that the machine malfunctioned preventing the baby from breathing normally.

Immediately after the accident, the Director of the Medical Lab at the hospital wanted to test the ventilator. I advised a delay long enough to notify each of the interested parties and to give them an opportunity to be present. The manufacturer of the ventilator and the parents of the baby were notified.

The test is scheduled to begin at 9:00 but I get there early. This will allow me to become familiar with the machine and interview the hospital's personnel who were on duty when the incident occurred. Arriving at 8:15, I talk to the respiratory technician, the nurse on duty and the medical lab technician who will do the testing. By 8:45 I have a general idea of how the machine works, of the suspected problem and of what happened the day in question. I also learn that the hospital coffee gets old after the second cup.

The first person to arrive for the meeting is an investigator from the County Medical Examiner's Office. The family asked that office to be present and to determine the cause of the baby's death. We exchange pleasantries. I am a little anxious and apprehensive because I really do not know what the tests will reveal. My hidden hope is that the tests will prove my client blameless.

The manufacturer is sending someone from its national headquarters in Texas. It is now 9:00 and we receive a call advising us that the manufacturer's rep will be late. The small talk and anxiousness continue. At 9:30, the manufacturer's representative arrives. There is an immediate disagreement over the tests that should be run and who should run them. After discussion, ground rules are laid and pictures are taken to verify and preserve settings on dowels and pressure gauges. Each test is run carefully and meticulously. The pressure gauge is saved for last because it is the suspected culprit. It proves faulty.

Further tests are necessary to determine why the system failed but that necessitates a breakdown of the unit. Moreover, the necessary equipment is not available. The manufacturer's representative wants to take the machine back to the factory for further testing. I disagree. I feel that the machine should be stored in a place where no one can get to it without my knowledge and prior approval. Besides, there should be no destructive testing without giving every interested party an opportunity to be present along with an expert. I suggest that since the Medical Examiner's Office is involved, it should store the machine at its facility. The Medical Examiner's investigator nixes that idea but recommends that it be placed in the Police Department's storage room. We agree and the police are called.

When I arrive in my office around 3:30, I find thirteen telephone messages, most of which require a return call. I learn that two cases were settled and a person with a 2:30 appointment showed up and left after waiting about one-half hour. My secretary says that she was very angry.

I dictate a memo to the file concerning the test because I am certain that a lawsuit will be filed. I sort through the telephone messages and mail so I can arrange them according to some priority.

At 4:30 I receive a telephone call from a friend who is being investigated by the FBI. He wants my advice. I make an appointment for the next day. Next I receive a call from a representative of Farmers Insurance Group. He has a question concerning the value of a case and what should be paid to settle it. I recommend a figure. I answer a few letters and review tomorrow's schedule. I realize that I have a deposition scheduled at the same time that I set the appointment for my friend. I call him back but there is no answer. My calendar indicates that I have a trial next week and there are some things that I must do to be ready for it. I make a list. It is now 6:10 and it is dark outside. There is still a lot of work to be done but it will have to wait until tomorrow.

BARBARA SATTLER

Criminal Defense, Solo Practice

Growing up in the 50's, I used to watch Perry Mason and think about how great it must be to be a criminal defense attorney. At the time it was only a dream because I didn't know any lawyers, no one in my family had ever graduated from college, and all the lawyers I saw on TV were men. By the mid–70's the world had changed considerably. After living through the 60's and earning a BA and MA, I found myself working as a counselor in a state agency feeling extremely frustrated because my efforts to help people seemed fruitless due to bureaucracy and regulations.

At the old age of 29, I revived the long-dormant idea to going to law school. Now fifteen years later, after trying over a hundred cases including murder, terrorism, and dog abuse, I am a sole-practitioner doing criminal defense, and trying to raise a child. To my surprise I often do more counseling than legal work and still butt my head against a system that seems unresponsive, hostile and unconcerned with individual justice. Often my most valuable service to a client is listening or hand-holding, rather than giving legal services.

With all its frustrations, I wouldn't give up criminal defense or private practice.

Criminal defense work is fasted-paced and exhilarating. People ask me all the time, "How can you represent those people and sleep at night?" Although sometimes the people I represent are stupid, uneducated, and may have committed a heinous act, the system is so badly skewed, to punish and to expedite, that the majority of the time the punishment so outweighs the crime that representation is easy. Someone once said a criminal defense lawyer sees "bad" people at their best; a divorce lawyer sees "good" people at their worst. What is difficult for me is dealing with prosecutors who seem more concerned with statistics, and judges who seem more concerned with expediting their calendar than with finding what justice is, or trying to solve a real social problem.

At the end of a trial which didn't go well, I may question my performance (perhaps I could have been better), but I never question that my client deserves my best.

On a typical day, before going to the office, I have to figure out with my husband who will take and pick up our son at daycare and arrange for his other daily activities. Because I run a business (and employ a full-time secretary, part-time attorney, and other support staff), often many hours in the day are filled with administrative matters such as paying bills, deciding what books and supplies are needed or can be put off, fighting with the IRS, and my version of billable hours. These are problems neither law school nor my five years as a public defender ever prepared me for.

I usually handle around twenty active cases (not including inactive appeals or cases which are in other stages of waiting) which typically include DUI's, drug cases, child molestation and rape, domestic violence, and murder. On a typical day I talk to clients (this is where the counseling comes in), write motions, write letters begging for, or explaining why a certain deal or plea bargain should be given, go to court hearings, interview witnesses, do research and speak with other lawyers, probation officers, or police officers. Sometimes I don't have time to eat lunch or make a personal call.

I will never forget the first time I head the words "not guilty" nor the first time I heard "not guilty" in a murder case. I still feel a thrill seeing my name in print or my picture on TV (at least on a good hair day) and, of course, winning a case. However, over time what has provided the most satisfaction and pride is receiving cards from clients who are writing to thank me, not because of the result (which sometimes is not good), but because they know I fought hard, did my best, and, most importantly, cared.

THERESA GABALDON

Law Professor: Large Law Firm

My sister, who is a romance novelist, has the best job in the world. This is largely because she has self-defined it to involve working at night, getting up very late, and eating chocolates for breakfast.

I, a law professor have the second best job in the world; if eating chocolates were a necessary part of the job description, it would clearly rival my sister's. As it is, I have enormous flexibility about what I do and, within reasonable bounds, when I do it. The highlights, and only strictly scheduled events of the week are, of course, classroom appearances. I currently teach to an average class size of around 120 students; put a microphone in my hand and I become Oprah Winfrey. Coming up with different ways to cover the material is part of the fun, and if I choose to play a game of "Jeopardy" with corporate law topics, none of my teaching colleagues will object (at least not to my face.) My students are good-natured and appreciate whatever effort is expended in their behalf.

Performing scholarly research and writing is another important part of my task, and it is here that the possibilities for marching to one's own drumbeat are most unlimited. I choose my own topics for inquiry, and simply work on them until I have said what I have to say. My most productive "thinking time" starts at 4:00 a.m. and I try to take advantage of it. This may lead to a lull later in the day, but a quick trip to aerobics class recharges my batteries.

Although the description thus far may suggest that the law professor leads a life that is somewhat distanced from others this is only true if he or she decrees it. If you display any disposition to listen, as well as to impart, students will be by to chat about a truly breath-taking assortment of subjects. Your colleagues can, if you choose, be your sounding boards, your confidantes, your matchmakers, and, every now and then, your bowling partners.

My immediately prior incarnation was as a partner in a large law firm. As such, I had the third best job in the world. In all honesty, flexibility was not one of the things that commended it. Rather, it was the technical challenge—present also in law teaching—and the sense of command. Frankly, the money wasn't bad, either; in ten years of teaching I have yet to achieve my salary in my last year of practice.

I specialized in corporate and securities law, and these are the areas that have carried over into my teaching and my scholarship. It was, at the time, something of a "glamour" practice. The deals were huge, the pace was fast, and the travel arrangements were luxurious. The pressure, however, was intense, and I can remember the feeling in my chest as I realized that a deadline was approaching and that the legal judgement being brought to bear on a multi-million dollar deal was mine. I have no regrets about having lived that life or about having left it, simply because I have found something I like more.

Because I have truly enjoyed both of my law-related professions, I have to believe that there is something about the law that has "worked" for me.

I know that it has not, and does not, "work" for everybody. I enjoy the solving-the-maze aspects and the challenges of communicating my solutions to others. I suspect, however, that I lack the passion for justice, fairness, etc., that motivates some— and that's probably just as well for a corporate lawyer. In fact, from my observations, it is passion of this sort, combined with some type of corporate law-practice, that frequently leads to dissatisfaction with the law. There is fulfillment in serving particular clients well, in teaching, and in being an upstanding citizen and contributing member of society, but it will still leave some people feeling that there should be something more.

ANDY SILVERMAN

Legal Aid

It is 9 a.m. I arrived at work awhile ago. The waiting room is filling up and it is my day to be "on".

Being "on" in the legal services parlance signifies your day to do intake interviews. It is the first time the client talks to a lawyer. Such days generally amount to 10 to 15 of these encounters * * * the real guts of a legal services practice. I know it is a day that I will get no other work done but seeing clients.

The phone rings * * * it is the intake worker informing me that my first client is ready. I am now officially "on" and the stream of clients may go on all day * * * one right after another.

A young woman with a three-year-old tagging along walks into my office. After the introductions, I go for the extra legal pad and colored pens I always have ready and hand them to the child. I know that if the interview is going to be at all meaningful I have to keep the child happy and busy.

The woman tells me that she is two months behind in rent and the landlord has sent her an eviction notice. She has been out-of-work for the past four months and her ex-husband who she cannot find has not paid child support for the past year. Her problems sound overwhelming * * * where do I start * * * is there anything legally I can do?

Well, being a lawyer, my initial reaction is to think of legal remedies * * * the law school approach to the problem. Is there a violation of the landlord-tenant law? Is the eviction notice proper? Will she have any defenses to a possible unlawful detainer action? I start going down this road and quickly realize she can no longer afford this apartment and all she wants is time to find suitable but cheaper housing for her and her child. A phone call to the landlord from me, the lawyer, might do it. She tried the day before and failed. I call and the landlord reluctantly agrees. And another call to a friend in the public housing office helps her cut through the bureaucratic maze to find new housing. She leaves a bit relieved.

Before my next client I think about whether I am a lawyer or a social worker. Did my last client need a lawyer? Or did I do for her just what a corporate attorney does for the corporation president: identify the true problem and find the easiest and fastest way to resolve it. Well, it does not matter, I helped someone and that's all that really counts.

No more time to reflect, the next client is standing at the door. He is a man in his 50's who works part-time as a laborer. He had purchased an insurance policy because of a newspaper advertisement that had made generous promises. But when he became ill, the company said his claim was not covered. Sounds like a legal problem and one that another lawyer in the office may be interested in pursuing. She has handled similar problems and is looking for "the" case to litigate. This may be the one. I get the facts and tell the client we will be in contact. I will talk to the other lawyer tomorrow when I am "off" intake.

Legal problems keep flowing in all day. Food stamp cutoffs, car repossessions, housing foreclosures, there is no end. They have one common ingredient: a person in trouble that needs help. That personal side of legal services keeps me going. It is frustrating * * * it is gratifying * * * it is being a legal services attorney.

At the end of the day an older woman walks into my office as my final intake of the day. She does not speak English well but gets across that her son is in the county jail. My first reaction is that she has a criminal problem which legal aid lawyers do not handle. In my tired state I think that I may be able to get rid of this problem quickly. But I hear her out and become fascinated. I remain after closing hours talking to her about her son's complaints about the conditions in the jail. I have heard about that "awful jail" for years but now may have a real, live client that wants to do something about it. She tells me that her son and others in the jail would like to talk to a lawyer about such a suit. I promise her I will see her son tomorrow. It all seems worth it.

LESLIE COHEN

Public Interest

When I decided to go to law school, it was always to become a "peoples" lawyer. I always wanted to fight for individuals civil rights. However, when I went to law school, I perceived that fight to involve struggling against racism and sexism, and encroachments on first amendment rights. At that time, little did I know, that 12 years later I would actually be fighting discrimination, but for a different group of people—one of the last groups to gain civil rights in our society—persons with serious disabilities or mental illness.

For the last three years, I have been working for a public interest law firm which is the recipient of several federal grants to represent persons with disabilities to be free from abuse and neglect, free from discrimination and to promote access to adequate services and programs. No day is a typical day, but any day could include part of the following:

I strategize with an advocate on how to approach a school district's failure to provide a child with traumatic brain injury appropriate services. Under the federal Individuals with Disabilities Education Act, all school districts are required to provide children with special needs a free and appropriate education including any related services they may need. Should we request a hearing to get the school district to pay for the services of a cognitive trainer to help the child? We decide to submit our expert's report and let the school district respond.

I next speak with an attorney in our office about a pending Americans with Disabilities Act case. Her client, who is deaf, has not been provided interpreter services during required training and in-service meetings at his job. The client is frustrated and feels he can't learn how to do his job better or advance because he is not receiving the technical assistance other workers are. We are in negotiations with the employer and discuss whether providing the client with interpreter services in the future will be enough, or should he receive remedial trainings and/or compensation for being denied an interpreter for so long.

I receive a phone call that a former client, who had been inappropriately institutionalized at the state hospital for many years. Now he might be returned. Evidently, through lack of appropriate care at a local mental health agency, the client has deteriorated and is in need of hospitalization. I dash off a letter to the local mental health agency apprising them of the situation and demanding that they stabilize our client's care so the he can be returned to his community placement.

I then rush off to a meeting of persons discussing proposed legislative changes to the criminal rules concerning the competency to stand trial law. I am concerned that proposed changes may result in incarceration of individuals with mental disability for long periods of time unnecessarily and in contravention of constitutional principles.

There are just a few of the issues I will address on any given day. Representing persons with disabilities involves important civil rights issues. As our jurisprudence begins to address the rights of persons in the United States who have been previously ignored, such as persons with disabilities, gays and lesbians, immigrants, and children, there should be lots of exciting opportunities available for law students to enter public interest law.

RITA A. MEISER

Large Firm

The practice of law in a "large" law firm varies dramatically depending upon the firm and the city. In many, people hate briefcases and consider lunch at McDonald's a gourmet delight. Each firm has its own personality, which is reflected in many ways, especially the manner in which it deals with associates. As a result, I describe my practice to you as a person who, while content in my role as a practitioner in my particular law firm, might also not be content in a different large law firm. I also write as a person whose initial perception envisioned a happier legal life in a small firm, and who has been pleasantly surprised at where I have ended up.

My primary orientation in becoming an attorney was to maximize my involvement with people. The areas of law in which I am mostly involved reflect this goal. Mostly I practice hospital law. This is one of those areas that you do not know exists when you are in law school. Hospital law encompasses a broad range of legal problems: removing from a hospital staff a physician who does not perform at the proper standard of care; determining what procedures must be followed when a physician decides that life support systems should be removed, and working through the administrative procedures necessary to have a hospital add a department or beds. The work appeals to me because it involves effecting positive, tangible change in a way that is often lacking in the practice of law.

My second area of practice is employment discrimination, primarily from a defense perspective. I find this work intriguing because of the variety of people and areas to which it exposes me. Processing a discrimination charge, I learn the business operations of the client, as well as meet and work with people involved in the world of business. It has not been my experience that practice from the defense posture necessarily mandates advocacy of personally offensive legal positions. Business people are generally fairly practical. If they recognize that a policy or practice is unlawful and will cause them continuing economic harm, they are generally receptive to changing it. The lawyer plays a role in advancing this recognition.

Finally, I represent two adoption agencies on a pro bono basis. The gratifications are obvious and the ability to participate in this type of activity is often a luxury less easily available in a small firm.

As can be seen, there is little correlation among my major areas of practice. Also, my practice in these areas is not to the exclusion of occasional work in other areas. This is an example of a difference in the personality of my law firm as opposed to some others. Large firms place differing emphasis upon the importance of an attorney specializing, how quickly specialization should occur, and how much pressure is placed upon the associate to specialize in a given area. My specialties evolved over the course of three years of exploring numerous legal areas.

A large firm offers a new lawyer diversity, not only in terms of the type of legal practice offered, but in the people themselves. I initially perceived this to be an advantage of a small firm, but I now find it to be one of the greatest attributes of a large firm. I assumed that I would have closer personal relationships and find the working atmosphere more pleasant and intimate in a small firm. I now believe that a large law firm incorporates numerous types of personalities, and its size permits this diversification not to generate conflict. In a small firm, a personality conflict between two members can create tension for the remaining members in a way which does not occur when 70 lawyers are involved. Also, to the extent one specializes, the pool of working relationships narrows, thereby promoting the more intimate working relationships.

There are advantages and disadvantages to large firm practice, and what those factors are is the function of the given firm. The emphasis upon time commitments, responsibility, and client contact are all variables which must be assessed in evaluating the personality of any firm. In my particular firm, client responsibility and contact came quickly; however, this is not true in every large firm. If you are considering work in a large firm, interview carefully, particularly for second year clerkships, and try to select the firm which you think has the personality with which you are most compatible. Use your second year clerkship at that firm not only to verify whether your perceptions were correct, but to develop your ability to analyze the makeup of other firms, so that if you interview at another firm, you will more quickly be able to assess whether it's for you.

MICHAEL SACKEN

Large Firm

Like many students who wander into law schools I was uncertain of my goals, beyond delaying my separation from the university environment and finding some meaningful occupation. At orientation, an old friend and I pledged our joint *non*-goal:

Never to work in a big, corporate law firm—not for political reasons ("selling out"), but because it sounded so distasteful and mercenary. Ultimately, we both abandoned our pledges, at least initially, and joined our destinies to large, institutional firms.

The first step on the primrose path was succeeding in law school, which is not a goal to be consequently jettisoned. After my first year, I was elected to the law review. After anointment, I was courted by various law firms, which always approached new review members. My circle of acquaintances during the second and third year included more review colleagues, because we worked together and were thrown or chose to join together in social activities.

There was an intoxicating and delusive sense of being the "best" of our class. Whatever diversity of goals originally existed among us, we experienced a coalescence. New mythologies were introduced regarding big firm practice. The really complex and challenging issues were encountered there; you worked in a collegial atmosphere, surrounded by individuals of comparable intellect and ambition ("your kind"); and you were proximate to and advisors of the powerful. Even the sweat-shop working hours were translated into a reasonable expectation. After all, *you* were used to interminable work for the review.

Even so, I retained enough skepticism to work with a small litigation firm during the key second summer, rather than accept the traditional big firm clerkship. This experience provided an unintended consequence: I returned for my third year irrevocably committed to a big firm, for new reasons. The lead attorney in this small stable was a superior trial lawyer (and, perhaps inevitably, an indifferent law student). Measuring my potential against his realized abilities, I feared that I would never be a "successful" litigator. For one who had the "right stuff," a lesser standard than excellence seemed inconceivable. I developed a disabling "won't" category: I won't litigate. Big firms offered specialized practices without litigation, and an ego assuagement as well (I am still among the best). It was absolutely the wrong decision for me.

My *worst* decision was to exclude advocacy categorically, because that narrowed extraordinarily my range of options. Unfortunately, in those antediluvian days, my school offered few trial practice or clinical courses, and I was too intimidated to take what was available. The single critical decision to make prior to seeking employment is to litigate or not to litigate. That decision defines your career alternatives as no other. Take trial practice or a clinical experience. For reluctant litigators the dread of the unknown is far worse than pedestrian reality.

My second poorest decision was to choose a large prestigious law firm, in part because I believed that it was expected of me and the only worthy choice. That practice turned out to be exactly what I suspected (and indeed somehow previously knew before I "learned" otherwise in law school): What I did not want to spend my life doing. Unfortunately, reviving that self-knowledge required an unfulfilling couple of years.

This is an idiosyncratic account, not a generalized indictment of big firms. What I experienced has a lot to do with me, and perhaps the firm that I chose, and perhaps little to do with you. At least, be cautious about rejecting such an opportunity because you see yourself as too idealistic, introspective or humanistic. The information system at law schools is riddled with explicit and implicit biases. Pursue these questions vigorously and extensively; then react on your own biases. And, a final bit of Polonian wisdom, never be afraid to admit your first decision was a mistake and move onto a preferable pasture.

JAMIE RATNER

Government Attorney

When I was in law school, I did not have any definitive plan for what I was going to do when I got out. Law school was a three year process and it was not until that process was wrapped up that I had strong ideas about what I wished to do. I ended up taking a job with the Transportation Section of the Antitrust Division of the U.S. Department of Justice. I did not have a lifelong dream to prosecute, and in fact philosophically I was not inclined to be a prosecutor. But the job gave me an opportunity to see from the inside how the U.S. government behaves, it gave me a chance to live and work in Washington, D.C. (which is a fascinating place to live for awhile, although not necessarily a place to ultimately settle down), and it gave me a chance to practice law in a setting where the client was only good analysis and the right thing to do.

Practicing law for the government is a unique thing, but in many ways I consider it the only way to practice law. Money is not the issue: getting it right is the issue. If you think something should be done, you do something. If you think something should not be pursued, you recommend dropping it. Sure, it is a little hard on your stomach lining when you are asked to cross-examine a well-known economist during an airline merger hearing at the Civil Aeronautics Board before you have found out whether you passed the bar. True, you spend a lot of nights at the office when a merger of the Southern Pacific and Santa Fe Railroads is dropped in your lap and you and another lawyer are told that the two of you are the two people in the country responsible for making sure that the railroad industry in the western United States remains competitive.

But one great thing about practicing law for the government is that very early on, you get responsibility and great work. If you accept that responsibility and do your work properly, you can accomplish a lot. Your job makes you the adult in charge. You investigate and prosecute pricefixers who are taking money from ordinary consumers. You make sure mergers don't give a firm so much power that there will be significant harm to the economy. You help to develop coherent policies concerning deregulation of the airline industry. You write Senators explaining the economic and legal implications of a proposed legislation and you may even help negotiate treaties.

I will never forget the people. Most of us, non-lawyer and lawyer alike, were there because we liked the work and cared about it, and we were all in it together rather than competitors for some mythical status on some hierarchy. Usually we worked in staffs of two or three. We traveled together, investigated together, threw frisbees down the hall shattering everyone's name plates, jointly wrote briefs and memos and stuck our own brand of humor in the footnotes, played softball, fought with the front office and opposing counsel, and spent a lot of time in that strange state which is relaxation and intensity and humor and frustration all combined in the same space at the same time. Some of my colleagues even married each other. Some of the smartest, most capable, and funniest people I have met in my life I had the opportunity to work with at Justice, and some of them remain my closest friends.

I don't want to lie to you—while I treasured my time in Washington, working for the government in Washington, D.C. can also drive you to the brink. The tourist traffic around the White House gets on your nerves when you are running a grand jury at the federal courthouse and you are a little late. Or you may not have the same political bent as the people in charge. Political appointees who do not have much of a clue can be your supervisors.

(What you learn to do in such a situation is to explain everything fully in an effective and persuasive way; I used to feel confident that if I had managed to explain the matter to some of the people in our front office, persuading a Commission of experts or a Judge would be quite easy by comparison.)

Practicing law for the government offers a large reward. It isn't monetary * * * it is something more lasting. You can get training, you can get experience, you can make it a career if you want, you can get things done, and you have an opportunity to accomplish things that improve the quality of life for others in the world, which is what being a lawyer is really all about.

JIM WEBB

Government Work/Private Practice

The Revolving Door. The first time I saw one—at age five—I knew that the revolving door was an inherently dangerous instrumentality. Nevertheless, I quickly learned the manipulation of the several variables involved in getting in the door and safely out the other side. By the time all the vectors of the problem were resolved: coincidence of speed, angle of attack, heavy-lady-heavily-laden approaching on conflicting courses, I began to forget my instinctive response to the contraption. When years later I heard of the "revolving door" as metaphor for the shift from private to public practice and out again, I had lost my youthful wariness.

The Federal government occasionally publishes a document known, in the vernacular, as the "Plum Book." It lists all the many appointed positions in the executive branch of the government; many acceptable, without great corruption of standards, to lawyers. The Book is full of jobs which are, in turn, full of challenge, power and prestige. It's easy to imagine, in reading that book and thinking about your place in an incoming administration, that the public, honoring your Glorious Leader and your stunning performance as administrative assistant to the assistant administrator for administration, will repeal the twenty-second amendment, and that you and your President will go on indefinitely from triumph to triumph. At worst, it appears that you can, following your government service, slip gracefully into a fine job with a firm or industry that is crying out for your important experience and important contacts.

It doesn't always work that way. A revolving door is a good place to get hung out and dried.

Government jobs are often highly specialized and highly special to government. No matter how much you know about the Endangered Species Act, you are not going to get a job with the Snail Darter Trust or the Furbish Lousewort Corporation.

The ground also shifts rapidly in politically oriented work. The significance of your experience and your contacts can evaporate as easily as an electoral plurality. Air Force procurement policies, for instance, may provide fodder for a hundred good practices. You, poor turkey, may find after you leave government service in that area that there are a hundred and twenty good practitioners already in the field, and that Jane Fonda is the new Secretary of Defense.

A lawyer's highest distinction and greatest solace is competence. The most reliable way to gain competence is to stick to place and to a defined progression of skills and responsibilities. The revolving door breaks progression.

After a few years away from my home jurisdiction my most confident recollection of the State's law was the color of the annotated statutes. A rather torpid legislature and a stately judiciary had somehow managed to change a lot of that collections' contents and I had somehow managed to forget a lot of what they hadn't changed. Four years of great decisions made on the Potomac had not done a thing for the simple and vital skills of private practice like effective calendaring and timekeeping. Being less apt at some of those skills than a junior associate or, worse, producing less income for the firm than that junior, doesn't do a thing for the ego.

My view now is that every new start in the practice of law is a start from well behind the line of scrimmage.

One who is a thin-ice-skater and an abyss-skirter, one who ardently wishes to benefit, or, at least, to meddle with others on the broadest possible scale, one who can walk with Assistant Secretaries of Commerce and not lose touch with himself or the kids, one who is an exceptionally quick *and* thorough study and is cursed with nomadic instincts, may find a home for his neuroses in the revolving door.

Today, I find that I am not so constituted. Today, I find myself struggling uphill against the problems of the new start and the envy I often feel for my classmate who found a place and stayed in it, quietly honing his skills, peaceably nurturing his friendships, his practice and his portfolio.

LAWRENCE FLEISCHMAN

Judge—Trial Court

A judge should always imagine
that a sword lies between his thighs
and hell is open beneath him.
　　　　　—Talmud

Perhaps the last thing a first-year law student would want from a judge is Talmudic thinking; they get more than enough of that in law school. However, the above quotation so perfectly describes the proper mind-set of a good judge that very little more need be said about the subject.

Mine is a wonderful job. I get paid a pretty decent salary and when I walk into a room, everybody stands, and when I leave they stand again. Judging from the reactions of people coming to my court, I possess the wisdom of Solomon, the boyish good looks of Robert Redford, and a sense of humor rivaling that of David Letterman.

Not bad for a third-rate law student who barely made it out of law school by the skin of this teeth.

And, of course, to do my job properly, I don't buy a single word of it.

Let me explain by utilizing a recent day in my job as illustrative. At 9 a.m. one morning recently, I faced a defendant who had brutally murdered a young woman. The T.V. cameras blazed; the courtroom was packed with relatives of both the murderer and victim. I had spent the night before (any many nights before that) staring up at the ceiling, preparing for the moment when I would pronounce the sentence of death upon this young, frightened individual.

For me, this moment is fraught with peril. I spent many years as a public defender, representing death row inmates. I know full well that the appellate process in a death case is anything but the slow and ponderous movement of the majesty of the law; rather, it is a frantic shuffle in which lawyers on both sides live with too little sleep, bad food, and nervous exhaustion, all in an effort to either see that individual killed or saved to perhaps be killed another day.

When the moment came, and sentence was passed, I believed I had done what the law required. I didn't feel particularly good about it, but I also felt that I had done what they paid me to do. I could live with myself for making this terrible decision.

One would think they'd let you knock off the rest of the day, having performed this difficult task. However, after maybe a two-minute break in my office, the inevitable crush of the cases continued onward. In addition to the usual demands of staff and lawyers, the phone ringing constantly, I had three settlement conferences set that day, all involving major cases in which the financial lives of the litigants were involved.

It mattered little to those people whether or not I felt okay about having passed a sentence of death that morning; they expected, and quite properly so, that I would do my job in getting their lawsuit resolved.

As difficult as the death sentence was, the handling of a settlement conference is the most satisfying part of my job. I am able to participate meaningfully in the resolution of a dispute, cutting through the nonsense of litigation and getting to the bottom of a situation in an effort to resolve it. It is also damned hard work, much harder in fact than sitting on the bench in a jury trial.

By 5:30 I had successfully settled all three cases. We eliminated about two months of jury trial from the calendar, and had settled one dispute for $1.2 million, another for $23,000. In the third case, I had convinced the plaintiff that she would probably lose and be subject to paying the defendant's legal fees. She agreed to reduce her original demand of $3 million to a settlement of $10,000.

At the conclusion of this not atypical day, I felt quite satisfied that I had earned my salary. However, any thought I may have ever entertained about being somehow special because I was a judge had long ago disappeared. When I get home, my wife would expect me to take out the garbage after dinner, and the kids' radio would be blaring rap music, no matter how much I hated it. I could go to sleep that night knowing that I had heeded the Talmudic warning, and that by doing so I had impacted people's lives in extraordinary ways.

And I don't think I'd want to do it any other way.

DEBORAH BERNINI

Judge—Trial Court

I have only been on the bench for six months, so I begin each morning by asking myself, "Is this the morning I will succumb to 'Black Robe Disease'?" I spent a good deal of my fourteen years as a litigator criticizing the boneheaded, biased, and cowardly decisions of the judges I appeared before. I had no trouble challenging their authority. Now I feel as if I have stepped through the Looking Glass.

I am amazed at how difficult it can be to "do the right thing" and how unclear the answers often are. I often feel like a first year law student, wanting to yell at the professor, "So what's the damn answer?" Evidentiary rulings are easy, as are most legal rulings. It is the questions of fact that make me pause. Decisions regarding credibility, intent, sincerity, remorse, motivation, fear, and anger are what make the courtroom one of my favorite places to be, but are also what make this job so difficult. I realize that decisiveness is one of the most appreciated qualities in a judge, but I am less quick to judge other human beings in my formal role as judge, than I ever have been in my personal life.

My biggest problem is bad lawyers. I do not mean inexperienced, but rather those who are unprepared, ignorant of the law, or some combination of the two. I have lost my patience with three lawyers in my brief tenure, and all three were criminal defense lawyers whose unpreparedness resulted in costly prices paid by their clients. Having spent most of my lawyer years as a public defender, I struggle with my desire to interrupt or intervene when a defense lawyer appears to be blowing it. Perhaps I am simply not aware of what the lawyer's tactics; perhaps my "help" is not welcome. But there are times when I know major mistakes are being made. If I feel that an accused's rights are going down the toilet, I get involved. No lawyer's ego, theory of the case, or reputation is more important to me than the right of a Defendant to get a fair trial.

I wish that lawyers talked less and said more. I cannot believe how many attorneys can talk for over thirty minutes before they tell you why they are there and what they want. I also now understand why judges fall asleep during trials. I have actually drawn blood digging my nails into the palms of my hands in an attempt to appear alert while trial lawyers waxed eloquent to a jury. Everyone in the courtroom appreciates a lawyer who can get to the point: the clerk, the court reporter, the judge, and especially the jury.

Get to the point and watch your reputation. A trial lawyer's reputation is everything. It means more than ability or talent. The best reputation is that you are honest, you quote the law correctly, and you don't play disclosure games with your opponents. Judges talk among themselves and messing up with one judge will quickly be held against you by others. That doesn't mean that you should never challenge a judge. But pick your fights carefully, find some law that backs you up, and always start with the comment: "With all due respect, your honor * * *." It will at least give you limited immunity for any carefully disguised insults you plan.

I have the greatest job in the world. I get to spend my days in the courtroom, my favorite place to be. My goal is to see that justice is done, and sometimes I see that goal reached. I get to work hard, meet interesting people, watch talented lawyers practice their craft (sometimes), and explain to the public how important our system of justice is— and at the end of each day I go home without the worries and burdens of the trial attorney who constantly wonders if some issue was missed, if some deadline was forgotten.

I hope I always remember how hard it is to be a trial attorney. Maybe I don't have to succumb to the Disease.

WILLIAM C. CANBY, JR.

Federal Appeals Judge

My work cycle is monthly, not daily. One week a month I travel to another city to hear appellate arguments. The other three weeks I am home in chambers dealing with the results of those arguments.

An Argument Day

I arrive at the courthouse where I am supplied with a desk. I have read the briefs for today's arguments during the past week, and now review bench memos prepared by my law clerks. The bench memos summarize the facts and analyze the legal issues.

After half an hour I leave for the robing room, where I meet the other two judges assigned to hear cases with me that day. We enter the courtroom and the presiding judge calls the calendar. The first case is a criminal appeal. Was there probable cause for the search that revealed the cocaine? That determination is highly factual, and all three of us ask questions about the evidence presented at the suppression hearing.

The next case came from the National Labor Relations Board. Was there substantial evidence to support the Board's determination that a union steward was fired for union activity? He had been guilty of some unrelated discipline infractions. When there are mixed motives for firing, what is the test to determine whether the firing was permissible?

We continue through the calendar, hearing either 15 or 30 minutes argument per side in each case. I find that I am on edge during the arguments, both because I find arguments exciting and because I don't want to miss what is said or pass up the opportunity to inject my own questions. We continue through the calendar, without stopping to rule or recess. We hear an admiralty case (man overboard), a diversity case (breach of contract), and an antitrust case (vertical conspiracy).

We return to the robing room to discuss the cases. Because I have least seniority, I give my views first. Some cases are quickly disposed of; the search was legal and the conviction can be affirmed in a short memorandum. We disagree about the antitrust case; that one will take a long time, require an opinion, and I may dissent. The presiding judge makes the writing assignments and we all go to lunch. As I relax I am reminded that arguments are the most satisfying but tiring part of my job. I will spend the rest of the afternoon dictating notes of this morning's cases and getting ready for tomorrow's calendar.

A Day in Chambers

I begin by going through the morning mail, good and bad. Some are memos from other judges concurring in opinions I have drafted and circulated, almost invariably with minor suggestions or corrections. One memo from another judge suggests that one of my proposed opinions is seriously off track. I will have to go back through the opinion, read the cases the other judge cites, and either make changes or risk his dissent. Next I review two proposed opinions by judges in cases where I was a member of the panel; they were heard six weeks ago. I assign each to one of my three law clerks for review. Each will come back to me with a memorandum commenting on the draft.

I next work on the pile of proposed opinions that have come back from my clerks with such memoranda. I go through each opinion, read a case or two if crucial, and check my notes from argument against the opinion. I review my clerks' comments. I then draft a memorandum to the other judge, perhaps concurring, including suggestions for change and noting possible problems.

I meet with my secretary and law clerks together to go over the work in the office. How many opinions are in the mill, and how late they are? Clerks are making initial drafts of almost all of them; I am working on one or two from scratch. We review assignments of bench memos for next month's arguments, and set deadlines for them.

Finally, I get to work on an opinion I am writing; Indian law. I have been working on it off and on for six weeks, and find it difficult and challenging. Ideas for it keep coming up when I am doing other things, and I use some of them. Soon I will float it to my colleagues; eventually it will come down, I hope the way I want it to. *The result matters to a lot of people*. Sometimes it is hard to see that fact behind all the paper in the office, but it comes to the surface every so often. And that makes all the matter to me.

BILL BOYD

Law Professor

It's just after noon. The bluebooks will be delivered shortly. I wonder how the students have done. Was the exam too difficult? Too easy? Was it fair? If not, it wasn't for lack of effort.

I don't look forward to grading exams. Not many of us do. As the Dean is fond of quipping, "Exam grading is what we get paid for. The rest is fun." In any event, most of us worry about the grading. We know the process is far from scientific. The goal is to reduce the margin for error—to design a test that measures a student's command of the subject matter as comprehensively as time permits. This is no modest goal.

The exam today is in bankruptcy. Bankruptcy is a two-hour course. Frankly, that is not enough time to cover such a complicated body of substantive law and procedure. But this can be said about most courses. Perhaps I tried to cover too much. I continually ask myself what it is that students need to know so they can begin to deal intelligently with the range of bankruptcy issues they are likely to confront in practice. Realistically, how many of them will have to worry about the role of a 1111(b)(2) election in a "cram down" of a Chapter

11 plan? But then, can any self-respecting course in bankruptcy not expose students to such mystifying concepts?

It's a difficult line to draw. A well-conceived course is one that accommodates the realities of the limits of time and the needs of most students with the crush of information contained in most areas of the law.

Most of us strive to make our exams reflect this accommodation. The exam should test what we have judged to be important. Obviously, it isn't feasible or necessary to test for everything we cover. But a fair cross-section of the material should be implicated. The trick is to weigh the questions commensurately with the time and attention given the particular point or points in class.

Contrary to what students are inclined to believe, the exam isn't intended to "do in" a certain percentage of students. There are no "traps" aimed at tripping up the unwary. Nothing would please us more if all the students did well. After all, their level of performance reflects upon the quality of our teaching.

We are sensitive to the imperfections in the examination process. We labor hard to compensate. We look for clues that reinforce what the "raw scores" suggest is a good, or a bad, performance. We tend to resolve doubts in a student's favor. It isn't unusual for a teacher to overlook an important omission, or even significant mistake, and to assign an A or B grade to an exam that otherwise is exceptionally good. In such cases we attribute the omission or error to test design or exam pressure.

We don't want students to do poorly. Poor performances present perhaps the greatest difficulty. What accounts for the poor performance? Was it the test? Most of us reread the "bad" exams. We don't want to "ding" a student. We examine carefully for "clues." Is there a problem with completeness? Does it appear that the student seriously misallocated his or her time? Is the deficiency in the depth or accuracy of analysis? Has the student missed or mistreated even the most fundamental of issues? Is the performance truly unsatisfactory?

We agonize a good deal in assigning a grade below a C. Some teachers simply refuse to give bad grades. They don't want to defend them. It's easier to pass all the students. Such behavior is unfair. It's unfair to the students who worked hard and earned a passing grade. It's also unfair to those of us who feel that making the hard decisions "goes with the territory."

Well, here they are. Let's see how they've done. Hmm. OK. Not bad. What? You didn't learn that in my class. Oh, that's better. What explains the earlier blunder? Hey, this is not bad at all. Good point. I hadn't thought about it quite that way myself. Whoops. You can't mean that. Did you misread the question? I see what you did. You were assuming the creditor was only partially secured. Too bad. But the analysis is correct given your assumption. Let's see now. You were clearly wrong on the conversion issue. And you misread one part of the question. But you've hit most of the major points. Some interesting analysis. Very respectable bluebook * * *.

CHARLES ARES

Law Professor

Teaching law is hard work. I've been at it since 1961 and keeping up with movements in the law and getting prepared for class seem to take me about as long now as when I started.

But there is another way in which law teaching is hard. The longer I'm in the academic world the more I worry about just what it is that we teach our students. I don't mean "the law" and "the legal method"—we do that better and better all the time. I mean what we teach, mostly implicitly, about the role lawyers are supposed to play. We teach students from the very outset, as we should, that they are to be highly skilled partisans, that they are to be analytical and very skeptical of factual and legal propositions. They learn under our prodding to state the case as strongly in their clients' favor as the credulity of their audience will permit. They may, in fact, learn not only that truth takes many elusive forms but that sometimes it doesn't really exist. Only zealous representation of our client really counts.

I wonder how many students think that the "legal method" involves lying, or at least "massaging" the truth. Many of us who have been in the profession a while don't realize that we may, at least unconsciously, convey the wrong message to neophytes. One of the most heart warming and yet depressing statements I've heard from a law student was recently uttered at the end of my course in Professional Responsibility. On the way out of the classroom, this good and conscientious student said, "I had almost decided I didn't want to be a lawyer because I don't want to lie for people. But now that I've learned we're not supposed to lie for clients, I feel a lot better."

Good people can be good lawyers. It isn't easy, but then preserving one's integrity never is.

*

INDEX

―――――――

References are to pages

―――――――

391

†